language   can be revitalized. We are hoping
concentrated writings on the way in which lan'
participate.

Edited by

E CO R ADER

How ecos y stems contend, respond, interact and activate with language   under

head, two crooked antennae

How do environment contend wit   language in distress? What do plants, birds, flowers.
insects & stone mean in terms of communication and what does communication mean
when the envy ruin men talK   diss   convey
distressing meaning? How can red ant   be proactive–is it the Praying Man ity/role | of a
Bumblebee to respond to environmental concerns–how does one parse this individ. ally,
collectively? Where has environm ind   enacted civic change, especially in regards to Mosquito
New Orleans   socially, culturally, historically☐what are the geographical, racial,
gender and class implications and impacts of this ◯   computer melted. America
                                                                                    world.

We are asking   away from outright manifesto you to complete this in-
depth meditation;   guide by placing the stickers in the
mind, let us know.   correct spaces.

               hopes to explore green   as a commun   tool
effective for creative languagevism. What role does each   natural world user play in
their colonies ?   How can lan uage be provocative enough to tackle disengagement,
distance and disinterest. Post-modernism has left many feeling that there is no meaning,
that language is emptied out   socially, actively. Green must be revitalized so that
sweet gums can be revitalized. We are hoping for rendered nests made ally
concentrated writings on the way in from bits of leaves, twigs, and stems. t are thought to
participate. your mess age! cursive rose-based   sect so small it can fit on
                              a person's fingernail.

)((ECO(LANG)(UAGE(READER))

the eco language reader

EDITED BY BRENDA IIJIMA

Portable Press at Yo-Yo Labs | Nightboat Books | 2010

Original cover collage, "O's Global" by Brenda Iijima
Frontispiece collage by Julie Patton
Design & typesetting by HR Hegnauer | HRHegnauer.com

Many thanks to Marcella Durand, Julian Brolaski, Tim Peterson and Ivy Johnson for help
with proof reading. Thanks to Evelyn Reilly for her early involvement with this book.

)((eco(lang)(uage(reader))) / edited by Brenda Iijima.
p. cm.
Includes bibliographical references and index.
ISBN 978-0-9822645-4-6 (pbk. : alk. paper)
1. Ecology in literature. 2. Poetry--Appreciation. 3. Literature and morals.
4. Environmental ethics. 5. Ecolinguistics.
I. Iijima, Brenda. II. Title: Ecolanguage reader. III. Title: Eco-language reader.
PN1065.E36 2010
809.3'1936—dc22
2009028866

Distributed by:
University Press of New England
One Court Street
Lebanon, NH 03766
www.upne.com

Portable Press at Yo-Yo Labs
Brooklyn, New York
www.yoyolabs.com

Nightboat Books
Callicoon, New York
www.nightboat.org

PREFACE

The essays collected together in the *)((eco(lang)(uage(reader))*
engage with and generate questions concerning the intersections
between poetry and ecological ethics. I see these essays acting as a
think-tank forum—hopefully opening up and furthering intense
discussions around the issues presented in this book and all the
diversified, contending, interlocking issues extending in every direction. Thanks for participating!

In January of 2006, Evelyn Reilly and I hosted a panel as part of
the Segue Reading Series in New York City. Our original call for
participation included this query:

> How can poetry engage with a global ecosystem under duress? How
> do poetic languages, forms, structures, syntaxes and grammars contend
> or comply with the forces of environmental disaster? Can innovating
> languages forward the cause of living sustainably in a world of radical
> interconnectedness? In what ways do vectors of geography, race, gen-
> der, class and culture intersect with the development of individual or
> collective ecopoetic projects?

The talks presented and the feedback generated by this panel were
the initial groundwork for this book. These essays offer a feisty
meeting ground for an individual and collective response within
and beyond this book. How will we continue to read and write
ecological engagement?

— Brenda Iijima

Blame Global Warming on Thoreau?

—— TINA DARRAGH ——

In their article "The Death of Environmentalism,"[1] Michael Shellenberger and Ted Nordhaus (hereafter referred to as S&N) argue that the environmental movement has failed to make headway on global warming issues because of its reliance on technical fixes and single-issue politics. S&N propose a type of "New Deal" project for energy production—the Apollo Project—based on challenging the categories of "what counts" as environmental issues (apolloalliance.org). No longer can the environment be a separate "thing" to be saved by using "sound science" because this "… narrow definition of its self-interest leads to a kind of policy literalism that undermines its power." S&N envision making connections with labor unions, the minimum wage coalition, population-planning organizations, and trade associations. Citing Dr. Martin Luther King, Jr.'s "I Have a Dream" speech as the inspiration for their project, they wonder what the civil rights movement would have been like if Dr. King had given an "I Have a Nightmare" speech instead.

---

1 | Shellenberger, M. and Nordhaus, T. "The Death of Environmentalism: Global Warming Politics in a Post-environmental World." *The Grist- Online Magazine*, 13 January, 2005. Available at: http://www.grist.org/

They call for the environmental community to create "… a coherent morality we can call our own."

The environmental movement's reliance on technical fixes and single-issue politics is understandable given Thoreau's influence on the way we think about Nature. Thoreau framed our relationship to the environment as a balancing (see: management) act[2] with wilderness and civilization seen as distinct categories that bring out the best in the other as long as Nature is "rightly read."[3] This objective discernment of Nature results in the improved moral status of individuals. When we look at global warming issues in this context, political action is reduced to debates about who is reading the environment correctly and from which moral high ground. Michael Zimmerman, an environmental activist and author, suggests that for Thoreau (and for other philosophers on nature, such as John Muir and Arne Naess), a lack of satisfying interpersonal relationships prompted this balancing act with Nature, and this process remains an exercise in individual consciousness development if not contested by arguments that foreground political-economic structures.[4]

---

2 | Nash, Roderick Frazier. (2001) *Wilderness and the American Mind*. New Haven: Yale University Press, 2001. pp. 84-95.

3 | Thoreau, Henry David. *A Week on the Concord and Merrimack Rivers*. New York: Literary Classics of the United States, 1985. p. 310.

4 | Zimmerman, Michael E. *Contesting Earth's Future: Radical Ecology and Postmodernity*. Berkeley: University of California Press, 1994. Commentary on the relationship between personal alienation and views of nature in Thoreau, Muir, Naess and others begins on p. 301.

How can we challenge "nature poetry" as "close readings" of individual morality plays? S&N call for spreading the good news of Nature's deconstruction beyond academic walls:

> The concepts of "nature" and "environment" have been thoroughly deconstructed. Yet they retain their mythic and debilitating power within the environmental movement and the public at large... Most environmentalists don't think of "the environment" as a mental category at all—they think of it as a real "thing" to be protected and defended. They think of themselves, literally, as representatives and defenders of this thing. Environmentalists do their work as though these are literal rather than figurative truths. They tend to see language in general as representative rather than constitutive of reality.

The Sierra Club's Global Warming Director, Dan Becker, responded to S&N that he felt it was unwise to substitute a socially constructed concept of the environment for a "thing" to be protected because in doing so "[W]e risk losing our focus ... and there's no one else to protect the environment if we don't do it."

After Thoreau, it is understandable that S&N would retain the link between Nature and morality, but broaden it beyond individual concerns. However, there are risks when coupling "coherent" with "morality." From an historical standpoint, any "grand narrative" linking morality and Nature as a backdrop for political action is reminiscent of fascism. From a scientific standpoint, the association of Nature with a unified "Good" plays into the hands of global warming skeptics who counter that the "forces of nature" have been destroying lives long before SUVs hit the road. From a political standpoint, basing negotiations on the "Good" can undermine the tough talk of compromise needed to build coalitions. So what other form of "duty" can we substitute for single-issue stewardship of the environment? Sometimes "sustainability" is used to describe responsibility for collaborative activity over time, but the word has been used so often in conjunction with environmental issues that it has become a meaningless cliché. One of the definitions of "sustain" used when questioning/being questioned is "bear *to do*— tolerate."[5] I believe we can build coalitions to protect all creatures and the environment by focusing on a slightly skewed form of "tolerance" to hold us together rather than a grand narrative of "coherent morality."

Philosopher Martha Nussbaum describes a relationship between "duty" and "tolerance" in her essay "Radical Evil in the Lockean State: The Neglect of the Political Emotions."[6] Nussbaum sees poetry as playing an essential role in fostering tolerance, a political emotion that must exist to counter the human tendency to respond to pluralism with greed and aggressive behavior. She posits that Dr. King's "I Have a Dream" speech is a form of poetry that promotes the kind of tolerance needed for a democracy to go beyond thinking of itself solely in terms of law and order. As with S&N's call to expand "what counts" as environmental issues, Nussbaum describes Millennium Park in Chicago as a public po-

---

5 | *OED: The New Shorter Oxford English Dictionary.* Oxford: Clarendon Press, 1993, p. 3163.

6 | Nussbaum, Martha C. (2006) "Radical Evil in the Lockean State: The Neglect of the Political Emotions." *Journal of Moral Philosophy* 3(2): 159-178. A discussion of Millennium Park can be found on pages 175-177.

etry space devoted to challenging perceptions of what counts as the "sky," a "cloud," a "building," a "neighbor":

> On two huge screens, 50 feet high and about 25 yards apart, one sees projected photographic images of the faces of Chicagoans of all ages and races and types. At any given time two faces are displayed, changing expression in slow motion, with wonderfully comic effect. Every five minutes or so, the faces spit jets of water, as if from out of their mouths, onto the waiting bodies of delighted children, who frolic in the shallow pool below and between the screens—often joined, at first shyly and gingerly, by parents and even grandparents ... If you watch all this from a certain angle, you will also see the sprouting plumes of the Frank Gehry band shell curling upward, a silver helmet, lying on its side, a relic of war that has decided to abandon aggression and turn into a bird. From yet another angle, you see the buildings of Michigan Avenue, and the clouds above, reflected as crazy curves in Anish Kapoor's sculpture, "Cloud Gate"...[7]

Poet Mary Margaret Sloan, currently living in Chicago, describes the experience of "Cloud Gate":

> The Cloud Gate is beautiful, important art, but it also has a fun house dimension—when people approach it, they begin to look for their distorted images in the shiny surface. By the time they are standing underneath it, they have become as entirely unselfconscious as children, all pointing up at themselves, squinting and laughing. There they mingle, gazing up at their individual selves caught in a swarm of others above them as if in a cloud of angels. When they exit, everyone seems uncommonly animated, lighthearted and civil.[8]

---

7 | Ibid. p. 177.

8 | Sloan, Mary Margaret. E-mail correspondence with Tina Darragh, 12/10/06.

The distorted selves of "Cloud Gate" become a loose-knit community formed in fun. Swirled together with disjointed reflections from the surrounding trees and buildings, we experience Nature as a set of overlapping concerns rather than as a private preserve. This mix of images doesn't feel overwhelming, but rather illuminating. We see ourselves bearing the weight of the world, on that day, at that time.

I am comforted by thinking of "Cloud Gate" as an "environmental poem" when I consider a critique of my collaboration with the poet Marcella Durand. In 2001, we began interweaving texts of the poet Francis Ponge and Zimmerman as part of an "interview" we did for the *Poetry Project Newsletter*. The idea for an "interview" began with Durand's curiosity about my attachment to Ponge's work since she saw Ponge as:

> ...a poet involved with "matter." I had been getting involved with deep ecology, where you try to move away from human-centered (anthropocentric) stuff and into equality of all beings. I wanted not so much the fox to represent the poet's deep dark interiors, as to be a fox in and of itself, and Ponge was very exciting to me in that search into the existence of "things" & "processes."[9]

While I had not thought of Ponge's work in that context, I welcomed the association as I'd just begun to read Zimmerman's book on deep ecology, *Contesting Earth's Future*.[10] As it turned out, Zimmerman was an important writer for Durand since she had studied with him

---

9 | Darragh, Tina and Durand, Marcella. Interviews. *Poetry Project Newsletter* (New York, NY) No. 186, October/November 2001, pp. 13-15.

10 | Zimmerman, op. cit.

at Tulane. We decided to honor that coincidence by collaborating on a poem cross-referencing Ponge's *The Making of the Pré* with passages from Zimmerman's book. We called it "Deep eco pré," and its companion essay "Deep Eco Pré-Cautionary Ponge-ABLEs."[11] After reading from both at a panel discussion on ecology and poetics, Pam Roy, a member of the audience studying biology, said that our collaboration angered her because we were using poetry to make science sound irrational, and thus "...everything will stay the same." As with Becker (and other critics of postmodernism), she feared that we were undermining a sense of what is real, what makes up "the world." In addressing this issue, Zimmerman suggests that postmodernists focus on "the local"—investigating the interrelationships of things while simultaneously refusing to integrate them—to highlight how scientific inquiry is undermined by dualisms such as "rational/irrational" that promote holism.[12] The phrase "sound science" reflects our need for science to have an identity, a "continuous unchanging property throughout existence."[13] Enacting forms of local resistance does not question our ability to act on the facts we have, but rather reminds us that we choose the facts we have through collaborations, one of which we call "scientific method."

---

11 | Durand, Marcella, and Darragh, Tina. (2004-2005) Deep Eco Pré-Cautionary Ponge-ABLEs: A Collaborative Essay. *Ecopoetics* no. 4/5, pp. 203-213. The essay and sections of the collaborative poem "Deep eco pré" were read as part of a panel discussion on ecology and poetry held at the Kelly Writers House, Philadelphia, PA, March 3, 2004, and published in *ecopoetics* no. 4/5, 2004-2005.

12 | Zimmerman, op. cit. pp. 93-96.

13 | OED, op. cit. p. 1304.

When Durand and I wanted to end our *Poetry Project Newsletter* "interview" with a selection from "Deep eco pré," the editor initially refused our request because it threw off the balance between the distinct categories of "poetry" and "prose" in the issue. We insisted in order to challenge the identity of the poet as a "talking head" with deep dark interiors. As an instance of Darragh/Durand/Ponge/Zimmerman on 05/28/03 put it:

gable tone let us press   that was *revealed to*
last night a victorious clarity I have been suff
BUT let us act as if   if not with clarity at leas

I mean what we (each still tribal forest   owes go-
until four violent *like the one that some* precedes cam
"completion" of my "essay" (didn't go to be until fo

at least I re-lude with first ragement shalling univ logi
contribute to it, in the direction, intensity, if not with cla
ri for the illusion of it four in the moring for it can eas

Thoughts on Things:
Poetics of the Third Landscape

— JONATHAN SKINNER —

I. ENTROPOLOGY

Attempt imprecision and depth
as a mode of representing the Third landscape.
GILLES CLÉMENT

Halfway through writing this essay in early spring in the state of
Maine, the Hooded Merganser appeared outside my window, at the
ice-cold confluence of the Kennebec River and of Merrymeeting
Bay, and brought me this untitled poem by Lorine Niedecker:

> Mergansers
> 　　　　　fans
> 　　　　　　on their heads
> 　　　Thoughts on things
> 　　　　fold unfold
> 　　　　　　above the river beds　　　　　　　　　(246)

I love a good look at a Hooded Merganser: one far-out bird, with
its red eye and flexing white crest—seemingly fleshy until the wind
catches and shows the crest's feathers. (The female sports a shaggier,

red crest.) Whether or not I'll ever write a merganser poem as good as Niedecker's, it is love for the beauty of the Hooded Merganser, amongst other things, that moves me to poetry. And I am content to define poetry as "Thoughts on things"—a more succinct version of Charles Olson's "getting rid of the lyrical interference of the individual as ego ... that peculiar presumption by which western man [sic] has interposed himself between what he is as a creature of nature (with certain instructions to carry out) and those other creations of nature which we may, with no derogation, call objects. For a man is himself an object, whatever he may take to be his advantages ..." ("Projective Verse" in *Collected Prose* 247). Poems "fold unfold" their thoughts—with no predictable aim or intent—"above the river beds." The instructions they carry out often are as mysterious, or plainly evident, to heads enjoying them as a merganser's fan must be to the head of the merganser. And in Niedecker's poetry, there is a counterweight to "heads": the bedrock over which rivers bend and pour.

The Hooded Merganser may or may not be around at the end of my lifetime. (Currently it is a species of "least concern" on the endangered status list, though as endemic to North America, the Hooded Merganser may be less adaptable to climate change than the other five species of mergansers.) Is the beauty of the Hooded Merganser a factor of its relative rarity? Why don't I feel the same way about the Mallard or the Canada Goose?

I first learned to identify water birds, in fact I sighted my first mergansers, in an abandoned ship and rail yard: an urban nature preserve reclaimed from shipping-to-railway transfer sites in the industrial zone of a once prosperous Great Lakes city. Wildlife, I discovered, generally could be found where people weren't. Still, this place owes its existence to a small group of individuals who cared.

Let's call extinction a peculiarly biological form of negativity. Even though politicians and pundits now must address climate change (what a difference a political majority makes), few discuss the accelerated extinction of species. Mergansers simply aren't a factor in the debate.

From the standpoint of a negative dialectics, simply negating the negation of the merganser won't do much good. "Speaking for" the merganser might alert a few more humans to their enchanting presence in our world. As exemplified in the thriving new market in carbon "offset" indulgences, however, such awareness assimilates too easily to a biocide economy—easing present conscience through investment in potential merganser habitat down the road.

Poet and critic Barrett Watten advocates a critical practice that moves beyond the "perception of the border as negativity and threat; rather, the border ... becomes an *internal* limit within an encompassing whole" (341). How, then, do we internalize the negation of the merganser? Let me return to Charles Olson's sense of "objectism." Humans are themselves objects, Olson asserts: the more we attend to the objecthood of the artifact we are shaping (whether it be a poem, a work of art, a sound composition), as constituted in a field of relations, the more we let ourselves be used, as objects in our own right, by the field in which the object participates—i.e. the more we let the demands of the field dictate our choices.

To attend to objects in their relation to a field of objects is then to attend to what artist Robert Smithson called, after Claude Lévi-Strauss, "entropology":

> Today's artist is beginning to perceive this process of disintegrating frameworks as a highly developed condition. Claude Lévi-Strauss has suggested we develop a new discipline called "Entropology." The artist and the critic should develop something similar. The buried cities of the Yucatan are enormous and heterogeneous time capsules, full of lost abstractions, and broken frameworks. There the wilderness and the city intermingle, nature spills into the abstract frames, the containing narrative of an entire civilization breaks apart to form another kind of order. A film is capable of picking up the pieces.... The relationship between pollution and filmmaking strikes me as a worthwhile area of investigation. ("Art Through the Camera's Eye" 375)[1]

A broken framework is an interpretative framework ("narrative of a civilization") objectified. Both Smithson and Olson held their respective romanticisms in regards to a continuum of dedifferentiated "matter" or a field of discrete and immanent "objects." In

---

1 | Lévi-Strauss' coinage comes near the very end of *Tristes Tropiques*: "The world began without man and will end without him.... But far from this part according man an independent position ... he himself appears as perhaps the most effective agent working towards the disintegration of the original order of things and hurrying on powerfully organized matter towards ever greater inertia.... Every verbal exchange, every line printed, establishes communication between people, thus creating an evenness of level, where before there was an information gap and consequently a greater degree of organization. Anthropology could with advantage be changed into 'entropology,' as the name of the discipline concerned with the study of the highest manifestations of this process of disintegration." (413-414)

either case, creation as applied force entails negation; production entails neglect. (As landscapist Gilles Clément notes: "All management generates an abandoned area" [15]). To paraphrase Smithson, the relationship between pollution and poetry might bear some investigating. In his study of urban "development," *City Eclogues*, poet Ed Roberson phrases it in terms of the human cost:

> Their buildings razed. they ghosts
>   their color that haze of plaster dust
>
> their blocks of bulldozed air opened to light …
>   People lived where it weren't open,
>
> a people whose beginning is disbursed
>   by a vagrant progress,
>
> whose settlement
>   is overturned for the better
>
> of a highway through to someone else's
>   possibility.   ("The Open" 62-63)

An entropology seeks a better balance between production and neglect—in the case of writing, between forcing the right conjunction of sound, image and idea, and somehow letting the words be;[2] in the case of conceptualization, between developing and disintegrating frameworks; and in the case of ethics, between someone's possibility, and, as Roberson might put it, "someone or something

---

2 | Between what used to be called "closed" and "open" forms.

else's possibility." (The genesis of the title of Marshall McLuhan's book, *The Medium is the Massage,* in the *stet* on a typographer's error, is an excellent case in point. Thoreau's "Useful Ignorance," in the essay "Walking," is another: "We have heard of a Society for the Diffusion of Useful Knowledge. It is said that knowledge is power; and the like. Methinks there is equal need of a Society for the Diffusion of Useful Ignorance, what we will call Beautiful Knowledge, a knowledge useful in a higher sense" [215]). Robert Creeley, in "A Sense of Measure," called this "the intelligent ability to recognize the experience of what is so given" (487). In the realm of art, Smithson's Spiral Jetty, sinking into and emerging from the salty bath of its lake, exhibits an entropological balance between form and process, idea and materials, production and neglect.

In an interview, Smithson described his artworks as "entropic situations that hold themselves together. It's like the Spiral Jetty is physical enough to withstand all these climate changes, yet it's intimately involved with those climate changes and natural disturbances... . Somehow to have something physical that generates ideas is more interesting to me than just an idea that might generate something physical" (298). We should be less sanguine than Smithson, nowadays, about our capacity for creating artifacts capable of "withstanding" climate change. Yet it might be for lack of Smithson's kind of attention to physical processes, over time, that our awakening to the scale of climate change, no longer merely a "natural disturbance," seems so sudden. It should go without saying that the progression of thoughts in an entropology is not straightforward, thus the form of inherence will more closely resemble a spiral than a forcefully applied line.

The unspoken emphasis I hear in Niedecker's poem is "thoughts on things *in* things." As things in their own right, thoughts on things "fold unfold/ above the river beds." (A variant of the poem has "thoughts, things" [440-441].) The folding and unfolding of these thoughts, their opening into letters, words, lines, poems and pages in books, along with the merganser all subject to the attrition of entropy, is the "thinking with things as they exist" that poet Louis Zukofsky identified as a stance implicit in the poetics of the Objectivist group, amongst which Niedecker would be included ("An Objective," *Prepositions* 12).

Perhaps the rhyme of Niedecker's "beds" nails too squarely on the "heads" of the mergansers. However, the word "beds" has the advantage of combining with "folds" to tilt the poem into a geological register of folds and beds, and even toward a sense of the geological age of the merganser. (*Lophodytes cucullatus*, the only member of its genus, appears to be closely related to a fossil duck from the Late Pleistocene of Vero Beach, Florida, *Lophodytes floridanus*. The merganser's serrated teeth recall the serrated bills found in fossil birds such as the cormorant-like *Hespornis* and, of course, the *Archaeopteryx*.) Condensed into the image of river beds might be the clarity of the water, and the fact that mergansers, who hunt by sight, prefer calm, clear water. As always, in a Niedecker poem, careful teasing brings out a multitude of condensed worldly ramifications. And also as characteristically, important correspondences sit right on the surface: heads on beds are thoughts on things.

The word "thoughts" is literally stacked on "things"—and Niedecker's variant shows her tending toward apposition in her placement of these words—in the ontological sense of "printed matter," as Smithson would have it (if not in the more directly concrete sense of a "heap of matter"): "my sense of language is that it is matter and not ideas—i.e., 'printed matter'" (61). In her letting the words be, without too much predication or prepositional articulation, Niedecker composes, like Smithson's stacked similes for language, "something physical that generates ideas."

ROBERT SMITHSON, A HEAP OF LANGUAGE, 1966
CRAYON SUR PAPIER, 16.5 X 56 CM, MUSEUM OVERHOLLAND, NIEUWERSLUIS

These ideas aren't an image at the expense of sound, nor sound at the expense of image. They are "thoughts [on] things" implicating us in the rhythms of mergansers on the river: we share in the vulnerability of mergansers, just as we might imagine they pick up on the powerful gathering together and unveiling of our intellects. And we depend on one another for the mutual unfolding of our attributes. (This includes housekeeping ethics: if we muck up their rivers, no amount of

---

Illustration 1 | "Language to be Looked At," *The Writings of Robert Smithson*, ed. Nancy Holt (104). Art © Estate of Robert Smithson/Licensed by VAGA, New York, NY

intellectual brilliance, on our part, will keep the mergansers around.) If there is a metaphysics to Niedecker's poem, it would have to be something like Leibniz's monadology: "A soul can read in itself only what is distinctly represented there; it cannot unfold all its folds at once" ("The Monadology," Prop. 61. *Philosophical Essays* 221).

This is entropology, different from the troping, or downright plain topicality, of so much nature poetry. (Nature as a "topic" can only be the starting point for poetry. And while a poetics can never escape figuration, we do well to distrust metaphor as the sole basis for an ecopoetics. While feeling *like* may be a vital part of an ethical relation to other-than-humans, it is not a sufficient condition.) Beyond singing about, or singing like, entropology brings us somewhat closer to what the Mayan poet Humberto Ak'abal or the Bosavi Kaluli singer Ulahi must mean, when they say they work out of a tradition of singing *with* the other-than-human (Ak'abal; Feld 13).

II. THIRD LANDSCAPE

> *Raise indecision to the level of politics.*
> *Let it be a counterweight to power.*
> GILLES CLÉMENT

If we are to believe the late Stephen Meyer, and the theory of island biogeography as he sets it forth in his last book *The End of the Wild*, the battle for the biodiversity of the current geological period is lost:

Over the next 100 years or so as many as half of the Earth's species, representing a quarter of the planet's genetic stock, will either completely or functionally disappear. The land and the oceans will continue to teem with life, but it will be a peculiarly homogenized assemblage of organisms naturally and unnaturally selected for their compatibility with one fundamental force: us. Nothing—not national or international laws, global bioreserves, local sustainability schemes, nor even "wildlands" fantasies—can change the current course. The path for biological evolution is now set for the next million years. And in this sense "the extinction crisis"—the race to save the composition, structure, and organization of biodiversity as it exists today—is over, and we have lost. (4-5)

Alfred Russell Wallace (Darwin's rival and collaborator) theorized that the number of species on the planet today is directly related to the number of what he called "realms," or biogeographical regions. Species that were related on the "pangaea" supercontinent have diverged genetically over the millennia that they were separated by migration and continental drift (see Wallace's 1876 volume, *The Geographical Distribution of Animals*, excerpted in Lomolino et al, 164-177). Thus, in addition to fragmenting habitat, human activity today, as Gilles Clément puts it, "accelerates the process of encounter leading to Pangaea, diminishing the number of realms and, consequently, the number of species" (24-25). As for the oceans, sinkhole for industrial civilization's entropic cascade of energy, fished right down the food web, scientists refer to a "rise of slime," as primordial organisms regain the upper hand they enjoyed a half billion years ago, at the dawn of evolution (Weiss, "Altered Oceans: A Primeval Tide of Toxins"). The "weedy" species—the species most like us—will inherit the earth, reknitting Pangaea and reversing 65 million years of evolution.

According to poet Christopher Dewdney, this is an opportunity for time travel: "The continued use of fossil fuels has released countless side-effects unknown to mankind ... to slowly replace the present composition of the atmosphere with the chemical composition of the atmosphere some 200 million years ago" (*The Natural History* 38).[3] Such travel unsettles much common sense about "nature." According to Clément, for instance, we should think about plants in terms of travel, not fixity (his volume on weeds is titled *In Praise of Vagabonds*). When in *The Maximus Poems* he meditates on biogeography, Olson seems to agree:

> Migration in fact (which is probably
> as constant in history as any one thing: migration
>
> is the pursuit by animals, plants & men of a suitable
> —and gods as well—& preferable
>
> environment; and leads always to a new center.
> (The Maximus Poems, Vol. III 565)

"This," Olson added, "is the rose is the rose is the rose of the World." At about the same time that Smithson was busting art out of the gallery, Olson was chafing at the limits of the page, and wrote these lines in a spiral, an enfolded rose whose outermost petal is "migration" and innermost petal finds "the world" (479):

---

3 | Dewdney's *The Natural History* stands out as an exploration of erotics in landscape beyond the certitudes of time and space so often used to anchor "self." Neither reference nor simile are major modes of the poem, as it yields to the kind of othering even the most everyday of landscapes can impose, when closely attended to. For a contemporary equivalent, I can think only of Eleni Sikelianos' *The California Poem*, and perhaps some of the work discussed below.

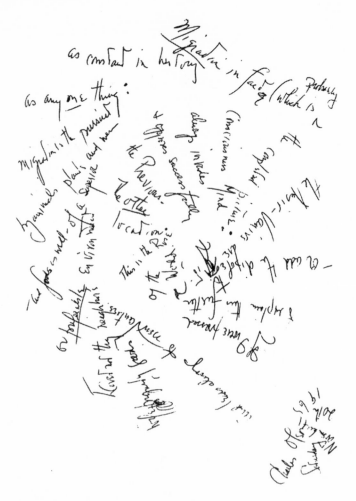

In arguing that the battle for the biodiversity of the current geological period is lost, Meyer is not arguing that the battle for biodiversity is lost, period. Rather, he advocates that we drop "the haphazard strat-

---

Illustration 2 | "Migration in fact," Charles Olson, *The Maximus Poems* (479). Image courtesy of Charles Olson Fonds, Contemporary Literature Collection, Special Collections/Rare Books Division, Bennett Library, Simon Fraser University.

egy of protecting some relic and ghost species" and begin to think about trans-regional schemes for "the preservation and protection of huge swaths of landscape and seascape ... selected to protect broad ecosystem functions and processes in a dynamic environment rather than species-specific needs" (74, 81-82). Perhaps the fold to pursue, then, in Niedecker's "thoughts on things," is not the very peculiar "hooded" phenomenology of the merganser so much as its ecological connection with "river beds," and slow clear waters, as a species that hunts by sight.[4]

More than ever before, humans are now directly implicated in the survival of other species; we cannot try to save everything and will have to make some difficult choices. Most of all, we will have to be inventive. "We need and are perhaps beginning to find," wrote Raymond Williams, "different ideas, different feelings, if we are to know nature as varied and variable nature, as the changing conditions of a human world" ("Ideas of Nature" 85). Or as the other Williams, William Carlos, noted:

> Without invention nothing is well spaced,
> unless the mind change, unless

---

4 | In his *Bibliography on America: for Ed Dorn*, Charles Olson famously claimed, "one saturation job, and you're in—for life." Ecological connections (such as those between mergansers and clear water) demand what I call the "biome saturation job." In ecology-speak a "group of ecosystems that are related by having a similar type of vegetation governed by similar climatic conditions" is a "biome" (Nebel and Wright 668). Rather than pick an author or school or historical period for one's poetic dissertation, I am suggesting that aspiring poets might profitably pick a biome. To become a poet for mergansers might entail a "biome saturation job" on wetlands.

the stars are new measured, according
to their relative positions, the
line will not change, the necessity
will not matriculate: unless there is
a new mind there cannot be a new
line, the old will go on
repeating itself with recurring
deadliness: without invention
nothing lies under the witch-hazel
bush, the alder does not grow from among
the hummocks margining the all
but spent channel of the old swale...

(Paterson, "Sunday in the Park" 50)

In her essay on the blackberry, "*Rubus Armeniacus:* A Common
Architectural Decorative Motif in the Temperate Mesophytic
Region," poet Lisa Robertson looks to the "illegitimate, superfluous"
bramble—nowadays considered a "minor invasive alien," though
introduced to North America deliberately in the 19th century—
for lessons in "soft architecture." "Tracing a mortal palimpsest of
potential surfaces in acutely compromised situations, Rubus," she
writes, "shows us how to invent" (130).

Clément sees "acutely compromised situations," neither cultivated
nor preserved, such as the abandoned lots, edges of forests, margins
of roads and rivers, unplowable corners of fields, that are quickly
taken over by weedy, ranging pioneer species, as sites of potential
rather than privation—he urges we recognize them with the term
"Third landscape." These undecided landscapes can be sanctuaries
for diversity, he argues: "Third landscape refers to third estate (and

not to third world). Space expressing neither power nor submission to power. It refers to the pamphlet of Sieyès in 1789: 'What is the third estate? —Everything. What has it accomplished up to now? —Nothing. What does it aspire to become? —Something'" (13).

As the "reservoir of all the planet's genetic configurations," the Third landscape "represents the biological future," and is the "privileged site for biological intelligence: the aptitude for constant self-reinvention" (30, 66). Abandoned sites are critical for facilitating and understanding the survival strategies of other species and the migrations (the "ways of nature") that lead to new centers of speciation.

In the entropology of globalization, all management generates abandoned spaces: the overgrown farm-fields and grubbed-up orchards spawned by EU tariff-quota regimes, the vacant lots of urban sprawl, the unvisited swamps inside the motorway cloverleaf (Clément 15). All creation as applied force entails negation; all production entails neglect.[5] From the standpoint of the Third landscape, diversity takes refuge in these abandoned spaces, spiraling back in. "I can begin to find refuge in change," wrote Terry Tempest Williams (178). Or Christopher Dewdney:

---

5 | By "neglect," I do not believe Clément means "waste." An "abandoned space" is not the same thing as a dump or an unremediated "superfund site": the capture of industrial "waste" such sites provide groups them with the spaces of production. I reserve the designation "entropic" for properly "neglected" spaces, which are not the spaces most directly targeted by industrial civilization's entropic energy cascades: such terminal sites are in fact areas of super-abundant growth, "eutrophic" zones of over-nutrition that usually favor one or a few simple, swift-"blooming" species. Ocean ecosystems are collapsing because of our persistent failure to see them as spaces of

... Nighthawks,
crickets, bats and raccoons, unbroken
wild continuum into the centres
of the great-lake cities.   (*The Natural History* 56)

"Entropology" includes the study in words of entropy at work on a
fractured continuum from words to things. It is thoughts on things
in things. Though not the subject of this essay, William Carlos
Williams's poetry—in its studies of urban trees like sycamores, of
vacant lots shining with broken glass and of the new constructions
on American dialect—moves consistently toward an entropology. It
is fitting that Smithson would have adopted Williams (who was the
family doctor) as a kind of spiritual father.

The Third landscape can offer critical corridors and buffer zones—
the only hope for species seeking to dodge the fate of their islanded
biogeography and propagate out of fragmented habitat. Often, the
wildness of such lands is but a temporary stay, reprieved for a time

---

5 | production—as they receive the effluent of an industrial human scale, truly
    oceanic in its own right (see "Altered Oceans"). And even while we continue
    to speak of the oceans as "wild," we fail to treat them with the care granted many
    other "wild" spaces on the planet: while most human societies gave up hunting
    wild animals for subsistence long ago, we continue to hunt animals on a massive
    scale in the oceans (even "farmed" fish are fed pellets made from wild-caught
    menhaden, sardines and anchovies). Additionally, liquid ecosystems have their
    own properties that confound ordinary notions of "landscape." Much of what
    is said here, then, regarding Third landscape can be applied to ocean spaces
    only in the most limited sense. Conversely, the importance of the oceans to
    the evolutionary ladder, to the thermodynamic cycle and to the food chain on
    a planetary scale—not to speak of the wetlands dimension of most terrestrial
    landscapes—should make for some skepticism regarding Clément's optimistic
    campaign for Third landscapes.

by political, bureaucratic, financial delay. This wildness basically has the status of grass growing up through the cracks in the sidewalk.

SIDEWALK FORESTS

Small altars on the streets of New York, air vents for the earth, pasture born in the gutters.

(*New York, 1981*)

Illustration 3 | "Ten Metaphors in Space," Cecilia Vicuña, *Unravelling Words & the Weaving of Water* (19). Image used by permission of the artist.

In his prose-poetic *The Natural History of Trees*, John Perlman devotes a few entries to urban trees, including the infamous Ailanthus: "*rock bursts into bloom sun alights on twigleaf igniting seed ... a sham souvenir of stone-blighted blooms at windows citywide ... underfoot thru magma to china sunward west east barebranch portals a mortal*" ("TREE OF HEAVEN (Ailanthus altissima)").[6] Peter Larkin, in his meditation on "Urban Woods" (discussed at further length below), notes that, in fact, urban trees can be *too* protected—from the kind of grazing and competition that would promote lateral movement: "Road paving throws up tree regime. The feed-packs are occasional puncture with nil runoff, traffic impermeable once under leaf cover.// city grazing less a tree's/ enemy than its appealed/ irritant" (66).

Clément points out that the official "designation" of Third landscapes, as heritage "preserves," inevitably subtracts from their status as Third landscape. He also notes, however, that institutional abandonment of the Third landscape does not signify total abandonment: "the non-institutional use of the Third landscape partakes in the oldest of spatial customs" (57). Presumably Clément is alluding to the traditions of the "commons," to sustainable sharing of resources that resists the (il)logic of capitalist extraction. As a "spatial custom" he may be thinking of Lefebvre's "spatial practice,"

---

6 | Barrett Watten sees the "cunning of capitalist unreason, the conditions of its reproduction" in "zones of disuse and unprofitability as particularly motivated ... the negativity of profit as loss" (348). Witness the fate of many of New York City's Lower East Side "pocket gardens" under the Giuliani administration, or the current "millennial" redevelopment of downtown Detroit.

or of DeCerteau's connection of "the practice of the everyday" with "walking rhetorics" and "phatic topoi."

A poetics such as I have outlined, however sketchily, as "entropology," or "thoughts on things in things," attentive to a balance between production and neglect, may be particularly suited to the non-institutional use of the Third landscape Clément calls for. At the very least, students of the Third landscape might attend to how they are *developing* it in their uses of reference and of metaphor. Can the grass share the space between the cracks with our metaphors that so constantly ply the interstices between words and things?

III. In Weeds is the Preservation of the World

> *What is a weed?*
> *A plant whose virtues have not yet been discovered.*
> Ralph Waldo Emerson

In the scale of desirability, opposite threatened species, we find weeds: rabbit, Colorado potato beetle, African mosquito, cactus moth, elm bark beetle, European starling, North American muskrat, cord-grass, giant African land snail, sea lamprey, Chinese mitten crab, zebra mussel, purple loosestrife, pampas grass, buffelgrass, garlic mustard, Asian tamarisk, caulerpa, Africanized honeybee, Argentine ant, Asian long-horned beetle, European gypsy moth, fire ant, bighead carp, northern snakehead, Asian swamp eel, brown tree snake, nutria, house sparrow, Japanese knotweed, marijuana, kudzu, common reed, Norway maple, Russian olive, tree of heaven, ice plant, datura, water hyacinth, giant salvinia, mynas, goat, cane toad, leafy spurge, cat, nile perch, comb jelly, house mouse, flatworm, Amur river clam, mesquite, tumbleweed, red-vented bulbul, gray squirrel, fox, Australian paperbark tree, empress tree, mallard, mosquito fish, water chestnut, giant hogweed …

What is a weed? In the "Weeds" poem of his final completed sequence, *80 Flowers* (a collaboration with Celia Zukofsky, who did the gardening), Louis Zukofsky takes on the question: "Founderous wilding weeds endear paradise/ … smallhead *bluecurls* blue-wool'd *romero* defer-ah/ *bamboo*-such *downyrattlesnake* pact is pubescence/ feed talk bananas great maulin'/ … *goldenrod* solid-day go ponder otter …" (*Complete Short Poetry* 350)[7] *80 Flowers* ties energy up in concentrated knots of allusion: in her book-length reading of the poem, Michele Leggott teases out, over several pages, the John Adams celebration of cultivation, rather than wilderness, condensed into "founderous wilding weeds endear paradise" (*Reading* 304-317). But in addition to condensation, to borrow from Leggott's argument on Zukofsky's "late poetic," the poems are constantly

7 | Is "founderous" (*fundus*) an allusion to Shakespeare's Bottom? On the one hand, weeds "endear" paradise, are anathema to the highly cultivated, metafloristic *80 Flowers*, as contrary to them as "wilding" is to garden (in dear paradise)—where entropy only enters the picture as the reader untangles the intertwined allusions. Indeed, weeds are a form of "bottoming out." (Zukofsky had discovered "founderous" in the *Autobiography* of John Adams—as what causes something to founder.) On the other hand, they have their own wild needs that can only *endure* paradise. It may even be the case that "wildings," cultivars found in the wild, are like an extension of paradise beyond the garden walls.

feeding, and being fed by, "contingencies' flowers"—"those places where one voice had been, or seemed to have been, listening to another" (55). The aureate music inside these lines emerges, via phonetic transliteration (the "homophonic translation" method Louis and Celia Zukofsky deployed in their Catullus) of the Latinate terms for some of the "weeds" they explore: *bambusa* (bamboo) in *"bamboo*-such," *Epicactus pubescens* (downy rattlesnake plantain) in *"rattlesnake* pact is pubescence," *Solidago* (goldenrod) in "solid-day go," *Ipomoea pandurata* (bindweed) in "ponder otter."

If condensation is the centripetal force of these poems, gathered into five words per line (five being the most common number of petals in flowers) and eight lines per poem, the poems flee their centers on contingencies: sonic horizons that accumulate a persistent sound of history (Leggott 56). Thus *pandurata* ("ponder otter") leads to *pandura*, a three-stringed musical instrument invented by the god Pan, which Leggott speculates may have suggested "otter," via that animal's Latin name, *Lutra: "goldenrod* solid-day go ponder otter." The line may offer a Thoreauvian injunction to go to the pond when goldenrod flowers and the bindweed runs, these solid days of July and August, to ponder the otter: "How retired an otter manages to live! He grows to be four feet long without any mortal getting a glimpse of him" (*Journal*, 30 Jan. 1854). Or it may be something else.

To read *80 Flowers*, by ear as well as by eyes and mind, with books and reference works at hand, is to enjoy a rhythm of expansion and contraction—pursuing rhizomatic contingencies of meaning, away from any evident center, *and* returning to the formal reproduction of meanings condensed into the seeds of words: entropic situations that hold themselves together. For the Zukofskys, "weeds dress earth" (in "Wild Geranium") as much as any human flowers garb gardens: Louis and Celia could hardly in good faith ignore the unruly, insubordinate, self-willed nature of these "wildings." Grasses, edibles and medicinals contribute to this poetry of knowledge. Thus a harvest of weeds, "ascending *tansy field-bindweed lady's-orchid-slipper* foison," makes for one of the pleasures of *80 Flowers*. Such pleasure and knowledge is especially concentrated in the weedy cluster of flowers halfway through the sequence, including Queen Anne's Lace ("topturfy gimp fiery oes eyes"), Chicory, and Dandelion ("madding sun mixen seeded rebus") (*Complete Short Poetry* 331, 339-340).

According to the Dictionary (American Heritage, 3rd Edition), a weed is "a plant considered undesirable, unattractive, or troublesome, especially one growing where it is not wanted, as in a garden." Meaning number three is "the leaves or stems of a plant as distinguished from the seeds." The word appears to be derived from the Old English *weod*, herb, grass, weed. Adventitious and asexual, weeds such as grass reproduce rhizomatically, through leaves and stems (and tubers) not seeds, bypassing a centralized reproductive system accessible to the breeder's shaping hands. Obviously it is the notion of "undesirability" that has permitted extending the designation to species other than plants. Weeds are nature ungirded, beyond the germ and girth of the gardener's yard—the negation of enclosure (see the family of words clustering around the Indo-European root *gher*). From the standpoint of weeds, even "wilderness areas" are a type of human gardening.

But another definition of weed is as a specialist of disturbed areas, or as the parasite on an ecosystem's more dominant species, a scavenger on the leavings of civilization. Here weeds would seem to be disliked precisely because of their supposed dependency on us; in their opportunism they are too much like us, and so cannot teach us about being "wild and free." Wherever you find humans, pigeons and mice and rats and cockroaches and purple loosestrife are not far behind: they are our "footprints," the ubiquitous trace of our heavy touch, registering ecological imbalance.

From an ecological standpoint, however, weeds are a necessary part of the healing process. They are the first species to wager their genes in a disturbed area—the pioneers. How ironic to shun them for supposed "dependency." It may be the summit of arrogance to look on these species we are associated with only as passive followers, rather than, in the evolutionary scheme of things, seeing ourselves as the followers, the helpers, the hosts.[8] In any case, styling weeds after our domestic relationships blinds (and binds) us to their nature.

What if the wild, rather than offering a logocentric origin for human being, were simply where humans are not? Not the birthplace of our species or the final frontier, where humans came from or

---

8 | Ethnobotanists have speculated that our somewhat mysterious relationship with psychotropic plants and fungi may be an instance of coevolutionary adaptation: we get high and the weed gets a free ride. The same may go for some edible plants (see Gary Nabhan, "Sandfood" in *Gathering the Desert*). While our relatively recent arrival on the evolutionary timeline makes this unlikely—it is more likely insects played a role in the evolution of alkaloids in vascular plants and fungi—we cannot deny that weeds get a lot out of us.

where we are are heading, but where humans are not (or are no longer). More and more, the "wild" flourishes in places where humans have been—in abandoned, "post-human" places.[9]

There are places where people are not and there are times when people are not: one might speak, in regards to cities, of the "wilderness" of the night, a time dominated by the life of feral creatures and their associates:

> Trees, that spin their seeds on inhuman looms. Night flowers
> violated by the long tongues of bats. Perfumes, orchestrated
> rivers inscribed on the wings of moths.
> A host of false moons,
>   the outskirts of the city.
>   (Christopher Dewdney, *Predators of the Adoration* 35)

The wild might be right under our noses: more likely there, than in designated "wilderness areas." I first met the Hooded Mersanger not in the "back of the beyond" but along a quiet stretch of a relatively tame river, one that only eight years ago was so polluted one wouldn't swim there. Paradoxically, the window hiding me from the merganser allowed me to see it.

Thoreau says that "Life consists with wildness. The most alive is the wildest. Not yet subdued to man, its presence refreshes him." (As

---

9 | Taking "wildness" as distinct from "wilderness," which is more narrowly defined by its ability to sustain a maximal range of trophic levels, all the way up to the big, man-eating predators. Grizzlies, cougars and wolves are so managed, tagged and radio collared, that ironically they may be less "wild" than cockroaches—if by "wild" we mean to indicate a degree of autonomy.

one meaning of "wild," the OED has "Not under, or not submitting to, control ... unruly, insubordinate, wayward, self-willed.") Thoreau also connects the "Wild" with inexorable and manifest colonial destiny: "The West of which I speak is but another name for the Wild; and what I have been preparing to say is, that in Wildness is the preservation of the world. Every tree sends forth its fibres in search of the Wild" ("Walking" 206-207). The wild is space, freedom, suitable conditions for growth. It impels the migration Olson writes of, the "pursuit by animals, plants & men of a suitable/ —and gods as well—& preferable/ environment."

Both writers acknowledge the predatory, colonizing nature of life itself: life sends forth its fibres in search of the most alive. We seldom think of the creatures that come to devour us in the night—as in Christopher Dewdney's chant of the primitive sublime:

> Because it is a huge and silent underwater predator.
> Because it is huge and primitive.
> Because it cruises, hovering, long snouted crocodilian.
> Because it is primitive.
>
> ("Grid Erectile," *The Natural History* 88)

Or as in—at the other end of the spectrum—Annie Dillard's famous description of a frog being eaten by a giant water bug (5-7).

By turns index of autonomous wildness and index of an all-too-human landscape, weeds embody the contradictions in our relationship to "nature." As the preferred habitat of weeds, the Third landscape, like Olmsted's unkempt Central Park in the 1970s for

Robert Smithson, is a "carrier of the unexpected and of contradiction" ("Frederick Law Olmsted and the Dialectical Landscape" 119). Rather than the First landscapes of pastoral fantasy, this landscape of weeds seems an appropriate site for the entropology of a poetics radically, and rhizomatically, open to the flowers of contingency.

IV. POETRIES OF THE THIRD LANDSCAPE

Consider boundaries as a thickness rather than a line.
GILLES CLÉMENT

In the city of brotherly love, the purple, sweet blossoms of the royal paulownia, or empress tree, festoon a mile-long stretch of fenced-off viaduct, a wild oasis suspended above the decaying urban core (an expressway border vacuum just opposite Chinatown): "never to alight till nations sue for peace seedpods for excelsior stuffing crates of cathay porcelain castaways in shiphold broadcast over foreign soils" (John Perlman, "ROYAL PAULOWNIA (Paulownia tomentosa) Along the Hudson," n.p.). Perlman's prose poem alludes to the "non-native" status of these fast-growing trees, whose seed pods came over as packing for Chinese porcelain. Traditionally, Chinese families plant an empress tree at the birth of a daughter, to be harvested for dowry furniture when she is married. Paulownia trees currently enjoy a strong market in Japan. Wherever we find plants we find culture: the empress trees seem to have known where they were going, when they chose this abandoned railway bed convenient to Chinatown. A recent visit to the site uncovered evidence of selective cutting—perhaps some kind of "non-institutional use."

Peter Larkin's many-minded phenomenology of trees from the perspective of leaves, *Leaves of Field*, offers an astonishing entropology in its up-ending of grammatical (and arboreal) hierarchy, as if language were to be seen from the point of view of its words. The section of the book titled Open Woods, which moves in three parts from "Urban Woods" through "Ancient Woods" to "Opening Woods," ends with a meditation in prose and in verse on the Third landscape of secondary woodland (87-88). Reading Larkin is like guessing topography from canopy, and entails inventing a whole new method. Here the trunks of sentences seem to hang from their qualifying canopies, grammatical subjects depend on their predicates: "The composing process of secondary woodland *does* overstay when it rewrites the profile of pre-clearance vegetation" (81).

Illustration 4 | Reading Viaduct, Philadelphia, photo © J. Skinner

It is a sentence diagram in reverse: the mind gets a purchase on "secondary woodland" and "pre-clearance vegetation," but must speculate on the central predication, "the composing process [overstays]," even with the qualification, "when it rewrites the profile." What is a composing process, what does it have to do with staying or moving on—or with the overhanging we hear in 'overstay'—and what is a vegetation profile? In the next sentence, just where we expect predication to develop and narrow the meaning, it leafs out through butted appositions: "Being uneasily ajar is revision slighting climax of the arena: arena otherwise not patient with any cut-through not itself but a porch-approximation of horizons" (81).

Naming of unfamiliar structures and processes adds layers to predications that would feel familiar were the phrases more sequential (as if we were reading Paul Celan in the language of woodlots). Scale is almost impossible to judge, so that one doesn't yet have the frame or trunks of an overview. In its obdurate metaphrase language reaches for a space of time outstripping imagination, as seeds "scatter their seams of remission over disjunct successions, the trans-massive evanishment" (76). "Disjunct successions" entails a *very* long time (with multiple disturbances and returns to climax), while "evanishment" seems to imply an event more instantaneous: in the meantime, words, phrases and sentences await exploring.

We learn that Third landscape is not simply topographical, nor a matter of contiguous extension. We can find Third landscape, as an instance of "opening," in the midst of all woods: not extension but "brush gap insertions which woods strikingly put *below* canopy level: laterals not polar to verticals but winding between masts among the unreleasable poles of shelter" (87-88). "Land," originally a subdivision of a field, is measure of ground, while "scape" relates to sheaf, a collection of similar things: thus "landscape," a collection of lands, exceeds the aestheticized sense of "an expanse of scenery that can be seen in a single view" (Jackson 6-7). According to J.B. Jackson, landscape is "a space deliberately created to speed up or slow down the process of nature" (8). But temporalities of "nature" are not themselves uniform, nor can creation emerge from outside of "nature." Clément notes that, in successional landscapes, species come to occupy fragments of *time*, as much as or more than fragments of space (see Clément, "Le jardin comme index planétaire," in Roger 394). For Larkin, landscape is not so much a thing as a process, a kind of prosody marked by opening (which the prose poem enacts through clearings of verse) and by colonizing, to a rhythm not necessarily human. (The rhythm of Open Woods evokes the Japanese haibun's alternations of prose and haiku verse). "The highly open can never be *lightly* wooded" (93). It is a process whose articulations weedily colonize the poet-forester's abandoned grammars.

The Nature Conservancy pamphlet, *America's Least Wanted: Alien Species' Invasions of U.S. Ecosystems*, exemplifies the hysteria regarding "invasive" species:

> An invasion is under way that is undermining our nation's economy and endangering our most precious natural treasures. The intruders are alien species—non-native plants and animals introduced into this country either intentionally or by accident. Attention to the problem of alien, or exotic, species often centers on their costs to agriculture, ranching, forestry, and industry. The price they exact on the nation's forests, grasslands, and waterways, however, is at least as great. (1)

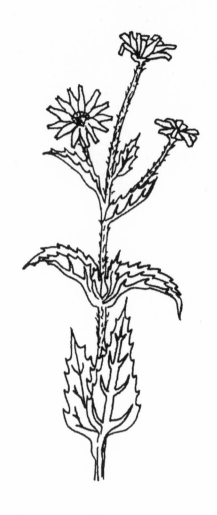

Heliopsis helianthoides

FALSE SUNFLOWER

Illustration 5 | James Thomas Stevens, "A Half-Breed's Guide to the Use of
Native Plants," *Combing the Snakes from His Hair* (24). Image used by
permission of the author.

Obviously, this language participates in the rhetorical hyperbole meant to catalyze political change. From a cultural standpoint, it is troubling language, indeed (and ironic to hear, coming from the heart of imperial America). Clément, who claims that movement, as opposed to fixity, is the nature of botanical species (see his *Éloge des vagabondes*), reads into such rhetoric, besides xenophobia, an unwillingness to think on the global scale. With Meyer, he urges that we abandon the fetishization of endemic species (many doomed to relictual status) and begin to think in terms of behaviors and functions, planetary ecosystem "services." ("What would happen/ if there were a terrific shortage of goldenrod/ in the world," Grace Paley wonders ["Thetford Poems" in *New and Collected Poems* 61]).

James Thomas Stevens' "A Half-Breed's Guide to the Use of Native Plants" negotiates settled-unsettled survival strategies, of yet not of the landscape: his Scurfy Peas that "keep shallow roots and break from base./ Dispersing in danger,/ to flee infestation." Or the False Sunflower, with a "forked tongue/ a fertile forked pistil.// Take note of his tendency to colonize" (25). The play with diagrams, Latin binomials, and overall détournement of the field guide format, disperses the tilt of figuration, with its romantic and erotic subtext.

The poems seem wary of colonizing their referent, looking to plants of the Midwest prairie, "for a key to surviving this new *old world*—a world that half my blood fought to obtain and the other half struggled to hold" (5). Stevens' series plays ironically with the frame of the "field guide," which is a genre for "going native," but also a taxonomic key

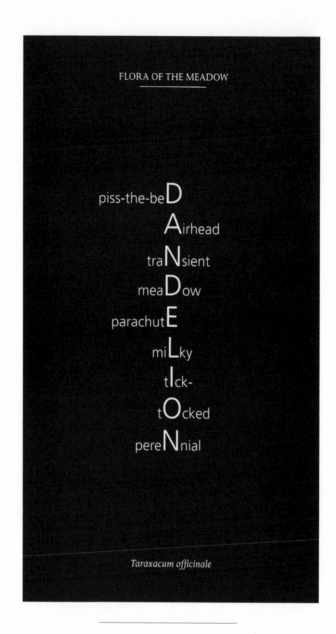

FLORA OF THE MEADOW

piss-the-beD
Airhead
traNsient
meaDow
parachutE
miLky
tIck-
tOcked
pereNnial

Taraxacum officinale

Illustration 6 | DANDELION Mesostic, Ken Cockburn, *Mesostic Herbarium*,
ed. Alec Finlay (n.p.) Image used by permission of the author.

that can serve a shallow sense of ownership. For Stevens, as for Roger Williams, a "key to the language of America" fits no door between self and other—opening, rather, onto self-reflection and complex zones of negotiation. Here specific rather than token knowledge, use rather than possession, offer the keys to survival.

The Mesostic Herbarium curated by Alec Finlay, "a phytological anthology by various amateurs of botany being a partial heterodox collection of mesostic poems on the names of flora arranged according to habitat" founds the movement in arts and letters Finlay cheekily dubs "petalisme" (n.p.). There is some exploration of Third landscape (as places of succession, transition, invasion) with entries on Flora of the Meadow, Flora of the Hedgerow, Flora of the Ashes, Exotics, and so on. It is a wonderful instance of entropology as the play between letter, name and properties leafs out with the reading eye down the page:

The letters in the name, turned on its axis, become "something physical that generates ideas"—with their aleatory suggestions, varied positioning of words along the stem, and vertical display of what Anne Carson has called "alphabetic edge," that pictorial outline of the invisible edges of sound (*Eros the Bittersweet* 53-61). Additionally, the "concrete" dimension of the work foregrounds the fact that writing takes place in space. The discursive articulation of the poem is governed by the contingent relations of marks left over from the economies taking them up as phonetic signs. Letters draw attention to the eloquence of what they are not. It is an ambient poetry that could easily become setting, in its own right, for a field of dandelions—recalling the garden works of Finlay's father, who might have set these poems outside, in glass, stone or wood.

Not all "weeds" are plants: consider the *"ELECTRIC CONTORTIONS"* of Maggie O'Sullivan's "Starlings": "Tipsy Bobbles, Dowdy/ wander. Halt upon// grinned jeers, gin's note." Considered as pests in America ever since they escaped Central Park—where they were introduced from England—starlings may disappoint their Shakespearean legacy, but as sound "the pitch meander ears// tune me gold/ Dulthie pods." As sight, they are "Ochre harled" ("Kinship with Animals," *In the House of the Shaman* 41). Charles Bernstein has noted the "visceral gesture" here, what he calls "colliderings": "not an idea of the body made concrete but a seismographic incarnation of language as organ-response to the minute, shifting interactive sum of place as tectonic, temporality as

> **grinned jeers, gin's note**
> **someone's in the leading**
> **of small & the pitch meander ears**
>
> **tune me gold**
> **Dulthie pods,**
>
> **Lipper**
> **"Ochre harled**
>
> ***ELECTRIC***
>
> ***CONTORTIONS —***

Illustration 7 | "Starlings," Maggie O'Sullivan, *In the House of the Shaman* (41).

temperament, self is as self does." O'Sullivan's poems "lend themselves to recitation, while resisting thematization" ("O'Sullivan's Medleyed Verse" 158). To carry out the instructions fixed on the page is a transformative way of discovering one's objective nature: as the breath, the tongue and lips, performing "Dulthie pods," undergo "kinship with animals."

This kind of listening-by-saying, "high up at the back of the palate"— "Ear-loads I Sing!"—seeks "ORigins/ ENtrances" of language, rather than fixations of similitude: "the Materiality of language: its actual contractions & expansions, potentialities, prolongments, assemblages—the acoustic, visual, oral & sculptural qualities within the physical: intervals between; in & beside." It is impossible to sing the poems and not in some sense *become* their matter, to get the "Tipsy Bobbles" as one sings "gin's note," in what O'Sullivan calls "a Mattering of Materials" ("Riverrunning (Realisations," *Palace of Reptiles* 61, 64). In addition to the changes of font, part of the physical here is the page, in its "intervals between" often an active part of the composition rather than neutral support. It is one of the "things" in which O'Sullivan pursues her "thoughts on things."

O'Sullivan's "books" emerged from her "bookworks" and "assemblages"—from her concern, after "shaman" artists Kurt Schwitters and Joseph Beuys, for "the retrieval of potentials within materials" (67).[10] Her starlings are promiscuous creatures, shape-

---

10 | O'Sullivan singles out Schwitters for his "superb use of the UN—the NON and the LESS—THE UNREGARDED, the found, the cast-offs, the dismembered materials." (67)

shifting minglers, not taxonomic isolates slated for preservation or extinction. With them O'Sullivan moves, "plundering, blundering, sounding" over the cast-off materials of English (including retrievals from Joyce's own word hoard in *Finnegan's Wake*), her "electric contortions" colonizing the places of dialect abandoned by "literature" (62). The landscape her assemblages engage is accordingly one of "collidering" and transformation rather than separation and preservation, a weedy, cosmopolitan place.

One might wonder whether the participation of other species is not more invoked than assured here. Can "thoughts on things" really occur "in things" by way of much more than a kind of ventriloquism? It was perhaps an attempt to push the possibilities, in the face of such skepticism, that led to my collaboration with Julie Patton, some hungry slugs, fallen leaves, and a silicone information-processing machine, in the cybertext "Slug Art" (*ecopoetics* 01). (I call it a "cyber" text in Donna Haraway's sense of machine-animal-human hybrid, not as computer-based writing, but in reference to a scanner, and Photoshop and QuarkXPress running on a Macintosh computer, helping me to align Patton's marks with the slugs' tracery.) Attention to "qualities within the physical," to "intervals between" things, becomes "performance as space," or "a) art of a body moving in b) the space in between" (87). Between the petals of the rose of the world move invertebrates; just as the word "slug" itself vibrates, in Patton's writing, between the registers of garden, print shop, and street.

The Third landscape, in the end, may be little more than this in-between space, this interstitial zone, found everywhere life is found

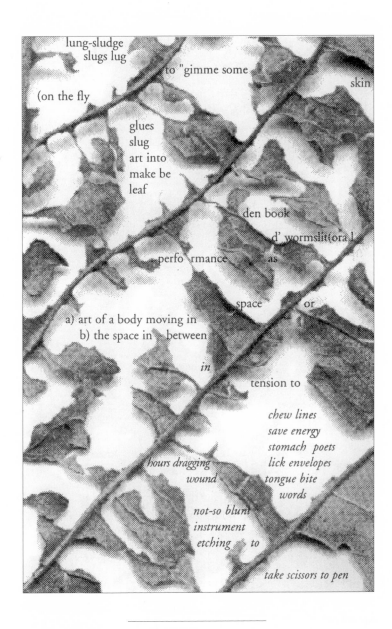

Illustration 8 | "Slug Art," Julie Patton, *ecopoetics 01* (87). Image used by permission of the author.

and, indeed, permitting further life. The specialists of such a zone, the entropologists or decay-givers, are also species of communication, good at shape-shifting, crossing borders, and sliding in-between. For poets to sing with them may entail little more than attending closely to what poets already do well. It is perfectly natural for a poet as attuned to the present moment of writing as Joanne Kyger to notice a grey squirrel "Descending nose down tall eucalyptus," and to migrate, after squirrel and eucalyptus, toward generational and hemispheric thoughts:

> It's Allen Ginsberg's medicine-tree squirrel
> followed me here from Boulder's Naropa campus

> Here to eat the neighbor's introduced Mexican oak
>   acorns from Chamula in Chiapas
>   where they boycotted the vote
> in recent election defying the ruling PRI
>   party which holds power by deception
>   repression & fraud. (143)

Along with attempting poems of merganser encounters—poems that hopefully spiral into an entropological singing with human language and the other species, and also spiral out to the world of that species' migration, and thus into a kind of saturation job on the biome-paths of that migration, as it intersects with our own global journeys—let us bring poetry to a renewal of the ancient customs of the Third landscape. This is the act of resistance poetry, as poetry, can offer to the institutionalized profit-as-loss of capital, a kind of attention that can lead to critically informed politics and modes of social organization. Only poetry can attend to the untended *as* the untended, essentially leaving it alone—"thoughts on things" without what Louis Zukofsky called the "predatory intent" of predication (*Prepositions* 16). Let's use poetry's care of language to strike the word "weed" from our vocabulary and begin to attend to *all* the species we are binding into our planetary future, with whom we *want* to travel into the future, even Ofelia Zepeda's tumbleweeds that "roll early into the village dance,/ semi-invited guests" ("People on Wayward Journeys (Russian Thistle, Russian Tumbleweed)" 58).

Then Vera stopped at the flower called fireweed ...

                                      ... Still we are the gardeners
of this world and often talk about giving wildness

its chance it's I who cut the field too late too
early right on time and therefore out of the earth which
is a darkness of timed seed and waiting root the sunlight

chose vervain jewel weed boneset just beyond
our woodchuck-argued garden a great nation of ants
has lived for fifteen years in a high sandy anthill
which I honor with looking and looking and never disrupt
(nor have I learned their lesson of stubborn industry)
they ask nothing except to be not bothered and I personally

agree (Grace Paley 64-65)

In apocalyptic thinking, the Third landscape signifies the end of biodiversity and an all-too-human future (see David Quammen, "Planet of Weeds"). But it also signifies beginning, the space where new species may be invented. Let's influence the production of this space.

Kamau Brathwaite's "Namsetoura" documents the delicate balance and the often agonizing struggle of a poet who literally has taken up residence in the Third landscape. His efforts to save his CowPastor from the airport expansion in Barbados, to make the State acknowledge poetry's non-institutional use of this abandoned land, have become a poem, or species-making species of making, in their own right:

> From what far cost of Africa to this brown strip
> of pasture on this coral limestone ridge
> cast up some three miles from the burning sea
>
> the grave
>
> hidden w/in the clump of prickly man
> -peabe. read cordea trees
> & countless clammacherry leaves
>
> the spider warn me of her entry

(118)

A major portion of the research for this essay was conducted on a fellowship with the Center for Humanities at Temple University (CHAT). Thanks are due to Richard Immerman, Jena Osman, and others at CHAT who supported this work.

WORKS CITED

Ak'abal, Humberto. "Xirixitem Chikop." Reading and talk for Dennis Tedlock's Poetics of the Americas seminar at SUNY Buffalo. 9 Oct. 2002. Minidisc. Collection of the author.

America's Least Wanted: Alien Species Invasions of U.S. Ecosystems. The Nature Conservancy, 1996.

Bernstein, Charles. "Colliderings: Maggie O'Sullivan's Medleyed Verse". *ecopoetics 04/05* (2005): 157-160.

Brathwaite, Kamau. *Born to Slow Horses.* Middletown, CT: Wesleyan UP, 2005.

Carson, Anne. *Eros the Bittersweet.* Princeton, NJ: Princeton UP, 1986.

Clément, Gilles. *Manifeste du tiers paysage.* Paris, France: Éditions Sujet/Objet, 2004.

Creeley, Robert. *Collected Essays.* Berkeley, CA: U of California P, 1989.

de Certeau, Michel. *The Practice of Everyday Life.* Trans. Steven F. Rendall. Berkeley, CA: U of California P, 1984.

Dewdney, Christopher. *The Natural History.* Toronto, CA: ECW P, 2002.

—. *Predators of the Adoration: Selected Poems 1972-82.* Toronto, CA: McClelland and Stewart, 1983.

ecopoetics 01 (2001) Ed. Jonathan Skinner. <http://www.ecopoetics.org>

Emerson, Ralph Waldo. "The Fortune of the Republic." Boston: Houghton, Osgood, 1878.

Faranda, Lisa Pater, ed. *"Between Your House and Mine": The Letters of Lorine Niedecker to Cid Corman, 1960 to 1970.* Durham, NC: Duke UP, 1986.

Feld, Steven. "From Ethnomusicology to Echo-Muse-Ecology: Reading R. Murray Schafer in the Papua New Guinea Rainforest." *The Soundscape Newsletter,* number 08, June, 1994: 12-13. <http://interact.uoregon.edu/Medialit/wfae/library/newsletter/SNL8.PDF>.

Jackson, John Brinckerhoff. *Discovering the Vernacular Landscape.* New Haven, CT: Yale UP, 1984.

Kyger, Joanne. *Again: Poems 1989-2000.* Albuquerque, NM: La Alameda P, 2001.

Larkin, Peter. *Leaves of Field.* Exeter, UK: Shearsman Books, 2006.

Lefebvre, Henri. *The Production of Space.* Trans. Donald Nicholson-Smith. Oxford, UK: Blackwell Publishing, 1991.

Leggott, Michele J. *Reading Zukofsky's* 80 Flowers. Baltimore, MD: The Johns
    Hopkins UP, 1989.

Leibniz, G.W. *Philosophical Essays.* Indianapolis: Hackett, 1989.

Lévi-Strauss, Claude. *Tristes Tropiques.* Trans. John and Doreen Weightman. New
    York, NY: Penguin, 1973 (1955).

Lomolino, Mark V., Dov F. Sax, and James H. Brown, eds. *Foundations of
    Biogeography.* Chicago, IL: U of Chicago P, 2004.

Meyer, Stephen M. *The End of the Wild.* Boston, MA: Boston Review Books, 2006.

Nabhan, Gary. *Gathering the Desert.* Tucson, AZ: U of Arizona P, 1985.

Niedecker, Lorine. *Collected Works.* Ed. Jenny Penberthy. Berkeley, CA: U of
    California P, 2002.

Olson, Charles. *Collected Prose.* Ed. Donald Allen and Benjamin Friedlander.
    Berkeley, CA: U of California P, 1997.

—. *The Maximus Poems.* Berkeley, CA: U of California P, 1983.

O'Sullivan, Maggie. *In the House of the Shaman.* London, UK: Reality Street, 1993.

—. *Palace of Reptiles.* Toronto, CA: The Gig, 2003.

Paley, Grace. *New and Collected Poems.* Gardiner, ME: Tilbury House, 1992.

Patton, Julie. "Slug Art." *ecopoetics* 01 (2001): 86-89.

Perlman, John. *The Natural History of Trees.* Bedford, MA: Potes & Poets P, 2003.

Quammen, David. "Planet of Weeds" *Harper's.* Oct. 1998: 57-69.

Roberson, Ed. *City Eclogues.* Atelos 23 (2006).

Robertson, Lisa. *Occasional Work and Seven Walks from the Office for Soft Architecture.*
    Astoria, OR: Clear Cut P, 2003.

Roger, Alain, ed. *La Théorie du Paysage en France (1974-1994).* Seyssel, France:
    Editions Champ Vallon, 1995.

Smithson, Robert. *The Collected Writings.* Ed. Jack Flam. Berkeley, CA: University of
    California Press, 1996.

Stevens, James Thomas. *Combing the Snakes from His Hair.* East Lansing, MI:
    Michigan State UP, 2002.

Thoreau, Henry David. "Walking." *This Incomperable Lande: A Book of American
    Nature Writing.* Ed. Thomas Lyon. Boston, MA: Houghton Mifflin, 1989:
    194-220.

—. *The Journal of Henry D. Thoreau.* New York, NY: Dover, 1962.

Vicuña, Cecilia. *Unravelling Words & the Weaving of Water.* Saint Paul, MN: Graywolf P, 1992.

Watten, Barrett. *The Constructivist Moment: From Material Text to Cultural Poetics.* Middletown, CT: Wesleyan UP, 2003.

Weiss, Kenneth R., and McFarling, Usha Lee. "Altered Oceans." *Los Angeles Times.* 2 Aug. 2006. 25 Aug. 2007 <http://www.latimes.com/news/local/oceans/la-oceans-series,0,7842752.special>.

Williams, Raymond. *Problems in Materialism and Culture: Selected Essays.* London, UK: Verso, 1980.

Williams, Terry Tempest. *Refuge: An Unnatural History of Family and Place.* New York, NY: Pantheon, 1991.

Williams, William Carlos. *Paterson.* New York, NY: New Directions, 1963.

Zepeda, Ofelia. *Ocean Power: Poems from the Desert.* Tucson, AZ: U of Arizona P, 1995.

Zukofsky, Louis. *Complete Short Poetry.* Baltimore, MD: The Johns Hopkins UP, 1991.

—. *Prepositions.* Hanover, NH: Wesleyan UP, 2000.

Fully From, All Scarce To

—— PETER LARKIN ——

Whether my work is strictly a variety of ecopoetry I can't say, but I'm certain it does impinge on things ecological. A concern for landscape is something looser and more mediate than a focus on the natural or non-human world as such, and my own writing quite directly descends from a tradition of loco-descriptive poetry, not to speak of Romantic pastoral naturalism. To the extent a compromised landscape is the "field" in which my sense of ecological dynamics has to operate though, there is considerable overlap, but also some tension. Landscape is also the (desiring) terrain across which questions of technology and geopolitics arise, which for me are refracted compulsively in the profile of the forest plantation: as arboreal configuration, industrial production. It is also the nostalgic trace of shelter or nurture, not where we live. But from the pain of home arises a responsibility of responding to what belongs alongside us.

I suppose I'm equally concerned with the phenomenology of landscape, or with an even looser landscape allegory, where notions of surface and depth, openness or closure, voluminosity and horizon, are fatefully implicated, together with a prevailing mythos of the horizontal and the vertical, a possible neighboring between infinite finitudes and an infinity for the finite.

I like to write about trees and plantations, and sometimes appear to readers to be doing that even when not. Neither *Seek Source Bid Sink* (1995) nor *Rings Resting the Circuit* (2004) relates to trees, but the earlier title, together with *Sprout Near Severing Close* (2004), are the closest I have come to working over specific ecological materials. During the past 15 years, I've been much taken with the notion of scarcity. This isn't so much a concept for me as a sourceful form of poetic thinking, one that arises from the word itself as it shifts from context to context. The term seems to bring together a number of key concerns, suggesting itself as both a way of addressing a disquiet and launching a critique, a mode of speculative consolation or contemplative discovery. It came about in an odd but highly concrete way. At work I was leafing through a publisher's catalogue and came across a title called *Social Philosophy and Ecological Scarcity* (by Keekok Lee, 1989) which, together with the blurb, set a chain of new (to me) thoughts. The idea of scarcity struck me as a way for poetry to offset the prevailing climate of desertion and absence and go toward the direction of a more problematic though rewarding sense of what we mean by the givenness of the natural world, of our origins within it. I was set off along a train of thought where I came to feel that our relation to what we are born into, or what absolutely precedes us in a mode of attraction and desire is indeed wholly given, nothing is held back, from an ethical, aesthetic, and spiritual standpoint; however, this given is not an elemental plenitude, but partakes of a complex assailing scarcity. We find ourselves called to mediate both the weak margins and potent horizons of a world that will always overtake us and which will always have started from where we cannot know ourselves. When the book I had seen eventually came out I found it less inspiring than I had hoped, but by then I had discovered Rufie Hueting's *New Scarcity and Economic Growth* (1980) and was to go on to read William Ophuls' *Ecology and the Politics of Scarcity Revisited* (1992) and Nicholas Xenos' *Scarcity and Modernity* (1989).

More often than not the ecological is presented in a postmodern context as a process of exemplary or renovatory turbulence, or what Eric Wilson in his study *Romantic Turbulence* (2000) calls (after Deleuze) a "chaosmic" ecology. This might be characterized as a defensive heterogeneity or vigilant counteranthropocentrism. Across this, my own work has tried (in a rather speculative and indirect way) to investigate possible paths and grounds of nurture, of shelter, or of aspirational belonging in which the relative notions of internal poverty and distance are also important. One great dread of the postmodern is the threat of closure, but it may be we need a more relative sense of the "closural," free to operate rather like the way in which the idea of the originary modifies our approach to any absolute origin. Luce Irigaray's writings have now familiarized us with the idea of the "half-open" and with the accompanying sense of filled rather than empty gaps. I've found in the writings of Michel Serres something equally nuanced and riskily ecological, opposing any unblinking idea of linear progression with a more complex understanding of the various "moods" (as one might say) of motion. Serres substitutes the idea of the homeorhetic (a stability of flow or circulation) as a better term than any reductive idea of the homeostatic within living self-regulating systems or bodies. He avoids a brittle unilinear innovation within which acceleration is often predatory of any more sustainable growth. And rather than just flow, he directs us to percolation, particularly in terms of the nature of time. Thus sudden crises or explosions neighbor periods of stagnation; burdensome or foolish regressions equally contribute to a fabric of rigorous linkage and sudden acceleration, all part of what he calls the intimacy of soul, no less present in the contour of a weather-front as in the pattern of a delta, or, I would add, in the un-dislocatory differentia of a branch (Serres, 1997; Conley, 1997).

For me this maps onto a preoccupation with "site," a setting itself compounded by the oscillations that make up the places we know, but also of those more problematic margins and creases inflecting the distance of domains we can't approach in the same way, not to speak of those obstructive microtextures of environment which come between us even before we identify with any sense of locality. How is a place stretched and folded, how is it ribbed and reinforced (lacking which it cannot project any horizon)? How does flexibility work within and around moments of local (or finitely vertical) rigidity? This is particularly relevant while trying to write about the architecture or variable tectonics of trees, themselves a compound of living and dead tissue. What is a threshold when encountering limit? How do apparently non-progressive links internalize or transfer differently a sort of filter that mediates or "digests" (i.e. transformatively re-absorbs) some of the deferrals and dissipations of threshold? Can the sublime abandonments of dissemination be partially countered by scarcer, more vulnerable sites of receptivity whose capacity for nurture will only ever have a minority effect? Our sense of flow needs to include coprimordial obstructions to flow, as well as the capacity of those obstructions to become part of a granulation which also configures, so that percolation is differentiated as much by carrying along with it elements enigmatically less than any pure process as the fragmentary traces of its own lining or enframing (Larkin, 1999, p. 173). It is this latter quality that may lead to margins, ecotones, horizons. At the level of writing, the importance of texture as distinct from text is signaled: the relative density or looseness of the weave is itself an "environment" grounding what sort of a figuring nexus a literary work can become.

Also helpful to me has been the writing of Robert Pogue Harrison and Edward S. Casey. In his book *Forests: the Shadow of Civilization* (1992), Harrison develops the idea of the "provincial," which is not a literally nostalgic periphery so much as a locus where human self-abstraction from the given world remains bound to the always surrounding, never circumscribed terrain from which it has drawn itself away. Such provinces are not so much dense fringes as primordial fragments at once opaque to our gaze, but persistently attached to what we take for the demarcations of our world. Casey, in books like *Getting Back into Place* (1993) and *The Fate of Place* (1997), plus many fascinating articles, has produced a rich phenomenology of the sensings of place, arguing that horizon "affords" depth as the outermost, circumambient edge of any givenness that can also offer a situatedness. Connected with this notion of horizon is for me a poetics of offering, of dedication.

The production surplus that sustains but also puts at risk a world of corporate capital carries with it a priority for product innovation as a means of the survival of the same, and this can leak into a generalized sense of accelerative postmodern cultural innovation, where "resistance" slips easily to the fore of other transmissible commodities. Paul Virilio, with his insight into the nature of virtuality as immobilism and his belief that acceleration and growth are often at opposite poles, has also grounded my sense of the importance of scarcity as a strategy. Scarcity is not stasis, as it is always in excess of any self-sufficient frugality, though it does not undermine such a basic economic discipline as that. Rather, scarcity resists modernity's sense of permanent climax and reverts to an ecological perception of the postclimactic, whereby urbanization itself is not definitive, but has to ride the geology and climate of a much deeper world it would be the articulated surface of (Davis, 2002). Being strategically "less" than these things, scarcity reaches out toward a horizon of desire that contextualizes consummation within a sense of hope and anticipation, at once immediate and remote, and touches on a theme in spirituality that the fifth-century monk John Cassian called "grand poverty." Scarcity also carries with it a sensation of the precarious: that the human, so adaptable and open to transformation on a productive level, depends in fact on a very delicate niche of interaction with the natural world, which is a world retaining the initiative of any subsequent human possibility and meaning (Larkin, 2000, p. 364). When it comes to spiritual-izing our capacity to be in this world, our window or interface is the merest chink, but it's through such a narrow defile, a startling glimpse between the enfilades of trees, that all genuinely rare an-swerability, the glade of participation, comes.

WORKS CITED

Conley, Verena A. *Ecopolitics: the Environment in Poststructuralist Thought.* London: Routledge, 1997.

Davis, Mike. *Dead Cities: a Natural History.* New York: New Press, 2002.

Larkin, Peter. "Innovation Contra Acceleration." *Boundary 2* 26.1, 1999, pp. 169-74.

Larkin, Peter. "Relations of Scarcity: Ecology and Eschatology in 'The Ruined Cottage,'" *Studies in Romanticism* 39, 2000, pp. 347-364.

Serres, Michel. "Science and the Humanities: the Case of Turner." *Sub/Stance* 83: 15, 1997.

This piece was written as a contribution to "Poetry Environments: an Ecopoetics Roundtable," organized and chaired by Jonathan Skinner for the conference on Contemporary Writing Environments at Brunel University, 8–10th July 2004. I am very grateful to him for encouraging me to write this up.

¹Eco-logic in Writing

—— LESLIE SCALAPINO ——

Considering the topic of ecological writing, I realized I don't have difficulty with the notion of conceptually placing together one's own language and the actions in the outside world; such as one's language-shapes (mine d) placed in relation to war in Iraq, however unrelated these outside actions are to one's own behavior, volition, desires, conflicts. That is, I don't find the relation of language to so-called 'political' events to be illogical.

In making a connection, I'm not proposing that one's language, sounds, conceptual shapes alter events outside. Rather, writing can note that one's/their sounds and conceptual shapes *are* events—that are also along with events in the outside. A poem may place these together. As such one's conceptions alter oneself and being, and alter their and one being outside. The individual (and any individual instance) occurs *as* reading. *As*: while, alongside, and being (reading is an act).

Positing a crucial relation between writing and the outside is not necessarily megalomania; it's specific and individual—and isn't the same as political action but could go along with it.

For example, in a long poem of mine titled "DeLay Rose," by writing scroll-like, vertical poems whose lines 'come to' a far right margin and drop off single words or end of phrases from that side into that held-edge, an unknown, I have the intent of placing the individual's and all mass actions on one line continually and their (they're) all starting together at one line which is 'coming up' starting again and again. One's being in this wild present [war, corruption, kindness]; one is in any case but may not notice it, therefore not be there because mind is it *then*—it's (mind's and anyone's) visionary language in the sense that what's included as that line (as all the present) is only 'what's happening,' outside. It's (the wild present's and the line's) any events. Hasn't outside. Hasn't oneself. The line (of writing) is only *there* on the page.

This doesn't save or alter citizens or soldiers. It *does* propose that the individual—who is reading—*is* action, present as future. It's to alter one.

Except in one poem, which I'll describe, I've not thought of the same relation of language to land, mountains, oceans, dumps, arctic, air, and other creatures who appear to us as languageless but aren't. For the most part I haven't seen these as susceptible to language (I've changed my mind reading Jack Collom but I'll consider that in a minute). In regard to other creatures: one'd have to interface with their languages that are not known and are (theirs) unknown mind formations.

In regard to land, Dogen said 'Mountains walk.' This is an accurate observation. One time when I observed this I was on a ferry on the

Yangtze River in China seeing a vast plain of cities of millions seen at the same time with river and mountains being destroyed for a dam in a polluted soup of flowing body of water (from which a fish rose and died before our eyes after which it fell back into the river), air (from which we returned home with pneumonia), and land in rubble, people in hovels of broken bricks with garbage everywhere, lines of laborers carrying huge sacks of coal up mountains while at once spouts of poison poured from factories night and day into the land and water. I wrote a poem called "Friendship" (which title I change now to "Resting lightning that's night" because "Friendship" is too fixed as a condition that's a result also, an imagined entity of exchange, and "Resting lightning that's night" is an optical sight, temporary phenomena and *also* imagined after and *then*).

The writing of "Resting lightning that's night" is notation of one's observing mountains walk—but are they doing that even in being destroyed forever? It was grief for mountains, though the grief was not the point in the sense of the stopping place—rather, I was making (as the syntax, sense of phenomenal space, use of dashes across which are changes) a conceptual level of time and space where any phenomena is dead only then when it has died, when it's in death *then*—a person is in death at the time when they have died, only then, but at a different time which is not when they've died, they are not in death—everything keeps going.

I had a dream while we were on the ferry (we were on the ferry for days) which got into the poem that my grandmother (who I'd usually dream with her face turned to the side and my aware in the dream that she had died) now had her face toward me and I was not aware of her being dead; I was trying to get her together for lunch with a friend whom in real life I hadn't seen for nine years whose face was turned to the side and he did not go to lunch. I woke fearing he was dead. When I returned from China, out-of-the-blue he called saying: "I had a dream about you; I dreamed we were going to go to lunch, but then we didn't." I realized from this that the dream was: not that the man was dead but that my grandmother was not in death *now*—or, not in death later, when not *at* the time when she has died. (Still, she's not alive here.) My dream was an examination of Dogen's theory of time and being, which I was reading and studying as we sailed on the Yangtze River seeing plains of action of people and natural phenomena at once. Dogen's theory, briefly, is that all times exist separately at once, present-future-past. Similar to Einstein.

Seeing at the moment of, or at the time of, writing, what difference does one's living make? What difference does one's living make in *'that'* space, and in relation to spaces all existing at once there? The extended poem is the sound of middles, waterfalls falling in the vast horizontal space (which I was seeing on the Yangtze River) where smoke stacks pour jets up into it birds flying—and the sense that people are that (are such as only 'in that'). The line goes past (falls/ the falls) in space, it surpasses falling creating middles. I was in the action of comparing phenomenal space (that I was in) to my mind's space (of conceiving of this space).

birds falls horizontal in the period when birds are up—[and] one is.

people not speaking—even—when—[as] birds horizontal (now)—
[or are]

[past] falls horizontal (space) is people—

———————

she is in 'the realm of death' when she died—but isn't now

—my mind is phenomena—as space in my dream—existing 'only'

—being 'on' water (past) now?—as her not being—is—one—now-
existing only

—is myself now, walking on water (past) in brown night there [on
water]?—only—at the same time—?

—'extreme' is existing only

thinking [my] the man had died was inaccurate—as the dream. It
was my grandmother wasn't (dead)

[that being happiness—as the dream being]—one isn't in death
except when one died

Though I was grieving for mountains, land, and water, whose destruction there (in China) utterly transforms the entire world (not
just China)—neither grief nor writing altering this—there *is* a
relation to people's action implied. Each can (do) act—at the same
time—on all plains and times. Unrelated actions. Actions and these
as mind phenomena change the space. *Anyway.*

not association but space changed

—black humps rainless—only

———————————

birds—wakes

cubicles tenements sides pouring factory chemicals from spout—
falls—.

brown small thorax fills—not being in oneself—or in them—falls
strand [and] flat water

only living having to die as being that isn't at the same time—one's
brown small thorax—is falls horizontal? There

only

what difference do mountains make?—

———————————

'at' night not carrying

one's walking 'brown' night—(walking on water)—people crawling
in lines up

what's the relation to its existing [at the same time]?

———————————

'can't face'—(in present is 'at the

same time') the lines of people crawling on coal

carrying—isn't 'facing' the night (?)

space

one doesn't overwhelm—brown tenements thorax

night's lightning—'facing'?

———————————

Perhaps the start of a sense of 'eco-logical writing,' for myself, is the phrase "my mind is phenomena," mind (as its phenomena/ subjects and as its body), not the same as land but alongside it. Writing enables the making of that spatial relation (of land and mind-phenomena, the two placed beside each other). It's a relation that's going on in every instant but writing can also 'make' it (future) by altering space, allowing one to see one's own joyful movement in space (making that) as well as being one's movement and seeing others' movements as joyful. The text is the altered space, sometimes one's to walk 3-D in it at jetting evening.

buttocks into evening walking at—/separate—evening

the flaps of the orchids at evening—not running—thighs

—then—[not at the same time]—'walk'

Writing "Resting lightning that's night" eventually caused another dream (a dream is an action outside the writing but produced by it) in which the dream produces an outside action: seeing that's being forest (thus not from oneself, not with eyes), forest that's at once white and green (two different colors that are at once the same, impossibility of existing together but they do *in the dream*).

The poem is always just mind phenomena and never (as it is separate as language) touches or exchanges with land or one's physical action in space—except making this as part of its mind phenomena.

"white green"—'no'—occur in one in dream in a forest

walking—there not to be any—separation between 'that'—being in
forest—there

only—but the dream is "whitish" rim, 'no eyes'—there—isn't in one

—is in the dream.—pair only—are 'that'.—"white green" night—is.

the two huge realms—not in one—occur

In *It's go in/quiet illumined grass/land*, I placed land and freezing sky
(so a line having a far right margin, set on my computer, reaching
the page's edge wherever it does slipped off onto the next line in
actual-space of page held on that far further-than-normal edge of
page) *beside* my mind-phenomena, on the far right edge of the page's
margin (gesture of my doing that and of perceptual faculties, sight,
thoughts) the intention was to place and hold 'one whole person'
beside the whole day or a night, there. No conflicts or psychology exist on that line! As I went along I thought of various events
in climate and day and was making as it happens a juxtaposition
of heaven and hell, the poem beginning to show the two were/are
part of the same space. Philip Whalen was still alive; he got into
the poem by being noted as just placing his mind (his nature and
mind-habits) by land-sky the-outside-heaven and just being that—
as one's thinking, just place it there again, just be that.

silver half freezing in day
elation the
outside
of the outside sky walking
rose

silver half freezing in day
                              moon's elation
              of the outside rose, his seeing
                        on both
                        'sides'
              seeing someone else at all and the
                              half freezing
              elation of the outside so that's even
                              with one
              continually over and over one/person

                        he will
              also now person dying? Is not

                        compared to
              space they're in outside silver freezing
                              half
              moon day now both walking rose
                              instant
              running—wall—wall

A person dying passes out of *that* (*there*/the) frame of seeing. That person being in place (phenomenal) when alive also intersects with other times at once. The poem makes plateaus seen conceptually.

Reading Jack Collom's poems in *Exchanges of Earth & Sky*, the reader experiences a porous exchange in which each poem being a paired structure is also sound giving the sense of the weight and lightness of birds *there* with one's reading in space-light.

Ecology: "The branch of biology dealing with the relations and interactions between organisms and their environment, including other organisms." I had been conceiving of this subject divisively (as ecocatastrophes), my sense having been that ecology pertains to the subject of our destroying the world—rather than: Nature *is* us as in language, yet Nature and language are not the same, are outside of each other. Poetry can be structures that are relations and interactions between spheres in spatial apprehension.

Jack Collom's poems in *Exchanges of Earth & Sky* are founded on this double exchange and their crossing: the fact that Nature is us as is language yet Nature and language are outside of each other. The poems are therefore their binary 'form' or occurrence, in each poem the factual naming of birds and naming of characteristics of each bird and an extension not of these characteristics but a tie of sound to one outside. The effect and perhaps the instigation in this poetry is the occurrence of joy by his text making, and reading being, a phenomenal space as duration.

In the beginning poems, "Western Grebe" and "Loon," physical sight sent to the brain before it's returned and seen, and language image (a bird a bolt from a crossbow as it flies underwater, and his language a crossbow) there is no night or day in language—nor is there any as phenomenally being portrayed in Collom's poem. He's cut across time and is on other layers at once.

A faculty is an orifice of perception or cognition. In Collom's poems, the *outside* is one's own sensations, one's faculty. It's a bird's faculty (Collom uses the word "faculty" in that instance) to lower its body in water submerged as suiting its fancy (choice of submerging?) as it swims or is stationary. There is no night or day in "black above below white": black is both above and below white, or black is above and white is below. Fair lighted filled bright white light black black (these) "fall" as motion and are maybe "fall" in (season) time. Yet the space and text have no time, are "before eyes": may be seeing occurrence in front of our eyes, or before there *are* eyes. A crossing divisions or/and as *no* divisions (except citing of the bird's name, there are not beginning markings of poems) is opening of space, phenomenal in the writing. Language reveals afterimages that are *in* the rolling landscape itself (and in the poem's space). Accumulation of light black filled open inhabited other birds in continuance: poems may appear to merge only separated by the appearance of a new bird (its name listed in the table of contents as apparently a new poem—or perhaps the list of contents isn't titles but listing of the appearance of birds?). Here are pages 3 and 4:

WESTERN GREBE

Aechmorphorus

black above below white

                                 nest a matted
        structure of tule—afloat—lightly
        fashioned to the living reeds so that it will move
        up and down—

                    eggs pale bluish green but stained
        light brown from the decomposed vegetable
        matter of the nest

for it possesses the wonderful faculty of lowering
                its body in the water to any desired stage of

submersion, and this it can do either
while swimming or while remaining
stationary, as may suit its fancy.

                    courtship
                            neck   arched
                                             beak
                                    downward
            some rubbed against
        each other, while others skimmed
    the surface, glide that sent the
                        water

                    flying

        & & & & & & &

    How did
                fair lighted filled bright
                bright fall fell
                white light
                black
                black
                black
                curvelit red-
                shine
                before eyes?

hard white skin
            scar
            hard white skin
    scar

miocene epoch/tertiary period
        distribution circumpolar   glossy purplish black with greenish

LOON

Gavia immer
     imber diver, ember goose, Walloon, guinea duck, greenhead

bill stout, straight, sharp-pointed and sharp-edged

nest: a hollow in the sand

its wolf-like cry is the wildest sound
     now heard in Massachusetts

cannot rise from the land

deep water
     where the bird can use its wings and fly underwater like a bolt
     from
          a crossbow

great northern diver
     mournful, mirthful, sinister, defiant, uncanny,
     demoniacal

        & & & & & & &

        language is like a weasel shot with scars
             diagonally, as if from far below, neon-
  seeming
             afterimages revealing bluish-white to be
             the formal speech of rolling landscape

Retaining the first captured fish (in the bird's mouth) while capturing a second or third (the characteristic of the bird, doing this)—the same as our reading. Collom's pressure of words in poetical structure is the birds' actions, later. The structure is later. As continuance in his apparently huge, endless space (as there are thousands of birds, so it *could* go on...) and as if beads that are his/a person's small actions, or a thought or color etc. in the paired mirroring space of each poem's continuance—Collom not only doesn't make hierarchies or urgent dilemmas (eschewing 'subjective'), one *being* the *outside* is, in exchange, joy.

Jack Collom interfaces with the birds' languages by making novel juxtapositions (novel by being *where* they are in structure) placed after the ampersands, so they are before other birds and after other birds—as if beside each bird, the space is completely open in effect. Page 9 after the ampersands of Great Black-Backed Gull:

> orange, lilac and dark brown almost black
>
> wolverine pudding

Or page 16, after the ampersand:

> the flat bright water usually hides...
>
> Abstract red headcheese rearing
>   cool, lilac-based in the icebox

Collom makes a zigzag continually "faster than eye can see"—because poetry can be a space allowing our minds to incorporate everything *at once simultaneously*. So, *Exchanges of Earth & Sky* produces what we're incorporating ahead of us, its (it's) grounded sound racing and being already ahead. In each poem the string of ampersands becomes a horizon, without above or below or middle by recurring. Although the string of ampersands tends to begin in the lower half of each poem, the impression is created that the horizon (of ampersands) begins everywhere in it and makes a limitless boundless space.

I asked Michael McClure which book of his is closest to ecological matter, he said *Rain Mirror*. The book has two parts, the first is a haiku stream, discrete poems in a series, the effect of the series being to hold the reader, being in a large increment in a condensed space and as such that space altered. We go through motions in which we're not mirrored (apparently, or are as 'our' seeing but not *in* people's events here) and we're at the same time as the plum or humming bird, *by not being mirrored*, altered.

OH,
HUM
MING
BIRD
SHAD
OW
on the black
plum
!

((No summer lightning
though))   (9)

A NOVEMBER
BLACKBERRY
all
red and sour
in
the
long
rain   (12)

                    WHY ARE
                  RED-BLACK
                      ROSES
                  on the table,
                     there's
                       hail
                    outside
                       ?   (13)

The second half of the book, *Crisis Blossoms*, is poems in a sequence
that are mind of an individual as coming apart and holding that
mind-formation as the line and gesture of the sequence's process,
to see that and as such be medicine (as in the section titled "After
the Solstice," beginning "'GIVE WAY OR BE SMITTEN INTO
NOTHINGNESS *and everlasting night*"/But I am here already,/
the tips of my fingers/ give off light.'

Both long poems in *Rain Mirror* are reader/writer being phenomena seeing phenomena. The second long poem, *Crisis Blossoms* is the
state of the person (the poet) having a "melt-down" in the process of
working on the problem of death and (their) impermanence.

    What matters is the cold skin of the python
            and her muscled ribs
    that ripple over the crate. One band
    of power preceding another. There is
                    ZERO,
    and the nonstructure of nada inside.   (70)

The self seeing its future as present: "All of the bodies/sculptured of
memory/are a gate/with/STAIRS/of/NAPALM/and/OPAL/I'M

THERE (79). The two long poems are as if pairs, a hologram. The unfolding of McClure's long poem—in individual poems and their duration—is like duplication of instruction of the fetus' DNA or DNA structures resembling each other in creatures widely different from each other. As reading, we're (readers) a motion from the outside in and from the inside out at once. It is as if one could place outside as hallucinations on top of one's inside as hallucinations and see something about seeing-or-mind-or-phenomena: "—I'm/ the ghost/of a baby/rabbit,/DON'T/ PUT YOUR HAND/ through me!" (78).

McClure described a young man in California (the poet Lewis MacAdams) who, concerned about a wild river that was going to be dammed and diverted to southern California, announced to the newspapers that he would chain himself to a rock in the bottom of the canyon that would be filled if they dammed the river. He chained himself to a rock where they couldn't find him, and they didn't dam the river.[1]

The last example of ecological structures in poems I would mention is M. Mara-Ann's long hybrid, hypnotic poem-theater work of spoken-music text, *Containment Scenario:/DisloInter/ MedTextId/ Entcation:/Horse Medicine.* The three center lines of the title contain by their capitals the words "text" and "dislocation."

---

1 | From personal interview with Michael McClure in Oakland, CA, June 2007.

M. Mara-Ann's poem-theater work is based on the national report on global warming. One element of the work's structure is the sections—introduction, prologue and director's notes— that are interruptions, extensions and meditations which go before and between Act I and Act II. These sections allow rest by variation in order to renew one's alighting concentration. Another element of structure is footnoting spots in the core text, which begin on the same page as the original text, to be read following the particular phrase of the original. The footnotes begin to extend longer than the original text, footnote-archipelagos from which one must turn back to the origin of the footnote to remember the origin and reorient one's reading, then turn back to the next passage or phrase in the original text, turning ahead to *its* footnote, and so on. This active reading becomes sustained attention, a holding of sounds like plateaus in the air, an inevitable letting go allowing the original's spot in the text and one's attention to it to be lost before one finds one's way back to resuming its reading process again. The poem's reading is exchange 'causing' the reader to hold a place in space as energy of comparing that place/sounds/thought to other place/event/sound. We must enlarge. The content is the transience of all life in its alteration, being itself as the sustained attention taking place. It is the imagination creating at the same time that life-forms outside—and the outsides and insides—are ending.

WORKS CITED

Collom, Jack. *Exchanges of Earth & Sky*. New York City: Fish Drum, 2006.

McClure, Michael. *Rain Mirror*. NewYork: New Directions, 1991.

Mara-Ann, M. *Containment Scenario:/DisloInter/ MedTextId/Entcation: / Horse Medicine*. Oakland, CA: O Books, forthcoming 2008.

Scalapino, Leslie. "The Forest is in the Euphrates River," *Day Ocean State of Stars' Night*. Kobenhavn, Denmark and Los Angeles, CA: Green Integer, 2007.

Scalapino, Leslie. "Friendship" (new title: "Resting lightning that's night"), *The Public World/Syntactically Impermanence*. Middletown, CT: Wesleyan University Press, 1996.

Scalapino, Leslie. *It's go in/quiet illumined grass/land*. Mill Valley, CA: The Post-Apollo Press, 2001; and Kobenhavn, Denmark and Los Angeles, CA: Green Integer, 2007.

Preface to *SECOND NATURE*: Poetry of Strained Relationality

— JACK COLLOM —

Note: This piece was written as Preface to a large, not-quite-finished manuscript of creative writing on/in/at/around nature.

> *The greatest amount of life can be supported*
> *by great diversification of structure*
> CHARLES DARWIN, *The Origin of Species*

Darwin was standing on a couple square feet of ground, good English turf, looking down. The turf "supported twenty species of plants, and these belonged to eighteen genera and to eight orders."

> I woke from a dream
> of heart worms, my chest
> seething with motion,
> muscle oozing.
> Was it the bloody turtle shell?
> The glazed-over eyes?
> I can't wash my hands fast enough.
> (Mary Crow, from "Iquitos Market")

I. Motivation aside, the rational excuse for *SECOND NATURE* is to provide some passage to an elaborated sense of nature

A. so that nature can be thought of as breathtaking variety

    1. of which we are but a tiny portion

        a. (while simultaneously it may be looked at as generalized, small, and even

B. unreal); thus our knowledge might blossom up and down a scale, as our powers have blossomed and continue to blossom, since

    1. it is the power/knowledge imbalance dissolving life.

I remember sitting at the window of my parents' bedroom in Western Springs, Illinois, one day, World War II, just two or three years into birding, seeing an immature chestnut-sided warbler come switching its way, feasting on bugs, up an elm twig—almost to the glass! Ah, thrill of spectatorship! It looked as perfect as a watch but twice as lively. Its colors were modest green and gray, but *what* green and gray! At that moment, I think I began to learn subtlety. Which is not to disdain vividness but to include processual increments *as well.* and also little acts and presences that don't point somewhere.

Which reminds me, contrariwise, of the precise way I was flung most conclusively over the apparent abyss between an adolescent sense of logical causality and an appreciation of abstract expressionist painting. I was working at a toilet paper factory in Seymour, Connecticut, and my job was to tend the huge machine that made the basic paper. The bottom part of this behemoth was a containment of "paper soup" circling and stirring about. In the center, a heated metal drum about nine feet long and six feet in diameter slowly whirled in place, positioned on its side. The lower whirl of it dipped into the "soup," and instantly a thin paper scum formed on the hot metal. When this scum moved up and out of the liquid, it dried quickly. Two feet up the curvature of the drum, a "doctor blade" had been aligned and bolted into place, from drum end to drum end. The paper was neatly scraped off and, since it had been hooked up already with a nine-foot roll of toilet paper winding itself up about twelve feet away, the new paper sailed thither, drying more completely as it flew. Every once in a while I'd flip the large roll off its bed and replace it, in the same motion, with a wooden core for the next roll. The Bunyanesque toilet roll would then be trundled to another part of the mill, to be cut into handy human-size products and wrapped with various brand names.

I got a lot of reading done between flips, but would also prowl the machine (which was as big as a house) looking for malfunctions and checking the "soup." I was paid $1.37½ an hour.

While prowling, I'd notice the inevitable dried spillage outside the lower tank portion. This was the era of colored toilet paper (a festive exit from the Eisenhower years?); we'd typically switch between green and blue and orange and pink several times a night. So the dried by-product was a papier-mâché concoction, abstractly concrete in both shape and hue. The colors swirled, blurted, formed extreme irrational symphonies of themselves. I was enchanted. And because it was an entirely natural process, I proceeded to feel a certain ease about accepting, also, whatever experimental art could come with.

(Then, of course, I had to clean it up.)

I was already familiar as a kid with the adult plumage of the chestnut-sided warbler. It's beautiful—a little more subdued than those of the Cape May or the Blackburnian. Golden crown over a raggedy but distinct robber's mask that zags down white cheek to thin, bright fox-red line that in turn runs along the side between dark (but double-wingbarred) wings and pale underparts. A bird of brushy second-growth woods. Cocks tail. Sings "Pleased pleased pleased to MEETCHA." One can think of it as allied to the abstract expressionists' work in regard to the impulses behind it: a few practical necessities developed into a basic scheme (warbler, or framed canvas), then aesthetics dynamically entwined with random play, enriched by feedback loops (either of evolution or painting), perhaps in both cases developmentally motivated by sexual display....

I'm emphasizing the play of nature and art. Criticism has, naturally, emphasized the role of (human) intentionality, as if critical thought generates nature and art.

SECOND NATURE consists of *poetry about nature.* The word "poetry" requires immediate qualification, since many of the pieces here include prose or are too experimental-seeming to fit any halfway normal sense of poetry. Then the word "nature"—well, even if one's hands were galaxy-sized, one could not throw them up high enough to express the appropriate discomfort with a space-chameleon word like "nature." Even worse, the word "about" appears to creep from word to thing like some gelid predator.

Start again. "Poetry about nature" may conjure up a certain (and/or uncertain) set of assumptions, since every large phrase (indeed, every word) in the world must wrestle its denotation with and against a vaporous but very real connotative spectrum. For example, one can define "fish" as "legless aquatic vertebrate" (with just a few necessary elaborations), and/or one can speak of The Fish as Elizabeth Bishop did in her famous poem:

> —the frightening gills
> fresh and crisp with blood…
> the coarse white flesh
> packed in like feathers…
> the pink swim bladder
> like a big peony.

climaxing with:

> I looked into his eyes…
> far larger than mine
> but shallower, and yellowed,
> the irises backed and packed
> with tarnished tinfoil
> seen through the lenses
> of old scratched isinglass.
>
> (Bishop, "The Fish")

(And within the music of, say, "shallower, and yellowed," "backed and packed," are the little white seeds of going *way* beyond description.)

"   @
Mulch seals.
Mulch guards.
Mulch covers.
Mulch retains.
       @

Though lacking the advantages of gas-powered mulchers in his rural English retreat, Samuel Taylor Coleridge's 1811 master aesthetic treatise, the *Biographia Literaria*, nonetheless foreshadowed contemporary mulching theory in its fundamental theoretical division between the aesomplastic and desynonymous aesthetic modes. The latter involves redeploying quasi recognizable pieces of experiences in the services of new wholes. Daily life and literature are in this mode broken into tiny, usable units that are then fitted into an evolving scheme in which their roles and functions have been radically transformed.

While the aesomplastic writer also begins with such raw material, his or her imaginative blade is faster and sharper resulting in a new, aesthetic whole that bears no immediate relationship to its constitutive parts.[1]

---

1 | "The most immediate analog is between the metamorphic and the igneous in geological terms; since the former involves sedimentary rocks undergoing transformation through heat; while the igneous involves a complete reconstitution of rock through extreme heat, a building from the ground up, that can only be experienced after the lava has cooled." —Lytle Shaw, from "Mulch: A Treatise."

One can divide voice according to mood or purpose. "Pass the salt" and Neruda's "Ode to Salt" are both beautiful instances of language. The difference between denotation and connotation seems to be "at best" a distinction between one image (which either remains technical or becomes a cliché) and many images (which remain confusing or become, ah, metonymy). But the history of writing about our surroundings (and our interweavings with them) has not usually been either precise or exploratory in terms of the subject itself. It's all too natural to deflate nature's geometry via anthropocentric suckage. Nature poetry has often become (though shamelessly generalized) a sort of specialty (as if nature were a hobby, or an acquired taste).

If we try a horizontal kind of classification, nature writing has tended to fall into just a few modes, like:

- Examination from Above, wherein a tweedy gentleman or bedizened lady rhapsodizes with genteel aplomb, through a distance of air meant to set up a comfy observational scale, about a rose, or other offering, as if nature were a dog holding up a shot goose.

- Projection of Our Cultural Concerns on This Conveniently Blank Screen That Nature Is. This includes Wolfman, Smokey the Bear, and a legion of cute rodents, tweety-birds, etc., as well as Come-Live-With-Me-and-Be-My-Love, *Animal Farm,* and many more talking pictures. Nature as sandwich boards.

• Nature as a Horrid Test of Our Resolve. "Hell, we'll beat down these African locusts, Bill, do a little cloud-seeding, then head for Utopia City."

I don't object to these as ancillary images; I just wanna maintain the energy of having options. I propose that even when nature is complimented (and at the same time poised beyond the tame glow of patronization), nature writings usually bespeak the assumption that nature is secondary. I further propose that even in writings more plainly sophisticated than the projections caricatured above—in writings, say, like those of Robert Frost and Mary Oliver—the principal energy seems presented with an undue emphasis on intellectual control of the writings (however bucolically flavored). That is, it seems to be taken for granted in such writings that language is above and mostly separate from its subject matter, that the formal concerns of creative writing are *not* intimately, causally, viscerally connected with their content, that there is such a geometry as "about" that liberates the shapes above the writing line (above the threshold of the paper) from those below it. In other words, that speech is not particularly, not importantly, a physical act.

I further propose that such ramification of the Intentional Fallacy doth continue into thee and me, that eternal vigilance is required to keep things natural (although everything is natural). Hear ye, Hear ye! Once and for All, the matter of Control is rather like Zeno's arrow, which in effect stutter-steps throughout eternity "until" it forestalls its own medium.

I propose that language should consider resembling nature.

John Ashbery writes a species of human nature. He's inside it so he has the right.

If we realize we're inside nature, we can write it, meaning get beyond (within) description.

I mean, we do give "lip service" to being one with nature, but we gotta give hip service (anatomy metonymy).

To that end, it's necessary to recognize the everything-scope of nature and, at the same time, to contradict infinity with a universe of finites. I admit this looks like "God," but the trouble with God is it becomes human. Becomes recognized as human. Nature can become human, too (Pan is only an obvious example, and so are you), but if all is seen as emanating from nature, the circle trips are voyages of discovery. Because, no limits.

Anyway, I thought postmodernism was gonna look this stuff over with an eye humbly ballooning up to a size and coverage from which it might admit the local by utterly transcending local limits, but I see PM's just another paradigmatic mousehole to work in.

I don't mean to be snippy (as if anybody does); I understood from some visual-artist friends that postmodernism would correct not the wrongness but the exclusivity of (what fell in) the modern. That the progress would be expansion rather than replacement.

Evolution, to me, represents a trustworthy soft template of how things work, and in nature Evolution has primarily expanded. Bacteria have not gone out of style in order to make way for birds of paradise. Maybe everything goes extinct (so far, not all at once) on a finite sphere-surface like life on Earth. But if art depends on resources that take advantage, in their scope, of the time-space indeterminacy of what we might call art's planet, then there needn't be the crowding (hence extinction) that pressures measurable space. Sure, art "feels" crowded, but there's a flexibility we may have to learn to roll around in. There's more room to ride, more "minerals and water" for creatures who function outside the pragmatic wave. Do I contradict myself?

Evolution is simple. Natural Selection is infinitely complex; it's not "just" dog eat dog, nor dog eat cat, nor even simple cat eat rat. To Eat is different on Earth than it is in art.[2] In "reality," to eat snatches away life (in order to extend it in the eater). It often seems that culture operates the same way, but I think the surreal connection system that is art can serve to conserve on/in/with its multiple spheres; memory can replace competition, can turn it into layered condition.

In nature, the dinosaurs live on as birds, physically (while psychically Tyrannosaurus rex becomes a capitalist—more organized). The passenger pigeon, vis-à-vis us, shape shifts to the chicken. More

---

2 | Not that art doesn't take place on Earth. It's important to emphasize the earthiness of art, just as it's important to emphasize the opposite. Etc.

ordinarily, giant sloths become shadows of themselves and are carried across the road hanging from a baseball bat.

As things happen, collage lies down happily with survival of the fittest, even in off-wilderness (the only wilderness extant), and we have all the accidental beauty of existence.

Something about strictures and
pictures.

———————

I think the basic point is Variety. (I also think the oxymoronic nature of that sentence should be no impediment.)

Some shy away from variety because it breaks up unity. I suggest there are more and better unities "out there." I suggest (and state) that any unity crumbled by variety itself is like the pre-Galilean unity of Geocentrism—encourages territorial hubris and internecine slaughter (you may think the collective Homo-sap-head swelled *now*; imagine if we still thought Earth the Center of the Universe!). Variety never hurt Shakespeare.

& true variety includes its oppositeopposite.

Variety's a gimmick by means of which to approach surprise (etymology, feminine of: upon—before—to seize).

In writing, it's more fun to play Earth than to play God.

This is not to claim that I, as poet, "play Earth" very well, or comprehensively. I make impatient leaps, even to the point of texture, and Earth is nothing if not patient. I line out clustersense but am secretly just linear. Lots of people are/appear earthier than I am, but there are many ways of reflecting or suggesting in writing the energies and shapes of nature. By being playful with language, I hope to bring out some of its own potentialities, unleash its unpredictable nerve rather than use it only as a transparency to register some skullbound logic. But these seemingly contradictory impulses overlap each other complexly.

I.e., a sonnet is, to an extent, nature poetry because of its structure (yes, that artificial structure). The call-and-response is like spring and summer. The contrast between iambic pentameter with rhyme scheme and all the little mouse-rushes within and around the actual line is like a forest—less and less homogeneous the further you stick your nose in. A good sonnet is like Pandora's box (the last two lines are the lid).

It's delight to pursue some semblance *in* language *of* nature. This pursuit tends to evoke true values of both. But chasing the language/nature identity isn't the only way to go. For one thing, brainplay's often anti-nature because it simplifies (which, of course, is part of nature). Many a light-filled goal's way off to the side of any logical question—it (they) just growed, like Topsy. Value precedes formulation (but is likely to include old formulas).

In the above paragraph, the language/nature resemblance has to do with residue curlicues on a mudflat. If I scant content I hope to compensate by piling things up.

I did walk along Salt Creek and around Long's Peak and did work a score of years in the manual ecosystems of factories; I can identify the olive-sided flycatcher; human nature lives somewhere along a sagging line between being a thought-up nut and just falling to the ground.

The tweed stance (Examination from Above) *can* elicit warm images; exposition *can* work like the hands or chisel of a sculptor.

Sheer wild-ass genius is *so* natural it doesn't write about "nature" (Pollock: "I *am* nature!").

———————

But we (people, Western people) can exemplify nature *much* more than we typically have in writing, and thereby learn more intimately and vastly "about" nature. & thereby be off and on joyous. & thereby not mess it up so fucking, fucking much!

We can represent the multifarious energy of the Earth, by experimenting and collecting.

We can verbally imitate the relational multiplicity of an ecosystem. (Some people might say, "Grammar does that already." But nature has a thousand and one &*@!=#( )+? times more options.)

We can help educate our children of whatever age to appreciate the dynamic immediacy of nature—to see, hear, feel, etc., that nature is "what's happening" *just* under the boring labels, even in/out Gotham windows. Maybe we can educate ourselves to perform a little inner time-lapse photography.

> i.e.   MT
> I met
> it (me).
> ....
> "Tie   M
> t(o)   'I'm E.'
> Emit
> sssss
> time
> time
> time."

Shit, even all this unnatural talk is natural.

- "Nature" is everything and something:
- It's the ocean in which culture floats like a handful of bubbles.
- It's that which is not manufactured.
- It's a stick. A ladybug.
- Ooooooooo.
- It's its logic.
- It's causal essence.
- It's a lost purity.
- It's a rose, and it's a photographed rose.
- It's the desire to smash something.

Therefore, it's an entity of great simultaneous scale.

Being a humble part of nature, I'd like to quote myself[3] (from a little "arse poetica," 1999):

In teaching and in my own poetry, I've been pursuing a sense of formal variety which seems to me to indicate a useful opening.

"Passage," written in the late '80s, details the extinction of the passenger pigeon, a story I only had from books but did have when I was a kid in the early '40s (i.e., quasi-organically). In a multitude of styles and voices (prose, collage, lune series, vers libre, limerick, vernacular, birdcall, freeform dimeter, chant, rhetoric), the attempt is made to lay out the history and ornithology in such a way as to let the language function like an ecosystem.

This approach isn't new—I'm inspired by Charles Olson's poem-as-field-of-energy ideas, perhaps even by (shudder) Carl Sandburg. Also by David Hockney's demonstrations of the multiple perspectives in Chinese scroll paintings. It's all tied in with the sense that, like it or not, writing does viscerally act out its own effects. We might as well transcend the pretense of linearity in writing, as Uncertainty and Chaos have helped us bust out of the ideal-forms mystical snobbery of Plato and Euclid.

In other poems I've employed or fallen into freeform haiku, anti-"poetic" language, notes, anagrams, concrete & visual notions,

---

3 | Life: that which quotes itself.

JACK COLLOM | 93

journal-style, sestinas, sonnets, acrostic varieties, rants, satires, *objet trouvé*, recipes, songs, "just plain" observations, arguments, lists, automatic writing, "I-remembers," slices (a type-space-based invention), yodels, surrealism, stories, and other shots-in-the-dark seeking a spark. All in humble imitation of *that* nature.

In teaching (often as artist in residence with elementary-age kids) I've tried to catalyze such variety and more. Even if the students take away no more than the sense that things can/must be looked at in many lights, I think their attitudes toward nature will be enriched as time goes on.

Meanwhile, Thoreau writes, "Last year's grasses and flower-stalks have been steeped in rain and snow, and now the brooks flow with meadow tea..."

And meanwhile, Elizabeth Bishop ends her poem by letting the fish go.

Just now, robinsong from a high branch.
Brewers and red-winged blackbirds
Pepper the scene for a twilit hour.
Fall yellow-rumped warblers love it here.

...

& I don't know why
I've carved the poem lines in 4s
when any number of things
blow down the valley

...

(Jack Collom, 2005-6-7)

! gON time BLOCKS !

—— JULIE PATTON ——

spelling be pee o ple o spit scat germ of thought ble blah blah ark
text phonic terms might have cosmos saw dust mandible handle bloc
heads spread unwelcome sheet scatter brains come post mos deft
beings housed in un dated...

"savage"

"queer"

"animal"

       (most native languages had no such separate... (block for...

"black"

"incoherent"

       (that *read...*

"primitive"

"[sk]inarticulate"

"bird brain"

"tweeted"

       (tweaked, animation thank shape-shafting shamaninalfauxbete,
change lingue)

"mumbo jumbo"

"gibberish"

"ill-literate"

"out of the mouths of babes"

> (No write? No rights. Rite? Wrong. Drum. Tongue.)

> *"hogwash"*

"monkey talk"

"quack"

> (lie buried, no ledge, fur tive, fix a tiff, signature, firm)

"gibberish"

"gobblety-gook"

> (geek to me.)

"moo"

"oink"

"batty"

"non sense"

> (ring shout)

"squawk"

> ("squaw"

"women's talk"

> (yo mother...

"bitch"

"trash-talk"

> (flood)

"has-been"

"dodo bird"

> (caca, scat...ter

"me ow"

"buzz"

(Katrina, what the "good" buck barks. In dia S ink (time in memOral

"dead languages"

(re

cAnt reasons CONNECTING dotes ant row promo fictions in specs beez in a bon mot drawing closed mind blinds dim ages fur get glow ball warnings currently b. linked squaring the word commons deconstructively so B. rend a selection from this "word in progress" de tailing her take on my imagination assembling graphic lack "in" ail paws bet re buzz codices and brace of birds herd armwing the void blook in cycles. Word. Initial blocs spell out narrative. Ecocurator s rap another, in part my own, meta spherically beaking some kind of tree template fur which to bend meaning. 'Nuff sad.

"The ants are a people not strong, yet they prepare their food in summer;
The rock badgers are a feeble folk, yet they make their homes in the crags;
The locusts have no kings, yet they advance in ranks,
The spider skillfully grasps with its hands and it is in kings' palaces

—Proverbs 30:24

PHOTOGRAPHS

These studies, small hand, languaging a-tudes were inspired in the winter of 2005 when Jonathan Skinner contacted me about collaborating on a Bates College Synergy Grant. I photographed approximately 300 assemblages. These photographs were taken in New York City and Cleveland, Ohio throughout 2005.

NEW ORLEANS
Louisiana
The Mardi-Gras — gayest
festival in the U.S. —
is held here annually.

GO BACK
ONE SPACE

French Quarter restaurants
and Chalmette National
Historical Park.

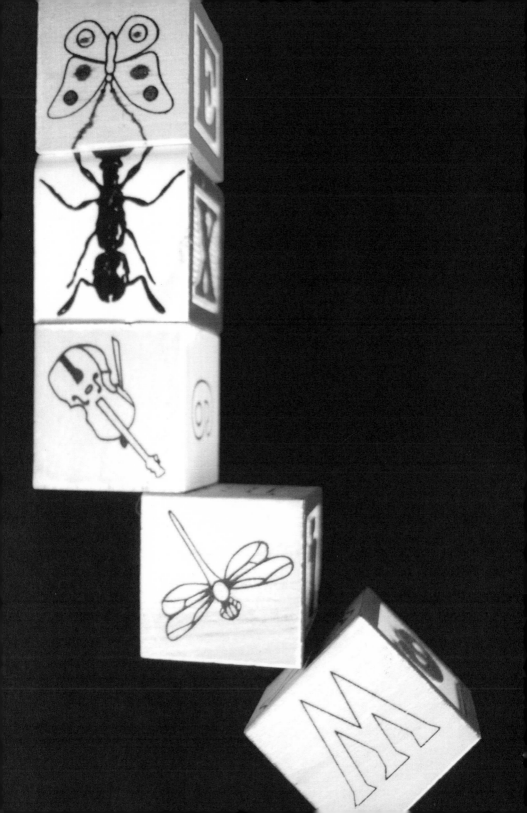

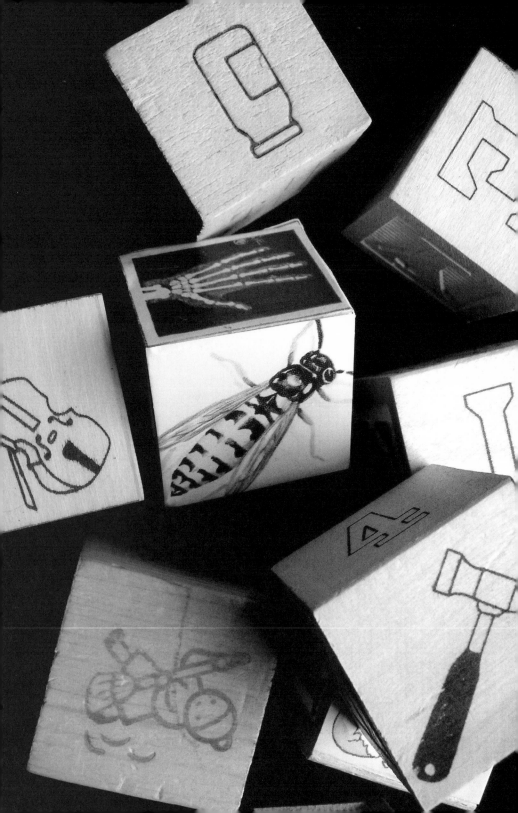

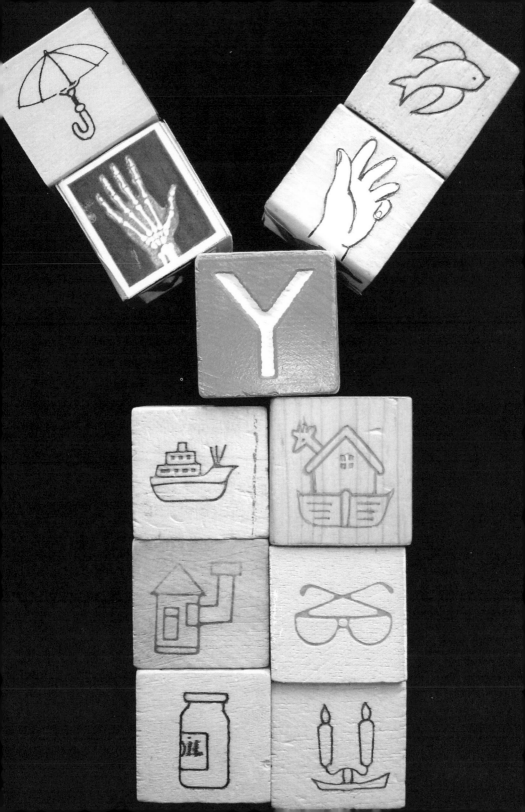

The Ecology of Poetry

—— MARCELLA DURAND ——

The first version of this essay was originally given as a talk at Small Press Traffic in San Francisco on September 21, 2002, as part of the "New Experiments" series, and was published in the journal *ecopoetics* in Fall 2002. Since then, I have revised the essay, with the revision appearing in 26 in 2004. This process was probably slightly different from the norm: because there was a good deal of audience participation during the talk, I decided that any revision should include a sense of that community response, which was also in keeping with my exploration of ecology, systems, and networks in poetry. As I write this, I find that I am having trouble even with the term "revision"—it implies a linear progress and idea of improvement. Per Jack Collom's concept of the spandrel in creative works[1] (drawn from Stephen Jay Gould's concept of the spandrel in natural evolution, which is drawn from the engineering concept of the spandrel as a seemingly useless, but necessary triangle of space created by the structure of an arch), perhaps this "revision" can be partly considered a spandrel, thrown off by the effort to understand the confluences between ecology, which is in itself the art of living in one's "house," and poetry, which could be defined as the art of living in one's language.

While driving cross-country to California to deliver this talk, we stopped at Yellowstone, a place that gave me a profound sense

---

1 | "Jack Collom Talks Spandrels, Foxes, and Receding Paths," *The Poetry Project Newsletter*. New York, October/November 2003.

of dis-ease. In a tedious downfall of cold rain, we dutifully took photographs of the "sights," which were for the most part located within an easy distance from the road. Our most vivid memory was driving on a seemingly endless figure 8, hemmed in by opaque forest. However, friends later exclaimed excitedly over our Yellowstone photos, declaring them the most beautiful over other photos taken of what we had found wilder and more spectacular places. Later, when reading more about Yellowstone, I discovered two things. The first was that scientists have discovered when an earthquake occurs in the Western United States, it can set off tremors in Yellowstone.[2] Somehow the complex "plumbing" (as so many tourist brochures refer to Yellowstone's active tectonic architecture) mirrors what is occurring in other areas of the continent. What had seemed to me a non-place was evidently some sort of connector to the rest of the continent. Perhaps, instead of the Great Plains, Yellowstone is the true quivery heart of America.

The second thing I learned was that viewpoints of the vistas that we (along with other millions and millions "served") had taken so many photos of had been artfully located, influenced by the 18th-century notion of framing and reflecting nature. Early tourists would hold up mirrors to the landscape, altering their direct perception of it. This reflective fad foreshadowed some of the current tensions of nature poetry, ecological poetry,

---

2 | See "Alaska Quake Seems to Trigger Yellowstone Jolts: Small Tremors Rattle National Park After Big Quake 2,000 Miles Away," released on November 4, 2002, by the University of Utah Seismograph Stations, http://www.seis.utah.edu/RecentNews/YNP-11042002.shtml.

and ecological issues. These tensions are linked to the perceived problems of contemporary experimental American poetry itself —that it is somehow out of touch, cloistered, urban, interior. As Jonathan Skinner says in his introduction in *ecopoetics*, "walks do not make it into the enclosed environments of today's best poetry."[3] However, Juliana Spahr has pointed out in recent readings that such poetry, the poetry of "walks," smacks of old-fashioned nature poetry, a poetry that, she says, does not include the "bulldozer" along with the "bird." But then there's the other extreme, a poetry that too obviously delineates the battles between bulldozer and bird, and expects deep yet instant change in human actions toward the environment, while making no deep and intrinsic change within its own poetic structure. Kaia Sand wrote to me that when confronted with such poetry, she wonders, *why poetry?*

Things have changed since the last burst of ecological poetry in the 1960s and 1970s, and I use the word *things* partly in the sense that the French poet Francis Ponge used it: exterior non-human objects neglected as subjects, that when concentrated upon intensely, can yield extraordinarily lucid writing. Traditional nature poetry, à la the human-subject meditating upon a natural object-landscape-animal that is supposed to function as a kind of doorway into meaning of the human subject's life, is simply no longer possible. "Appearing to serve a personally expressive function, the vocabulary of nature

---

3 | Jonathan Skinner, "Editor's Statement," *ecopoetics no. 1*, winter 2001.

screens a symbolic appropriation of the Land. Her cut sublimity grafts to the Human," says Lisa Robertson.[4] Nature has changed from an perceptually exploitable Other—most easily compared to a book to be decoded by the (human) reader—to something intrinsically affected by humans. We ourselves are the wilderness destroying the very systems of which we are a part, in a role we utterly do not understand.

I am not writing a manifesto, nor even a definition, of ecological poetry; however, I *am* interested, passionately so, in exploring the idea of a poetry that begins to take into itself ecological processes— a confluence of matter with perception, observation with process, concentration to transmission, that would most decisively turn what can seem nostalgic remnants of nature poetry into a more dynamic, affective, and pertinent poetry. "Pastoral Utopias have efficiently aestheticized and naturalized the political practices of genocide, misogyny, and class and race oppression. I consider that now pastoral's obvious obsolescence may offer a hybrid discursive potential to those who have been traditionally excluded from Utopia," says Robertson. Something obsolete recycled into something else— reclaimed by gleaners[5], junk turned into art. This could be poetry of which Sand would ask, *what besides poetry?* In my initial statement for the talk, I wrote: "Ecological poetry is much like ecological

---

4 | Lisa Robertson, "How Pastoral: A Manifesto." *A Poetics of Criticism*, edited by Juliana Spahr, Mark Wallace, Kristin Prevallet and Pam Rehm. Leave Books: Buffalo, New York, 1994.

5 | *The Gleaners and I*, Agnes Varda, 2001.

living—it recycles materials, functions with an intense awareness of space, seeks an equality of value between all living and unliving things, explores multiple perspectives as an attempt to subvert the dominant paradigms of mono-perception, consumption and hierarchy, and utilizes powers of concentration to increase lucidity and attain a more transparent, less anthropocentric mode of existence." How much more interesting is writing a poem that incorporates the incredibly complex discoveries about, say, global warming, into the very fabric of the poem itself? Close concentration upon systems *as systems* can lead to the animation of poetic processes. A lucid yet *wild* fusion of structure of poem with structure of matter/energy— *things*. And things not limited to those traditionally marked as "natural"—i.e., bears, foxes, woods, mountains—but expanded to include all beings, objects, systems, and locales—water reservoirs, the insides of televisions, invasive Purple Loosestrife, Africanized bee populations, cable networks—in a leveling of value between and of subject and object.

Rodrigo Toscano wrote me a lovely detailed letter in response to my talk, thoughtfully going through each category as I had set it forth. What he found most compelling was the idea of "equality of value between all living and unliving things." This idea of equality of value is essential for moving away from the exploitation and inertness of traditional nature poetry, toward Francis Ponge's revolutionary ideas of concentrating intensely upon *things* as *things*, and into the incipient and dynamic idea of poetry as ecosystem itself, instigated and animated through a Ponge-ian (or even Thoreau-ian) concentration upon exterior systems.

However, we came to the problem of "concentration," which Rodrigo felt was too vague and should be defined as a concentration of multiple perspectives "splayed" (his word) onto "new (or rather wished for/striven for spaces." In attempting to clarify—or justify—to Rodrigo what I had meant by concentration, which he felt could be mistaken as "mental acuity sense," which I have to admit was what I originally meant, I found that it was indeed a problem. However, since I think that problems are often fissures into further insights, I countered Rodrigo with Baudelaire's idea of surnatrualisme, "a state of perception which intensifies the existence of things, makes them hyperbolically themselves."[6] Upon further reflection, I also felt that "wished for/striven for" spaces were not as desirable as concentrating upon what was actually there, as wishing certainly entails a certain act of escape from and control over reality.

Rodrigo quite correctly felt that the idea of surnaturalism asserted the dominance of human as perceiving subject over things. After all, he wrote, "why would a worker's (or poem's) democracy social metabolic process (matter of matter) need <ideologically> to be made 'larger than life?' Answer: cause it's dead already—has been since rent asunder." Yet, while Rodrigo raises a most valid point, I'm still not ready to leave the original idea of concentrated mental acuity. First, such intense observation of *things* is one of the few doors humans have to escape our own overwhelming subject-being. How

---

6 | Clive Scott, "Symbolism, Decadence, and Impressionism." *Modernism: 1890–1930*, edited by Malcolm Bradbury and James McFarlane. Penguin Books: Middlesex, England, 1976.

else, besides perceiving, can we begin to disassemble ourselves? It is an absence of concentration upon the space around us that leads to ill-conceived housing developments that are monotonous and isolated from centers of interaction, forcing people to drive cars to work, shop or socialize (or even to enjoy the nature for which many people say they leave the city). For me the process is as such: concentration upon spaces and landscape leads to poetry; poetry leads to further concentration upon spaces and landscape. It is my poetic ecological system—self-sustaining, linguistically self-contained, recycling, and, if successful, animating both word and perception with the idea of action.

At the conclusion of my original talk, it was this concept of "concentration" that the audience debated most. Albert Flynn de Silver introduced the idea of "meditation" as a way to meditate "with" or "within" something as opposed to concentrating "on." To him, concentration seemed to imply a separation, wherein in meditation the subject and object could become more integrated. Laynie Browne thought that meditation could also be seen as a necessary second step in the process of writing ecological poetry—that it is "a skill of actually using all the senses very acutely and then before meditation there is a withdrawal of the senses…concentrate, meditate, and then the writing." Both Albert and Laynie agreed that Lisa Jarnot's *Sea Lyrics* would be an example of meditative ecological poetry, in which the recycling of the "I" becomes like a "mantra" in its incantatory quality, with the "I" being broken down into an equality with the objects with which it defines itself.

Kevin Killian questioned how to accommodate poetry that isn't overtly "ecological," that is one that wastes words, includes "unnecessary" language, "throws a lot of bottles away"—in other words, does following dictums make a better poem? I had to respond that following *any* dictum doesn't mean one will write a "good" poem; there is no "formula." However, I *am* exploring a few ideas that I *could* (speaking of "wished-for spaces") see animating the practice of poetry. Collom's idea of "spandrels" may in part answer Kevin's question: as Nature itself is not neat, and produces loads of unnecessary, even frivolous, things, ecological poetry is almost obligated to do the same. Giles Scott pointed out that the idea of concentrating on something in order to find the thing itself is actually a "wished-for space." In that the poet intentionally occupies and arranges linguistic space, is it possible *not* to wish for a space in poetry? Some kinds of plastic bottles are thrown out, while others can be recycled—the same with words. But does one have to be utopian to be ecological? Does being ecological mean having to wish for a space, even poetically?

At some point during the Q&A period, I jotted down "not oblivious to it," in that the concentration of the poet, debatable as it is, could perhaps counteract the obliviousness of developers, miners, politicians, drivers of SUVs. The idea of ecological poetry introduces a way in which one could write a poem so that the structure of the poem is animated by intense awareness, *not obliviousness.* Poetry written as "wished for spaces," or *intent*, is very problematic, but it's also inevitable to have intent as a certain catalyst. Here's a personal example: Tina Darragh and I have been writing a collaborative series of ecological poems[7] recycling words and ideas from Francis Ponge's *The Making of the Pré*[8] and Michael Zimmerman's *Contesting Earth's Future*[9], a book on the philosophies behind Deep Ecology. So, in this recycling, Tina and I intended to allow these texts, along with assorted articles on environmental issues found in *Scientific American*, *The New York Times*, and other media, to enter our own poetic structures, to see if we could shift perceptions of textual spaces and subsequently environmental spaces. But, while writing with moral intent, we also deliberately opened ourselves and the texts to a catalyzing equalization of subject and language. Our poetry recycled in form and process the "topics" we were writing on. So perhaps the resolution to intent is to only allow that intent to spark the poem into being—it's the key to the ignition, but then you let the car go (to use a completely un-ecological metaphor there).

This all relates to the current and insistent complaint of poets about how to make poetry comment on issues of the day while also retaining aesthetic integrity. This complaint finds some roots in the cultural and economic isolation of poets, but it can also stem from the atomizing tendency of experimental poetry. In order to fragment, you have to separate. In a dream that I had during the trip out to California, I got in a taxi with John Ashbery. So dur-

---

7 | Sections of this collaboration have been printed in *Anomaly*, Issue No. 1, Spring/Summer 2002.

8 | Francis Ponge, *The Making of the Pré (La Fabrique du Pré)*. Translated by Lee Fahnestock. University of Missouri Press: Columbia, Missouri, 1979.

9 | Michael E. Zimmerman, *Contesting Earth's Future: Radical Ecology and Postmodernity*. University of California Press: Berkeley, California, 1994.

ing this dreamy cab ride, we chatted about poetry, naturally. I said something about disjunctivity in contemporary poetry and John Ashbery said to me, "yes, but it's not the separate elements, it's how you stitch them together into a poem." I have long and fervently believed in the abstract composition of poetry, but in the context of ecological poetry, I have been thinking about the third and fourth dimensions of poetry, as well—that poetry has the ability to interact with events, objects, matter, reality, in a way that animates and alters its own medium—that is, language.[10] Experimental ecological poets are concerned with the links between words *and sentences, stanzas, paragraphs*, and how these systems link with energy and matter—that is, the exterior world. And to return to the idea of equality of value, such equalization of subject/object-object/subject frees up the poet's specialized abilities to associate. Association, juxtaposition, and metaphor are tools that the poet can use to address larger systems. The poet can legitimately juxtapose kelp beds with junkyards, or to get more intricate, she or he can reflect on the water reservoir system for a large city by utilizing the linguistic structure of

---

10 | More recently, I have been reading Eugene Ostashevsky's collection of translations of Russian OBERIU poets of the 1920s and 1930s. In his introduction, he writes that one of the poets, Vvedensky, "regards his poetry as an experimental inquiry into the relationship between normative language and the world. He has tested this relationship and found it wanting. Yet, as will become characteristic of the period after the dissolution of OBERIU, he no longer feels capable of fashioning a new linguistic system, one that adequately conveys reality." This sentence struck me for so many reasons: no doubt, Vvedensky, faced with horrible political pressures (many of the OBERIU poets were sentenced to prison or internal exile for their writings), at a certain point could not see into a more creative future for language. But did Vvedensky's "incapability" stem also from looking too much to language to "word" the outer world, rather than looking to (at) the "world" to refashion language? (Northwestern University Press, 2006).

repetitive water-associated words in a poem. Most other disciplines, such as biology, oceanography, mathematics are usually obliged to separate their data and observations into discrete topics. You're not really supposed to link your findings about sea birds nesting on a remote Arctic island with the drought in the West. But as a poet, you certainly can. And you can do it in a way that journalists can't—you can do it in a way that is concentrated, that alters perception, that permanently alters language or a linguistic structure. Because poets work in a medium that not only is in itself an art, but an art that interacts with the exterior world—with things, events, systems— and through this multidimensional aspect of poetry, poets can be an essential catalyst for increased perception, and increased change.

An Interview with Jed Rasula

——— EVELYN REILLY ———

Evelyn Reilly: What led you to write *This Compost?* How do you see it connected to other activities by poets who are exploring the notion of ecopoetics?

Jed Rasula: *This Compost* is an example of an emergent occasion. I didn't set out to write a book, it just came over me. For a year living in rustic circumstances in upstate New York in 1980-81, I'd brought a handful of books to reread with some care: *The Maximus Poems*, *"A"*, and *The Opening of the Field*. The links between Duncan and Olson were familiar, of course, but I was surprised to see how readily Zukofsky contributed to their open field matrix. The field kept expanding as I periodically took out the manuscript to revise it (1985, 1990, 1995, 2000). Because I was out of touch with contemporary American poetry during the 1990s (when ecopoetics emerged), I didn't foresee any connection to contemporary practice at all. So it's really serendipitous that what began as an utterly idiosyncratic exercise in 1980 found a welcoming environment when it was published in 2002.

ER: What, if any, is the relation between ecopoetics and so-called experimental or innovative poetry? You've written that "the bulk of modern poetry suggests a calamitous abandonment of the legacy of Whitman and Dickinson." Do you see any more hope in the experimental wing of the poetry scene today? Are there any current trends that seem interesting to you in this light?

JR: Whitman and Dickinson were experimental. That was the point of singling them out from, say, Longfellow and Whittier. They were like soil bacteria breaking down dead matter, rearranging the contents—standard procedure in nature, but an experiment in culture. In their case, the biodegradable material was poetry. I tend to regard as ecologically wholesome any activity in which decomposition is germane to composition. There is, of course, a completely different (un-American) legacy in this respect, with Mallarmé as resident guru ("Destruction was my Beatrice," he said), the urbanity of which is probably more immediately related to experimental poetry of the past couple of decades.

Jen Bervin's *Nets* is an encouraging instance of something that would be widely regarded as experimental, though I think the more accurate term is procedural for this rigorous trawl through Shakespeare's sonnets. I guess it might qualify as an experiment if her approach was, "Ronald Johnson succeeded in reducing the word count of the first four books of *Paradise Lost* in *RADI OS*, so let's see if I can do the same with Shakespeare." Likewise, Jenny Boully's *The Body* consists entirely of citations, clearly a compositional ordinance, not an experiment. But I'm probably beating a dead horse, insisting on this semantic distinction, but the whole category of procedural operations tend to be mis-categorized as experiments.

Insofar as there's any reason to speak of experiment, it's best to take an ecopoetic outlook. The danger is in looking for analogies from nature, assuming that cultural terms should be resolved with reference to natural cycles. I think culture as a whole is an extravagance, and an exorbitant experiment. And I mean, by culture, all human production, including the byproducts of natural functions (e.g. waste disposal). We make things: what are the consequences of our making? What do we make? From this perspective, possibly the most honest approach is Giacometti's insistence that he had no interest in producing sculptures. He just persisted with it because the more he did it the less competent he felt. Or he understood how unprepared he was to handle that material. That, to me, sounds like the very definition of being experimental. It also rings true with my own experience as a poet, which revealed itself long ago as that point of engagement I have with dysfunction where I am otherwise most functional: in language. I really hear Beckett when he says, in one of those dialogues with Georges Duthuit, "to be an artist is to fail." For the artist, "failure is his world" (a thesis tirelessly worked out by Maurice Blanchot). Beckett brandishes failure in this triumphant declaration, as if to embody the very condition he characterizes as: "Total object, complete with missing parts, instead of partial object."

ER: Although you have reservations about the use of the word experimental, can you talk a little about the Lucretian concept of the clinamen, the swerve or the deviation that might be compared to the genetic variation that potentially results in better adaptation to a changing environment?

JR: You're right, I do have reservations about the use of the term experimental, which is so casual and ungrounded as to be senseless, at least if it's to be understood as empirically derived from the verb to experiment. As things stand, anything is called experimental that won't be included in a forms and craft textbook. But by my reckoning, it's experimental to write a sonnet or a sestina: as in a laboratory experiment, you have carefully delimited parameters and a clear set of instructions. If these kinds of experiments have not interested legions of practicing poets, that's because it's a very old and familiar experiment, the results of which strike many as incapable of bearing news. Without a wholesale determination to reoccupy the form (I'm thinking of Ted Berrigan's sonnets), a sonnet says little more than "author X can write a sonnet," which is about as interesting as claiming the ability to walk through a doorway as a personal accomplishment. If you can attenuate statistical probability, though, so that getting through the door is a real challenge, then something interesting occurs—at least in a Charlie Chaplin movie. The clinamen is a wonderful concept in this respect; it opens the door on chances. It adds, to the confident expectation of going through the door, the propositional incertitude "I'll chance it." I'll take that risk, I'll bear the brunt of serendipity. Serendipity and catastrophe are twins in the domain of the clinamen.

Although the concept of the clinamen was just a shot in the dark, conceptually, on the part of Democritus (and propagated by Lucretius), it has very precise application in, say, genetics. Growth hormones in the embryo are synchronized with a molecule called IGF-1 (for "insulin-like growth factor"), but this molecule—which is like a green light on a traffic signal—can't promote growth all the time. It needs to be curbed by a protein (called PTEN). But if this protein "swerves"—or, in genetic terms, is defective—then we end up with that medical condition called the Proteus Syndrome, famously associated with James Merrick, the Elephant Man. Unchecked by the PTEN protein, the IGF-1 molecule continues to promote cell proliferation (particularly in bony matter—hence the huge skull) until the person is more or less suffocated by becoming a skeletal catastrophe.

When Steve McCaffery and I decided to use the clinamen as the defining concept for *Imagining Language*, we tended to think of it in its more positive, serendipitous aspect. But the multitude of "monstrous" examples included in the anthology retain some sense of malignant, catastrophic potential (e.g. the whole section called "Mania," as well as Francis Lodwick's "Forms of Distinctional Marks," or Urquart's universal language "Naudethaumata").

ER: Maybe the question of experimentalism is really a matter of more or less used—or overused—forms, so that certain writers find themselves deadened by the use of the sonnet or sestina but can embrace, say, Oulipean constraints. As for catastrophe, I've always thought that aesthetically the greater the risks taken, the worse the potential catastrophe, but also the greater the chance of "bearing news." Your description of author X who can write sonnets brings up the problem of "craft" as a way of thinking about the poem as well-made object, rather than, say, Lyn Hejinian's notion of poetry as "the language of inquiry." Is one or the other more or less likely to help in revealing our language's complicity in the abuse of our habitat?

JR: While I'm wary of the reverence accorded to craft in the creative writing world, it is an important term with broad associations. Craft, handicraft (Walter Benjamin links storytelling to handicrafts), manual labor, tilling and harvesting: these terms provide a continuum leading back to how we handle the earth. One school of poetic formalism (cf. anthropologist Victor Turner's son Frederick Turner, whose book *Natural Classicism* I wrote about in *Syncopations*) regards craft as an investment in those integral biological structures of hand-eye coordination that constitutes our ancestral heritage as a species. There is probably something to be said for strict metrics as a means of coordinating manual labor of a predictably repetitive sort. But I resist the notion that 4/4 time is more "natural" than any other meter. It's instructive—and in 1913 it was revelatory—that Stravinsky's *Rite of Spring* is a cascade of self-differentiating time signatures. The primal scene demands it. And this is in accord with Jerrome Rothenberg's longstanding insistence that primitive means complex. So on these grounds it makes sense to affirm Lyn's model of poetry as the language of inquiry with the understanding that "the language" is never a neutral term, nor a given artifact, but the medium in which to craft inquisitiveness.

Your reference to "language's complicity in the abuse of our habitat" implies that language operates as an independent agent, a bit like Christopher Dewdney's specter of language as parasite in *The Immaculate Perception*, or Jack Spicer's deathbed declaration, "My vocabulary did this to me." Does language really pull the wool over our eyes? Is language the primordial agent of ideology? If one were to believe that, then surely one would have to adopt music or visual art as preferential media—and, what's more, regard them as necessary antidotes to the poison of words. But then, painting would have to go, ecologically speaking, for its long investment in toxic pigments. Anyway, "language" is too general for our sociologically inflected modes of complicity; the more accurate term is idiolect. Consider the ruckus over global warming: I can't help but think that the term is close enough to "global warning" that the nay-sayers are motivated to protest because of the surreptitious provocation hanging over the whole thing.

ER: In *This Compost*, you put a particular emphasis on the Black Mountain school and its descendants, even though the notion they embraced of "organic form" now seems rather naïve to us. How useful are "organic" or "natural" metaphors in thinking about what an eco-poetics might be? I'm thinking not just of the notion of "poetic compost," but Retallack's "fractal coastlines" also come to mind. Are we risking a new kind of pathetic fallacy?

JR: I think it's important to distinguish between the implications of organic form among Black Mountain poets and the protocols of explication generated by the New Critics, from whom we derive the somewhat debased notion of organic form to which you refer. Black Mountain poetics understands organic form in a broader context that extends to cybernetics. (Somebody should write a big survey of the liberating effects of cybernetics on postwar American thought in the sciences and the arts, culminating with the '60s. You get a lot of it recapitulated by Thomas Pynchon in *Gravity's Rainbow*, but of course that's a phantasmagoria, not a chronicle.) In any case, I don't think you can dispense with organic form as long as poems have beginnings, middles, and ends—the terms of organic form as spelled out by Aristotle. How do you know when you've finished a poem? Whatever hunch is operative is "organic." That is, it arises from your nature, your being. Unless you're dealing with a prix fixe menu or with formal prosody—here's the dessert, here's the 14th line—how do you recognize where the end is? Organic form permeates every possibility except those indebted to chance operations. Even being arbitrary, in the psychologically willful sense, drags the organic along behind it, even if only as an unwanted third leg.

As for risking fallacy, let's consider ecologically what "pathetic fallacy" means: it signifies pathos, the feelings that are a necessary precipitate of their time and circumstance. I haven't seen any footage of it, but I'm pretty sure that the memorial in Blacksburg, Virginia, following the shooting at Virginia Tech was full of pathos, and that the pathos on display took many forms, from convulsive tears to the calculated rhetoric that Bush and any other delegated officials felt obliged to provide. The "fallacy" in John Ruskin's term is the attribution of feeling to the mechanical operations of "nature." It's basically an objection to anthropomorphism run amok. For the time being, anyway, I don't see any danger of organicism run amok. There are always instances of ideological fury, of course, holier-than-thou postures of rebuke and recrimination that pride themselves on their terminological choices. But here we get into the perennial problem of associating a concept with someone who espouses it (Hitler was a vegetarian, therefore vegetarians are pathological).

As to the use value of organic metaphors: any such use is limited to those for whom it's meaningful, and when the circumstance is ripe. I've deliberately put this in a colloquial form that makes an appeal to the organic, in order to remind you how metaphors are not always chosen but inherited in the vernacular. We're exhorted to "strike while the iron is hot," but how many of us are blacksmiths? This is the raw linguistic material Derrida anatomizes in his early essay "White Mythology." The danger, for ecopoetics, is to deliberately systematize analogies and metaphors and frames of reference in strictly organic terms, and then attempt to legislate those terms. Whereas I think the more responsible ecological approach is to be aware of the balance of passive and active in the choice of terms—that is, to be aware of all discourse as the promotion of what Kenneth Burke called "terministic screens."

ER: Well it's certainly true that there is no escaping the organic. And even chance operations connect to the random processes of nature. Although it strikes me that some entirely non-organic metaphors could potentially be just as useful as organic ones in helping us understand how language use feeds into environmental abuse. As you say, it's a matter of circumstance.

Can you say a bit more about the connection of organic form to cybernetics and also about Burke's notion of terministic screens?

JR: To speak of the organic is to refer to the conditions favorable on this planet for the propagation of carbon-based life forms. Cybernetics (from which we get the term "feedback") examines the interplay between organism and environment, which is such a rudimentary yet pervasive structure that cybernetics became the supreme science for a decade or so after World War II. Olson's poem "The Kingfishers" is a record of his encounter with Norbert Wiener's presentation of cybernetics (Wiener is quoted in section 4 of the poem). Adapted to the Central American setting, Olson comes up with this formulation of the principle of feedback:

> When the attentions change / the jungle
> leaps in
>   even the stones are split

I can't offer anything more precise than Don Byrd's observation, "Cybernetic thought is not a new paradigm. It is rather a science of paradigms... In light of it, no paradigm or archetype carries more than local significance." He's aware that this sounds dangerously like an incentive to solipsism: "Representations of the world are pragmatic, related to particular purposes, ideological. There is no common picture of the world." But his point is that "[t]he limit is not epistemological but environmental. Organic dignity is now founded neither on a transcendental source nor on the immediate intuition of being itself. Organisms are to be valued for their autonomy, for their existence through themselves, not for their origination in something Other. This is to say, organisms are the other."

To return to your question, "organic form" is a red herring where cybernetics is concerned. Rather, everything we know as form is to be ascertained in the cybernetic subject, organism-plus-environment. You don't get one without the other, and their mutuality means that neither can be regarded as a stable term. This is where facile exhortations like "back to nature" come undone. Back to what nature? Much of what people would identify as nature in California, for instance, consists of the ubiquitous eucalyptus, a tree imported from Australia in the 19th century. Humans are by no means the only species that migrates, and any large-scale migration rearranges habitat opportunities for other species. The impact of human behavior, given the imposing scale of our species population, is obviously of urgent concern because of the way local nudges expand exponentially into global consequence. Buzzards that used to be indigenous to the American southeast are now found in abundance in Ontario.

Why? Because the interstate highway system gives them an updraft of negotiable warm air currents, and the road kill gives them plenty to dine on during the trip.

Global warming has become an acceptable ecological topic (one of the few, in fact) I think because it rather comfortably succeeds previous paradigms of global malady like nuclear holocaust. Such paradigms invite, in turn, Big Fix solutions: nuclear detente via the SALT treaties, global warming via the Kyoto Protocol. In both cases we have available agents that can be approached like criminal culprits, nuclear powers and greenhouse gases. There's every reason to deal with them, of course, but the Big Fix options serve as terministic screens in Burke's sense, deflecting attention from the multitude of other contributing factors. The elimination (or at least stand-down) of nuclear threat has done nothing to abate militarism around the world; and the scale of environmental impact related to human activity is almost incalculable. "Impact" is constant, and it doesn't necessarily mean bad except from a romantic longing to live lives that can be easily mapped onto those of our predecessors. We live in a world that dates back only about 200 years, the point of a dramatic increase in human population (coincident with the industrial revolution) that Fernand Braudel calls the collapse of a biological *ancien régime*. So our biogenetic makeup is, historically speaking, an anomaly we drag around in the big sack of cultural anachronisms.

ER: To return to poetics, is there any reason to think that in eco-poetic terms metonymy, as a relational figure, might be preferable to metaphor?

JR: Of all the rhetorical tropes itemized by Quintillian in his immense catalogue, metaphor has no rivals (and he singles it out as most beautiful); the closest contender would be irony. Is it because we take pleasure in conversion? Is it symptomatic of the human intelligence to delight in metamorphosis? Is metaphor grounded in nature in some way—arising, for instance, from observing tadpoles turning into frogs, caterpillars becoming butterflies? If so, then the allure carries with it more than the simple act of comparison. As the tadpole becomes the frog, the metaphor suggests that X might actually become Y. (Wallace Stevens' poem "The Motive for Metaphor" concludes with an ominous evocation of "The vital, arrogant, fatal, dominant X"). The figural reckoning we as a species bring to our engagement with the world is of momentous consequence on a planetary scale. We can make a pewter spoon and we can make a hole in the ozone layer. Metaphor may fluctuate in poetic practice but it's a steady constant in vernacular speech, and this may reflect the propensity of the species for bending and shaping and changing things.

Metonymy raises different considerations altogether. Richard Lanham intriguingly suggests, "Perhaps metonymy has received attention in postmodern critical thinking because it is an affair finally of scale-manipulation, and manipulating scale in time and space undergirds much postmodern art and music." This strikes me as a fairly accurate characterization of a world increasingly known in the interplay between miniaturization and gigantism. That is, the global consequences of our species life are ever more apparent as a precipitously *ad hoc* collectivism that lies far beyond any inherited notions of political economy. By the same token, another form of globalism is evident in the Internet, which is based on microtechnologies. All this is unpremeditated or unintended, but when intended it does seem to reflect Lanham's notion of metonymy as scale-manipulation.

ER: Isn't there also a "proximity aspect" to metonymy that might connect to an ethics of "coexistence"?

JR: Good point. But it seems that coexistence within our own species is a challenge. Scale manipulation is something we're in the process of confronting in terms of population growth. In the past two centuries, each doubling of the global population has taken place in half the time of the previous doubling; since 1960 we've been getting an increase of a billion people every twelve years.

North America remains one of the less populated regions, but for someone of my generation the increase is palpable. No matter where I go now, I can't help asking myself where did all these people come from? It's that conspicuous. A century ago you'd have to attend a World's Fair to experience the throngs we now have even in suburbia. Then, it was part of a singular spectacle; now it's the public face of the inscrutable. I can't help but hear certain tendencies in public discourse in a diagnostic way. So, for example, the preoccupation with "the other" is really an exercise in nostalgia—a desire for when the other could be identified by way of immediate superficial indicators (race, gender, class). I don't mean to suggest that theorists of otherness long for a return to that: rather, the profusion of others now presses the issue of how one responds, and a reasonable response is to preach coexistence. But population growth hits us in unreasonable ways—specifically, it seems to provoke social attitudes based on flight or fight responses, namely religious fundamentalism. In the natural world there are recognized patterns of collective suicide or species abortion, as if a species were an incipient organism recognizing its inability to persevere on a certain scale. The phenomenon of global terrorism may have little to do with politics in the long run; rather, it might be an early warning signal of the stress of coexistence in the close proximity environs facing people whose cultural heritage is of no help in thinking about population growth.

ER: In *This Compost* you write of "the ability of humans to know themselves as their own matter," with the emphasis on "matter" as material substance. Can you discuss the implications of this kind of knowledge, including its implications for poetics?

JR: It's a question that clearly relates to what I've just been saying about population. We're approaching some limit at which humans numerically become sheer matter, and certain kinds of behavior reflect a panic response. It's like when you're hiking (here in Georgia, anyway) in the heat of the summer and keep walking into cobwebs. It gradually goes from aggravating to faint panic to potential freak-out, and I think that "other people" (I'm thinking of the line in Sartre's *No Exit*: "Hell is other people") increasingly provoke that response now.

But to return to your question, the passage in *This Compost* refers to Charles Olson's observation, in the wake of Buchenwald and Hiroshima, that the war had reduced people to so much raw material, and for him this led to a moral obligation whereby the ancient dictum "know thyself" had to include, in that knowledge, the expendability of yourself in the strategic reckoning others might bring to bear on you. The moral part of it, for Olson, is reflected in his use of the first person plural: it's "we" who need to attain this perspective. And I think that informs his poetics very precisely, in that the figure of Maximus is himself *plus* all possible others—an impossible challenge, but a necessary undertaking. It's quite a contrast with the studious replication of the Oedipal family you get in Zukofsky's *"A,"* not to mention the trans-historical paint-by-numbers bombast of *The Cantos*.

ER: In earlier essays you've expressed discontent about the nature and dynamics of the contemporary poetry scene. To what extent does *This Compost*, with its vision of a multigenerational "composting community" (manifested graphically by the juxtaposition of unattributed quotations from numerous poets across its pages), call for a new kind of poetry society? Does it generate a more collaborative, communal notion of how poetry happens, in contrast to the more hierarchical notion of individual genius?

JR: Careerism is the real *bête noir* in my observations on the contemporary scene. It's a byproduct of the success of creative writing programs, which have now been around long enough to have become thoroughly integrated into the institutional apparatus of the university system; the bottom line is the annual report to the dean on professional accomplishments. Just as you could observe procedural and thematic surges in scholarship in the past by looking at syllabi and publications—deconstruction in the '80s, postcolonialism in the '90s—it's now possible to discern holomovements in the body politic of poetry. It's a way of detecting a somewhat different kind of "composting community" than I focused on in *This Compost*. The alliance between Olson and Duncan and Creeley on the issue of open field composition, for instance, was deliberate but not programmatic, a matter of elective affinities that could extend to others without any question of membership, allegiance to party line, or even personal acquaintance. The poetry scene today constitutes an archipelago of sites where various alliances are made along similar lines, although, as far as I can tell, these sites don't seem to be broadcasting identifiable slogans like "open field" and "deep image" were 40 years ago. The scene is at a higher demographic level, in the university system, where we can see clumps of unelected affinities coagulating, disclosing trends and filtration patterns that radiate from a collective practice despite which, curiously, the issue of individuality seems not to suffer. As far as I can tell, your generation seems fairly comfortable with group dynamics, with a poetry scene from which the alpha male ego has been drained off to some extent, detoxified. I'm pretty sure this reflects the involvement of women poets. As I suggested in *Syncopations,* this is a decisive demographic transfiguration that has and will continue to create a very different sort of poetic community.

ER: At the beginning of your book, you quote Jerome Rothenberg's description of the poet as "defender of biological and psychological diversity" in the context of parallels between ethno- and ecopoetics. Does this view of the poet necessarily connect ecopoetics to an activist stance? You also write that "poetry is unique in favoring utopia as a transient occasion not universal city," which might imply the opposite.

JR: Why not see activism as the promotion of transient occasions? It's probably a consequence of utopian thinking that we tend to think of activism as pursuit of the greater good over the long haul, instantiating governance as transhistorical plebiscite without really considering what it's in our power to accomplish. Of course the key term is "our." Who are we? How many can "we" accommodate? To think on behalf of other people is, at one level, generous. It can also be presumptuous and, at another level, totalitarian (I know what's best for you).

This spectrum, from the egalitarian to the controlling, is evident in debates about ecology. To fully embrace the prospect of a globe in peril seems to lead to an absolutist response (we know what's good for us all), in which "take it or leave it" merges into "America: love it or leave it," so it's understandable that people seek some moderate position (think globally, act locally). At the largest level ecology is tantalizingly close to the Archimedean position: that is, in order to know all we need to know in order to act, we'd no longer be in or of this world. So it's useful to remember that the Greek root of ecology links up with economy in *oikos*, something like household management.

In that Confucian tag revered by Pound, if a man has not order within him, he cannot spread order about him. That's a little dictatorial, so let's make it more descriptive than prescriptive. The Confucian adage has conspicuous consequences for this society, simply in the fact that public life, such as it is, is dominated by what happens on television. The tremendous growth in forms of interactive media may be a reaction to the enforced passivity of the television legacy, but unfortunately that legacy remains the paradigm, the surrogate host, of the very models of interactivity that some see as replacing it. (For one thing, interaction invariably comes with a visual screening device, for which the television screen is the template). The diversity of transient occasions I'd advocate are not to be confused with the kind of diversity (viewing options) specific to a medium, and that means poetry as well as television. I have a certain phobia about generic experience as such, probably stemming from the expression "watching TV" which spooked me as a kid, when I realized that for most people it really was watching television, rather than watching something specific, making a choice ("watching TV" meant no choice, submitting to whatever was on). I continue to feel wary in the same way about, say, reading poetry, as if it were all the same. In the ecology of elected habitats, it may be beneficial to write poetry, or read it, but I disapprove of the urge to be a poet, which for many is the driving force. This is a posture almost indistinguishable from "watching TV"—as in, first I'll be a poet, then I'll find out what kind of poetry I'll write (or, again, read). As a defender of psychological diversity, I'd like to expunge the word "poet" from our vocabulary. Wouldn't it be wonderful to commend a piece of writing without the special pleading of genre marching alongside like the change of guards at Buckingham Palace?

This is why I've found it so expedient to draw on the literary theory of the German Romantics (the Jena group, especially Friedrich Schlegel), in which every venture in writing inaugurates its own species—the poem is at once an instance of poetry and "the poetry of poetry": that is, the act that includes reflections on its nature as act—amounting to a kind of evolutionary continuum in which the possibilities for change are accommodated to the medium without necessarily being the *raison d'être*. From that prospect, there's no need for "experimental" poetry because poetry is the name of an inevitable experiment in living.

ER: Having thus dispensed with the issue of "experimentalism," perhaps we can turn to another question: is an ecologically informed poetics necessarily a reaction against the Western rationalist tradition? A few of the essayists in our collection take that stance. I'm thinking of your phrase "the sanguine narcissism of the cogito."

JR: Merely to refer repugnant habits of behavior or styles of thought to the Western tradition has always struck me as a cop-out, a way of admitting, in effect, the problem is too big to think about, so dismiss something big as a kind of mental bait and switch. When I was twenty, "don't trust anyone over thirty" was the slogan; denigrations of "the West" (and its variants) derive from the same mindset. In both instances you willfully cut yourself off from your own experience, or potential. For baby boomers, it was a historically specific way to "go native" in one's own juvenescence (which is not the same as adolescence, it's not juvenile: it was a fascinated response to the demographic swell). We got over it, merely by virtue of biological consequence. But can we "get over"—let alone overcome—Western civilization? Far better, I think, to understand its complexities and not be swindled into thinking it's one big package deal. It's not a matter of either/or. What more instructive paragon of the Western rationalist tradition than Thoreau? The beat he heard emanating from a different drummer was as much indebted to Latin authors and Enlightenment botany as it was to Native American lore.

It's true that my phrase "the sanguine narcissism of the cogito" evokes Descartes, and Cartesian dualism can be held accountable for modern varieties of discourse that, pushed to a limit, provoked Jean-François Lyotard's instructive question, "[c]an thought go on without a body?" But, prodigious as the Cartesian legacy has been, I wouldn't conflate it with Western rationalism as such (is Hegel, then, part of Western rationalism?—it's a question to be heard in the spirit of David Antin's remark that if Robert Lowell is a poet, he's not interested, but if Socrates is a poet he'll consider it). So there's no way an ecologically informed poetics is a necessary reaction against Western rationalism, because "Western rationalism" is a figment of the impatient imagination. Somewhere in *This Compost* (maybe in draft, so it might not have made it into the published book) I referred to Western civilization as something one might plausibly characterize as a series of "gang-related incidents" in police lingo. I think that's much more accurate than talking about rationalism. In the end, it's not about what we "know," but what we do and what we've done that makes a difference. "Here error is all in the not done,/ all in the diffidence that faltered" Pound wrote at the end of Canto LXXXI, and I can never hear these lines without this juxtaposition from Canto CXVI: "To make Cosmos—/ To achieve the possible—." The m-dashes extend, conceptually, all the way to the horizon. And they join Cosmos with the possible in a gesture of unavoidable engagement.

An Interview with Tyrone Williams

—— BRENDA IIJIMA ——

Brenda Iijima: You grew up in Detroit and now make your home in Cincinnati. How has your relationship to these urban biomes shaped and informed your writing? Social landscapes: the local, situational, and experiential factor into your work in significant ways—perceptions, distortions, and dissonance filter the terms of engagement. The description for your book *On Spec* states, "these poems also implicate and illuminate the speculative enterprise that we venture into whenever we attempt to articulate what we see and what we believe about it." A long sequence in *On Spec* is titled, "Four Dialogues, Five Fish, One Bowl (interrogation procedures)," which points to the constructed aspects of the social-biome. From an ecopoetic standpoint, are there any subject-matters that you notice being left out of the contemporary writing called poetry?

Tyrone Williams: Growing up in Detroit in the late '50s and early '60s, I was fortunate to have a mother who indulged my early imaginative fantasies—supporting everything from science fiction series to mathematical theories, from *Highlights* subscriptions to a tiny organ and guitar. As a result, I was fairly isolated—my cousins nicknamed me Papa because I stayed inside a lot and read rather than playing outside with the other kids. Still, in my early teens, I became gradually aware of the Black Arts and Black Power movements. I sensed—rather than understood—these movements as challenges to the Civil Rights movement. In school I wrote editorials against busing, insisting that this punitive strategy against white suburbanites—and that's how Detroit seemed to me, stratified along race lines—only punished white taxpayers without really helping black kids. I didn't understand the tax-base foundation of public education, but I sensed that busing was not addressing the real issues. Although I still had a traditional concept of poetry and literature, growing up when I did under far-flung social and political conditions that did not appear to have any impact on my childhood gave me a sense of the social and political stakes. A sense of the aesthetic stakes would come later....

When I moved to Cincinnati, I was stunned by what I perceived to be the "backward" social, cultural, and political landscape of southern Ohio in general and the city in particular. As it turns out I wasn't wrong about Cincinnati, but I did realize that living in the Wayne State University area for so long had warped my perceptions of the rest of Detroit and of southeastern Michigan. Both southwestern Ohio and southeastern Michigan were more alike than I had realized. And so I defined myself "against" the region in which I found myself living. Nothing unusual about that for artists. It seemed strange to me, however, because in the WSU area—the Cass Corridor—there was a general sense of camaraderie and political solidarity even if the anarchists and Marxists were constantly at each other's throats. In short, those disputes—aesthetic, cultural, political—were family fights, were fought along the "left" side of the political spectrum. In

Cincinnati the battles were, and still are, fought along the right-to-center side of the spectrum. Aside from a few individuals here and there, there is no critical mass of leftists in Cincinnati. What complicates these regional issues even more are the suspicions directed toward "avant-garde" or "post-avant-garde" artistic practices by those from all positions on the political spectrum. I had—have had—a running dispute with some leftist organizations—organizations I support from a political perspective—in Detroit over "postmodernism." Part of the dispute, I'm sure, is related to how this term is defined. Is it an apolitical movement or a more radical movement than that of purportedly "radical" political organizations? Is it merely the aesthetic reflex of an attenuated avant-garde, its political significance irrelevant? These suspicions have, as we know, a long history, and I must acknowledge that they can not be dismissed as unfounded. Hence I like to think of the dispute as critical engagement, at least from my side of the discussion.

As for ecopoetics—it is a necessary adjunct to the overall critique of both late capitalism and fundamentalist Marxism. Aside from your work, Brenda, I'm interested in ecological critiques from figures as disparate as Mike Davis, Percival Everett, Marcella Durand, Leslie Marmon Silko, Lisa Jarnot, Taylor Brady, etc. However marginal or isolated a phenomenon vis-à-vis U.S.A. poetics, ecopoetics serves as an important mode of socioeconomic and cultural critique, not least against a "nature" poetics apparently resistant to extinction (though not, I should add, to being dislodged as the privileged species of a certain kind of poetry).

BI: Warning—this is going to be a chunky, convoluted series of questions within questions because there's so much I'd like to ask you to comment on!

I don't know if you come from a particularly religious background—if you attended church, were involved with a church community, etc. —but I am interested to know how you feel about the powerful language of religion that could be said to be poetic and how you see it shaping relationships and understandings of the environment. Biblical texts are evocative in bringing up notions of freedom, will, human power, the supernatural, human capacity and processes—how humans are capable of moving/removing mountains literally and figuratively. Here I think of mountaintop removal mining in places like West Virginia, Virginia, Tennessee, and Kentucky—the land and people's lives sustained and tainted in a contorted relationship of exploitation and value with megacompanies like the Anaconda Mining Company that have power over the land, environmental policy, humans, and all other animal's lives. Have you read Alena Hairston's book of poems, *The Logan Topographies*? It is situated within this triangulation of community, environment, and industry.

Your piece, *work/time=*, on the Critiphoria Website (http://www.critiphoria.org/Issue1.html), contains a hilarious and poignant mock interview between a mine pony and a possible equine impostor posing as a pony but maybe in fact a Trojan. The mine pony's historical account reads like a human miner's and we are reminded how systems of power (controlled by humans) don't make distinctions between human and animal in their allocations of cruelty toward "beasts of burden." I'm thinking not only of how in the Old Testament, man was given dominion over all of the animal kingdom, but how the idea of dominion is extended through the idiolect of the religious right evangelicals (and, it seems to have thoroughly permeated Western culture, for that matter). In this mode of eco-imperialism, resources are there for the taking regardless of the consequence to all other life forms.

I wonder how you feel about Hannah Arendt's understanding of human agency in the so-called natural world of so-called automatic processes. Here is a quote:

> We find in these parts of the New Testament an extraordinary under-standing of freedom, and particularly of the power inherent in human freedom; but the human capacity which corresponds to this power, which, in the words of the Gospel, is capable of removing mountains, is not will but faith. The work of faith, actually its product, is what the gospels called 'miracles,' a word with many meanings in the New Testament and difficult to understand. We can neglect the difficulties here and refer only to those passages where miracles are clearly not supernatural events but only what all miracles, those performed by men no less than those performed by a divine agent, always must be, namely, interruptions of some natural series of events, of some auto-matic process, in whose context they constitute the wholly unexpected. No doubt human life, placed on the earth, is surrounded by automatic processes—by the natural process of the earth, which, in turn, are sur-rounded by cosmic processes, and we ourselves are driven by similar forces insofar as we too are a part of organic nature. Our political life, moreover, despite its being in the realm of action, also takes place in the midst of processes which we call historical and tend to become as automatic as natural or cosmic processes, although they were started by men. The truth is that automatism is inherent in all processes, no mat-ter what their origin may be—which is why no single act, and no single

event can ever, once and for all, deliver and save a man or a nation, or mankind. It is in the nature of the automatic process to which man is subject, but within and against which he can assert himself through action that they can only spell ruin for human life.[1]

TW: I was raised as a Baptist and was made to attend church until about the age of 13 or so. I actually enjoy attending church—a Free Methodist one though denominations don't mean much to me. For me, theology in general is the twin brother of philosophy and they have been fighting it out for all of Western and Eastern history. Hence my concomitant interest in philosophy. Because of the influence of the Nation of Islam in Detroit when I was growing up—along with the bread-and-butter work of the Black Panthers in Detroit—I read the Koran in my teens and early twenties, along with Hindu and Buddhist texts. So my interest in religion, like my interest in philosophy, is ecumenical. I understand the history of the dominion, domination, and imperial linkage, though I would say that the Biblical texts are merely one instance—a privileged one within the West, but one instance nonetheless—of a more general "human" and pre-"human" tendency toward territorialism, encroachment, and conquest (the qualifying quotation marks indicate my suspicion that the word "human" has in fact authorized the historical processes you describe). To return to the specifics of your questions, I want to recall that the very concept of stewardship, of tending to, taking care of the "natural" world, is authorized by Biblical texts, which might account for the evangelical/apocalyptic

---

1 | Arendt, Hannah, "What is Freedom?" from *Between Past and Future* (New York, Viking, 1961). p. 168.

tone one often discerns in otherwise secular environmental/ecology-based texts and speeches. I know of Hairston's book but I have not read it; it might be interesting to juxtapose it with the work of Percival Everett... The piece *work/time=* you cite is part of my forthcoming Atelos book, which attempts to do just as you note— delineate the irrelevance of the human/animal distinction under capitalism, though the piece also alludes to the Civil Rights/Black Power dynamic coursing through, and often as, African American history. As for Hannah Arendt—I must confess I don't quite get it. I don't quite see what all the fuss is regarding her work, and this quote is a perfect example of why I remain puzzled. On the one hand she correctly notes that "miracles" are essentially disruptions of natural processes, though her distinction between "supernatural" and "human" events clouds the picture. The picture gets cloudier with an unwarranted conflation of "natural" and "automatic" processes, unwarranted because it isn't clear what the original distinction is between the two concepts. And then, in order to get to what we may read as a variation on her "banality of evil" hobbyhorse, she writes that "automatism is inherent in all processes"—that is, both natural and human processes. But the very historicity of human processes, which she asserts in this same passage, belies this statement. Is it not the specter of automatism in human processes that accounts for our belief that they are "natural" and, thus, inevitable? Human agency is possible precisely because of the gap between the specter of automatism and automatism *per se*, between what we might call "human history" and "natural history." This distinction is, as we know, ideological through and through. But so is the conflation of these two "histories" on the basis of an overarching or underlying "inherent" automatism. If we were to take this word "inherent" seriously in this context, would not doing so amount to the erasure of another word, one which accurately summarizes human processes that "tend to become as automatic as natural or cosmic processes"? That word, habit, has its own ideological baggage, of course; even so, it still serves as a corrective to the automatism underlying Arendt's project in general.

BI: How might your pet dog factor in to this discussion of the terms of eco? This question I'm asking in complete seriousness. In Donna Haraway's, *When Species Meet*, she faults Jacques Derrida in his critical overview of the animal-human divide, *The Animal That Therefore I Am,* for not endeavoring to understand what his actual pet cat might be thinking. Haraway writes, "[k]nowing that in the gaze of the cat was 'an existence that refuses to be conceptualized,' Derrida did not 'go on as if he had never been looked at,' never addressed, which was the fundamental gaffe he teased out of his canonical tradition."[2] The ontology of animal other—how do other animals act upon us? Is there interspecies communication? How do we shake loose the dichotomy of human and animal? How does language represent and present humans and all other animals?

TW: I'm unfamiliar with Haraway's critique of Derrida. I'm teaching some of her early work (*Simians, Cyborgs and Women* and *Primate Visions*) for the first time this semester (Fall 2008) so we

---

2 | Haraway, Donna, *When Species Meet* (Minnesota, University of Minnesota Press, 2008) p. 23.

will see. More generally, I suppose one could make a case for the inevitable anthropomorphic gesture that is initiated at the moment one speaks of "other animals" in terms of "act," in terms of "communication," etc., by noting that "human" "communication" also presupposes an anthropomorphism that is not, has never been, by definition, universally ascribed to other, only apparent humans. Even if anthropology attempts to reconceptualize its anthropomorphic matrix on the terra firma of scientific rigor, it does so, as Haraway demonstrates, by incorporating—by not expelling—its founding prejudice. It is on this basis, this necessary prejudice, that miscommunication and misunderstanding are possible. This relationship between the work of anthropology and anthropomorphism converts the human/animal dichotomy into the human/animal dyad, a fundamental inter-(intra-?) relationship that respects the otherness of the non-human animal (my qualifications concerning the word human still standing...) by reducing otherness to a mirror ("they" are just like us) or lamp (studying "them" enlightens us), and my allusion to M.H. Abrams' important study of Romanticism is deliberate.[3] As one of the dominant animal species currently above ground (unlike moles, say, or the remains of the dinosaurs), we get to name this epoch the reign of homo sapiens, but since we cannot say anything about the historical memory of other animals (we can only "test" their abilities to "recall" according to our understanding of memory, history, time, etc.), many of which live, on average, much longer than human beings, we cannot conceptualize their

---

3 | Abrams, M. H., *The Mirror and the Lamp* (Oxford, England, Oxford University Press, 1953).

conceptualizations of era, epoch, time, etc. None of this bars, much less forbids, interspecies communication as it actually exists, as we might wish for it to be, and so on. For most Americans, learning to communicate with their pet dogs is not only easier than learning Urdu, it is easier than learning how to read poems (contemporary or not) written in English, or deciphering the multilayered meanings of a rap lyric. That relative ease should give us pause regarding interspecies communication.

BI:

> As we talked of freedom and justice one day for all, we sat down to steaks. I am eating misery I thought, as I took the first bite. And spit it out.   —From *am I blue?* by Alice Walker

How do you respond to this provocative, powerful statement?

TW: I won't pretend to be familiar with the current arguments around the "problem" of sentience vis-à-vis animals and artificial intelligence (or its analogue in debates over abortion and the "beginning" of life), but Walker's statement only reinforces what I wrote above: anthropomorphism is inescapable the moment one believes one is communicating with an other (human or animal). Hence the controversy over issues concerning "freedom" (see Adorno's *Messages in a Bottle*, for one critique[4]), "justice," etc. Put another way, Walker's ability—and, why not, her privilege, our privilege—to eat "misery" must be respected no less—but no more—than the impoverished Rwandan, for example, who may never get to eat misery,

---

4 | Adorno, Theodor W., "Messages in a Bottle", edited by Slovoj Zizek (London, England, Verso, 1995) pp. 34-45.

much less "spit it out" in a gesture as ethical as it is narcissistic. I'm more convinced by ecological arguments—reducing the consumption of meat as a contribution to improving the environment for all animal and plant life—than the ascription of moral and ethical foundations—really, just mirrors and lamps—to others.

BI: At what point does an issue become ethical with all the clinging moral baggage? I think it is so hard to walk the line and separate out the moral/ethical. Even without stating as much a critique can be inferred. I'm constantly asking myself how an activist stance can be open and also un- or less-than-sanctimonious. I think your point about respect being a matter of consciousness—a matter of honoring a situation/set of terms goes a long way in finding a stance that is engaged but non-judgmental. How do you parse this?

TW: Obviously the separation of the moral and ethical as philosophical categories is largely heuristic; in practice we know that the ethical cannot be objectively determined and that it functions as an idealization or projection of the moral. And vice versa. Hence my reference to mirrors and lamps in a previous question, a reference that, though literary, illuminates a wider range of human activities. To be blunt, there is no engagement or disengagement that is not judgmental. The moral baggage is always clinging to an ethical stance. This is not to say, however, that some ethical or moral positions are not more conducive to biological survival—individually and collectively—than others. But as we know, biological survival is not always or primarily the most important value in a given context. Hence the debates over abortion, euthanasia, warfare, etc.

BI: Since WWII, at least 250 synthetic chemical compounds have been introduced into the environment. These new substances are interacting with and creating havoc in animal and human hormonal systems and disrupting body functions. There is a spike in reproductive complications, brain disturbances, cancers, etc. The names of these 250 chemical compounds are perhaps the least used words in our aesthetic lexicon. How can we uncover these disturbances in our art practices? Should we? Do poets have an eco-ethical role?

TW: Poets can, poets may "have an eco-ethical role" to play, a role no less and no more important than that of any conscientious citizen of the world. The level of engagement with critical issues confronting the earth and its inhabitants will obviously entail the absorption of lexicons from industries and institutions deemed hostile or, at best, indifferent to the effects of their products on terrestrial life. Having said that, I will insist that the introduction of synthetic compounds into the environment is, on some levels, structurally analogous to the ongoing development of life *per se*. That is, the development we call evolution is itself marked by disruptions, hostile encroachments, viral flare ups, and catastrophic events (volcano eruptions, floods, etc.). That these are natural—as opposed to synthetic—events is probably of little comfort to those on the losing side of this history. I understand the crucial difference—that we have some say so over synthetic or manmade events—and this difference must continue to be upheld as an ethical duty to the living and the lives we imagine extending beyond our own. But I think it is imperative to recall what this may mean: that in taking the side of life "as we know it," we may be taking a stand against a form of life we would never recognize as such. On the abstract level of life, this may still be an easy choice to make, but at more concrete levels things get a lot thornier. Let me invoke Alice Walker and her infamous campaign against ritual clitorectomies in the name of justice and freedom of choice. Or the protest against industrial development in the "third world" in the name of cleaner water and air and the end of exploiting child labor.[5] The problem is that there is no clear line between these concrete matters that may make taking sides complicated and the more abstract ones that may make taking sides relatively easy.

BI: The hybrid: as DNA is manipulated and cloning becomes a reality, conceivably in the future there may be hybridized humans— a human-animal-vegetable blend. I'm questioning notions of purity here—cultural, social, racial, and otherwise. How is language being hybridized? What are the implications?

TW: New life-forms will mean new forms of language—hardly a revelation, I know. I'm not sure I understand what you mean by "language being hybridized" since few languages in the world are "pure" in the sense of developing within isolated cultures. Certainly

---

5 | See Ellen Gruenbaum's *The Female Circumcision Controversy* (University of Pennsylvania Press, 2000) and Alice Walker and Pratibha Parmar, *Warrior Marks: Female Genital Mutilation and the Sexual Blinding of Women* (Diane Books Publishing Company, 1993). For the discussion of anti-industrialism in Third World contexts, see Takis Fotopoulos, "Globalisation, the Reformist left and the Anti-Globalisation Movement," *Democracy in Nature*, 7.3 (2001), 415-455, Kate Frieson, "The Political Nature of Democratic Kampuchea," *Pacific Affairs*, Fall 1998, 405-427, and Joel M. Halpern and John Brode, "Peasant Society: Economic Changes and Revolutionary Transformation," *Biennial Review of Anthropology*, Vol. 5 (1967), 46-139.

today all languages, to varying degrees, manifest themselves as hy-
brids of other languages. Globalization, in its broadest sense, is one
of the forces driving this process, though globalization, like hybrid-
ization, has been going on since the first humans set to sea. I don't
know if you mean to imply that with cloning and the concomitant
possibility of "human-animal-vegetable blends," attitudes toward
the environment might improve for self-interested reasons. I don't
think human-vegetable clones would necessarily be more inclined
to sympathize with vegetable life for the same reasons current human animals don't sympathize with other human animals.

BI: By using the word "hybrid" here, I'm thinking specifically
about the biological revolution that is taking place. In this sense,
DNA and RNA are new alphabets, able to be manipulated and
able to generate new forms and directly interact with other forms
of signage. For example, there's Christian Bök's experiment. On
November 17th, 2007, Bök introduced "The Xenotext Experiment"
at the One Origin, One Race, One Earth Conference. With the as-
sistance of the renowned geneticist Stuart Kauffman, Bök plans to
encipher a poem as a sequence of DNA and then implant it into the
genome of a bacterium called *Deinococcus radiodurans*, an organism
highly resistant to evolutionary drift. Bök notes that, because this
life-form can survive a nuclear attack, his poem might even outlast
human civilization itself: "I am hoping to write a poem that is still
here on Earth when the sun explodes." (http://www.shotgun-review.
ca/2007/11/spreading_and_preserving_poems.html). I'm wonder-
ing what you think the implications of this experiment might be.

TW: Hate to disappoint Christian, but when the sun explodes, the earth will be incinerated! Seriously, though, it's an intriguing experiment, though premised, perhaps, on a false assumption that this might be the first poem to outlast human civilization. That belief assumes that we "know" all the extant poems, that they have all been found and read, that there are no scrolls or books or scraps of papers or disks or postcard poems inside bloodied overcoats in some mass graveyard of human bodies, many of which may never be discovered and so will "outlast" human civilization.... I suppose, however, that intentionality is key here for Christian. Is this very different than Joyce's supposed quip that *Finnegan's Wake* was written to keep professors busy for centuries?

BI: Maybe he'll eventually build a mini-rocket device and send the organism out of the stratosphere—so it won't be incinerated...

The intention to plug a bacterium (some other life-form) with his poem is as flippant a gesture as intending to write a poem that will outlast human civilization—I want to appreciate the conceptual value of his experiment, but it is fraught with too many issues that aren't approached in his statement. On the other hand, maybe humans are a fading species (and the taxonomy of all other species too) in the face of technological innovation—meaning, the term "human" is no longer stable—terms are being hybridized. Life-forms are merging and blending (not evolutionarily but genetically) and so forms of communication will change dramatically, too. Maybe this is just a crude beginning of that. This is the

Dynamic Society model in action.[6] Bök is one of many using BioArt practices.[7]

TW: If the planet lasts long enough, humans, like every other species before them, will cease to exist. And genetic cloning may accelerate—or retard—that process. Ditto for the ingestion of elements we deem toxic. Still, let's not forget the lesson of the pharmakon[8]— that the difference between a remedy and a poison is a matter of scale. What interests me about Bök's project, what it reminds me of, is how much experimentation projected toward a possible future is part of the legacy of modernist (and some post-modernist) poetics, though I suppose you could argue that a certain tradition in Western poetics has, at least since Thomas Wyatt, projected itself against a present and toward a future it cannot envision…

BI: The greatest concentration of hazardous waste sites in the nation, 29 Superfund sites in total, exist in Silicon Valley, according to Rebecca Solnit in her essay, "The Garden of Merging Paths."[9] Solnit also states that technology is literally and historically a tool

---

6 | Snooks, Graeme D., *The Dynamic Society: Exploring the Source of Global Change* (London, England, Routledge, 1996).

7 | BioArt is an art practice in which the medium is living matter and the works of art are produced in laboratories and/or artists' studios. The tool is biotechnology, which includes such technologies as genetic engineering, tissue culture and cloning. See http://en.wikipedia.org/wiki/BioArt.

8 | Derrida, Jacques, "The Pharmakon" from *Dissemination* trans. by Barbara Johnson (Chicago, University of Chicago Press, 1981) pp. 95-116.

9 | Solnit, Rebecca, *Storming the Gates of Paradise: Landscapes for Politics* (Berkeley, University of California Press, 2007).

of power. She points to the social forces that control the development and use of machines and the social changes that might detour us from the current trajectory. She contrasts her position with Jerry Mander's stance in his book, *In the Absence of the Sacred*, where he thinks of technology as making an inevitable march toward consolidation, control and ultimately, ecocide. Language could be considered a technology and is perhaps the most effective tool to forward ideological constructs. How do you see language, especially poetic language, morphing into new technological forms?

TW: Yes, language is a technology, and the tools by which it is delivered reflect the history of human invention. So now the Internet opens up new possibilities, though many of these possibilities currently being enacted (e.g., hypertext, vispo, texting, etc.) represent a return to older modes of language—for example, an updated hieroglyphilia—that, perhaps inevitably, signal a certain nostalgia, however subconscious, for a less abstract, more phonetically based mode of communication. Of course, phonetics and phonology are just the tip of the iceberg if we want to dive into the controversies in which linguistics have been embroiled ever since the "invention" of this particular science...

BI: A complex ecology with lurking implications: landscape as repository for toxicity. A storage unit with an expiration date, no-man's land, no-go zone, barred regions, fenced-off zones, the border, wastelands, land mined fields, refugee camps that can never (seemingly) resettle, resource grabbing... But all of this too is cloaked and re-faced. Subdivisions, mixed-use appropriations, puppy mills housed in quaint barns—seemingly innocuous spaces contain hefty residue that starts to dictate. Pretty apple orchards are laden with noxious chemicals; the average American lawn is managed using chemicals designed as weapons in WWII combat (for example, Atrazine). A worker in an upstate New York apple orchard once told me he wouldn't dare eat the apples he picks. What's my question—I feel stunned. OK, I guess the general question that compelled me to think about the *)((eco (lang)(uage(reader))* is—how does language contend with the environment (that includes bodies) in duress—to combine poetry's engagement with these compounding issues?

TW: But this is an old story. When I was at Wayne State University in the '70s, my girlfriend and I stopped sitting on the grass when we witnessed the chemicals ChemLawn was using, and for years my father, who works for a bottled water company, has refused to drink tap water, the problem of his company's own plastic containers notwithstanding. Language, if you will, has been contending with this in the West at least since Blake ("London")—I mean, the English Romantic enterprise contends with this issue if only by negation. Another way to view technology is to return to Locke, Hume, Hobbes, et al, who link the origins of human society with the desire to master nature and other humans, not simply out of a desire to master (Hobbes notwithstanding) but also out of a desire to improve, as is said, the quality of human life. Everything depends, of course, on how one defines quality, but note, too, that no one was under the illusion that the movement toward mastery was motivated by the desire to improve the quality of all forms of life. And I'm not just talking about flora and fauna. The invocation of the "human" has historically always meant the simultaneous demonization or, at best, bracketing of all considered non human. In the West we are familiar with the Native American and African experiences, just to name two groups once considered non human.

Human Views of Nature

—— JAMES SHERRY ——

During the past few years I have written and published a few poems and essays based on an idea I call environmental poetics. The central theme is to show how poetic arts can adopt an environmental model without losing the reader's interest or regressing to natural pietism. The overall book is entitled *Sorry*, but each individual chapter of the book, whether poem or essay, is modeled as an environmental niche with dependent and independent themes rather than as an argument as found in the European essay form developed by Montaigne or Bacon. In some ways these niches can stand alone and in some ways they are dependent on the other niches. For example, the niche on the World Trade Center and terrorism links in interesting ways to the niche on the use of passive voice in literature, but the story about counting all the fish in the sea stands as an independent piece of literature whose topics are merely reflected elsewhere. The following niche talks about the separation of ecology from environmentalism, suggesting that the analysis of the environmental problems requires rethinking the structure of our relationship to the other components of the planet rather than criticizing other people's behavior. "Human Views of Nature" shows how each individual has many relations to the environment depending on his or her role and that no essential relation can be established in advance. What does this imply for the future of our human society?

The time is ripe for a project to better organise information in articles related to Environment. This page and its subpages contain the suggestions; it is hoped that this project will help to focus the efforts of other Wikipedians. If you would like to help, please inquire on the talk page and see the to-do list there.   –Wikipedia

If, as most scientists suspect, there will be a significant change in global climate during the current century, then we will likely see a concomitant change in social structure. (Michael Thompson's article "Man and Nature as a Single but Complex System"[1] is the inspiration for these ideas). In the same way that weather will be the news, the social structure will focus on nature. Rather than defining nature in one way, the new social organization will accommodate several myths of nature for different types of people in different social roles and environmental situations. A cab driver in New York, for example, will have a different picture of the value and scope of nature than a Tutsi warrior will. Further, as a person's role changes, their view of nature changes as well. In my role as a poet and critic, I view nature differently than I do in my role as a father and husband trying to feed my family.

In my role as a poet, I am writing from the viewpoint of one or more singular myths about poetry (poetry styles or schools typically posit themselves as independent of other styles). I may be concerned with:

- how I feel and what happened to me and my group (expressive and personal poetry)
- how I communicate and make you feel about events (communications model)
- how I make meaning (philosophical poetry)
- the subjects I write about, which may be primary (political poetries such as romanticism)
- how I use language (various experimental poetries)

---

1 | Thompson and Price, *Newsletter of the International Human Dimensions Programme on Global Environmental Change*, 2002.

If, for example, I write from the viewpoint of my personal identity (expressive), is that poetry irrevocably different than if I write poetry based on the myth that it is about the materials of poetic composition—language, form, and other non-lexical meanings? What is my poetry when I mix the two or include a third set of components? Does such composite poetry lack rigor in that it uses inconsistent components to drive its meaning? Does poetry need to use a mode of expression that is consistent with its themes? Can it, like an environmental niche, incorporate a variety of functions, expressed differently? Writers and critics have been fighting about this subject for 30 years or more, perhaps forever, in an effort to gain acclaim for their own viewpoint. The net effect of such discussions has been to marginalize poetics. Politicized poetries from both sides of the "aisle" have been linked to each other rather than to the larger culture from which they sprung, with the result that the focus of poetry (and other arts) has been made increasingly less central to the larger culture. My current approach is to work on ideas about the environment and to push poetries and arts into environmental models so that a larger and more coherent policy around poetry can be established, a more inclusive poetry and poetics can be imagined and written, and poetry can establish a current place in the epistemology of our society.

As environmental processes become less predictable, change will occur in the social, the political, and the cultural spheres. (The projected changes in poetics, outlined in the preceding paragraph, are exemplary). Individuals will be expected to take a stand, have a point of view. But as Wikipedia points out, we don't have a clear idea of what our environment is or how to make changes through the study of ecology. If we are not clear about environment and ecology, then we are even less clear about nature. Is nature all that is the case, the ceiling of reality, or are there supernatural forces that control nature? Does nature include humanity or is humanity irrevocably opposed to nature by virtue of self-interest and special capabilities (reason and reflection) that allow us to "rise above" nature in special and important ways? Is nature the material world, the essential characteristics of things, the forces and phenomena that produce all that is, the world of living things, the total of reality, a primitive state that we seek to exceed—or is all of the above couched as a confusing multiple-choice question that can only be answered by avoiding any semblance of essentialism?

Each role that a person takes has an inherent myth about nature that is not well defined today, but that will be defined in excruciating detail as the problems of environmental change make themselves felt and further discussion is "marketed." In one sense, the need for a word like nature is a result of the disintegration of our relationship to the rest of the planet, especially if we think that nature is all that is the case, and no "supernatural" forces can be confirmed beyond our internal constructions. In another sense, nature is a very useful way to describe the overall presence of our world. One danger, especially in a poetic discussion of nature, is to take nature is a noun, which makes us think it's a thing, when it's also a set of processes, relationships, and non-things, that is, where there is no object we can point to. Given this level of multiplicity and uncertainty around what is nature, how can we use the term and make sense of it? In order to understand nature we need to understand the relationship between other organisms, our environment, and ourselves. But again the path to that understanding is circuitous and not well understood.

Wikipedia defines ecology as the study of the interactions of organisms with their environment and with each other, while environment is defined as the combination of all the conditions external to the genome that potentially affects its expression and its structure (strange assumption and not one that I'd suggest supporting; this may be one of the reasons Wikipedia needs to change as of this writing). Environmentalism advocates the preservation, restoration, or improvement of the natural environment, especially regarding the control of industrial and other pollution. Other issues of concern also include species extinction and preservation of biodiversity, responsible waste management, recycling, the threat of global climate change, ozone depletion, and genetically engineered organisms. But all these ideas are up for grabs because Wikipedia is proposing reorganizing its eco/enviro pages. I suggest below one way to start changing it and ourselves.

This niche attempts to reconcile a few issues that are not well defined in the top down version of Wikipedia's definitions. Other niches attempt (sic) to reconcile some of the bottom up issues that arise from epistemological considerations and specific problems arising from the simultaneous discussion of poetry and the environment.

The key, to this author from the viewpoint of poetics, is the failure of both ecologists and environmentalists to reconcile cultural issues in a new environmentally oriented model, as opposed to couching all planetary activity within an existing humanist/scientific model or within a pre-humanist/deistic model. Each group's effort to define the essential fabric of reality misguides us down a single path, whereas many paths will lead us to fruitful results. While both deist and humanist environmentalists and ecologists promote social change based on environmental issues, neither of them is willing to question their myths about nature, and as such are always in a state of internal contradiction from which they have to argue a defense that becomes the fabric of their reality instead of clarifying or understanding nature. Further, the two groups are not definitively separated, as many scientists continue with an essentialist viewpoint that is associated with deism, and the deists for their part continue to use scientific jargon and method to reinforce concepts of deity. (This subject has been dealt with extensively in other essays of mine in *Sorry*. Also see Michael Pollan's *The Omnivore's Dilemma*).

From the essentialist viewpoint, all human activity around ecological and environmental issues is conditioned by one or more myths about nature. For example, in science, nature is the ceiling beyond which speculation is fruitless, because assertions cannot be proven false. For deists, there are supernatural views and values (based on prior texts like the Koran, Bible, or Bhagavad-Gita) that will impact their choices regarding how we should treat humans, animals, plants, and non-organic components of our environment. These assumptions are inconsistent with data about the environment, whether fact-based (earth temperatures, for example, are increasing) or belief-based (god is continually re-engineering the planet to improve human conditions so long as humans continue to follow his rules, so any changes are god's will). The problem for us is that we cannot at once dismiss our assumptions about nature or society. Remember how hard it was in 1970 to talk about the shift from a univeral male pronoun? How many fights were started by questioning something as simple as a pronoun? Any essential view of nature will be as difficult or more so to change.

A non-essential view (and I would like to become a proponent of this view if I can figure out what it might be and how to write about it) implies that the complexity of interactions among all these components drives a cultural model of the environment that includes, but also goes beyond the science of ecology or a set of statements about the environment. And to avoid lumping all these values and studies together, we need a cultural model of nature to help us condition our modes of action. In this way, scientists can act as scientists, politicians can legislate, and cultural workers can create while acknowledging the values of the other workers. Thompson takes it a step further by pointing out how we each will subscribe to different myths of nature, depending on our role of the moment.

Yet so important is this set of cultural issues that I hesitate to accept my division of knowledge in this paragraph into science, politics, and culture because of its basis in the enlightenment and the larger humanist set of assumptions that I am trying to replace. As an environmentalist (and I mean that I am trying to see my assumptions within the architecture of an environment rather than from the viewpoint of only one myth about nature), I look for a planetary model that includes viewpoints that may be illogical, but which exist and have a significant impact on the forum of discussion. I also want to propose a multifaceted view of nature. A useful activity might include imagining an environmentally oriented social structure like my high school English teacher did with Chaucer's *Canterbury Tales*, where he imagined that the pilgrims and their relationships represented civil society in the 14th century.

I suggest that the issue of social structure may need to be dealt with because of the lack of conviction in the popular press around environmental problems, as opposed to the general agreement of the scientific communities about the largest environmental threats. (Several writers, including Al Gore, have pointed to how differently the popular press depicts the greenhouse effect, as opposed to the near 100 percent concurrence in the professional scientific press). I further suggest that there's a big difference between the external, fact-based approach and the belief-based approach. Then there is the question whether we should prioritize the scientific fact-based or gut-held belief approaches when making decisions about our lives, our communities, and our planet. Finally, I'd like to ask whether we can extend data and metaphors from microbiology/genetics to ecosystems and larger frames, or if there are different models that must be applied to bigger and smaller scale stuff and where the breakpoint is—organism or gene pool or niche or ecosystem or entire planet.

From the viewpoint of poetry then, the question of the value of metaphor becomes strikingly less trivial when posed in this way. If our myths of nature make us behave in ways that are contrary to our individual and collective self-interest, then these essentialist metaphors pose as great a danger to civilization as nuclear weapons do. In addition, their long-running impact at a very low level renders them nearly invisible as a threat to society. I hope this makes an argument for continual investigation and creation of messages about society from all levels rather than just the top. It makes an argument for the shifting values of art, science, and politics, and it makes an argument for seeking ways to promote problems in their complexity rather than reified to an essentialist misrepresentation of the major problems confronting us right now and just over the horizon.

It's likely, based my own introspection, that we need to avoid prioritizing along the fault lines of belief and fact so that we can simultaneously address both the fact- and belief-based approaches. The advantage of such a method would be that each of us (almost all in any case) has both a fact-based and a belief-based set of biases that need to be addressed before personal and social change occurs. A real solution, from the human perspective as well as from the environmental one, would simultaneously accommodate both biases. Otherwise, we will forever second-guess decisions depending on which set of biases we are focused on at the moment. (Of course, we can and will continue to have essentialism in our culture because we sometimes need that kind of reassurance and that is one of the approaches that needs to be conditioned in our solution set. But maybe I'll deal with that issue later).

The result of these discussions about essentialism (fact and belief) all direct me to a non-humanist, non-deistic construction of the world based on our view of nature. God and humanity can fit in, but they are neither the center nor the focus of our endeavor. I am talking about environment and ecology, which, regardless of any human or godly plan, are views of nature. As a result, a view of nature that takes us into the parallel world that I am proposing is a pre-requisite, so that we carry as few assumptions forward as are useful and proper to such a discussion and ultimately to such action. (If these conclusions are not clear, I need to rewrite or extend these ideas in other niches).

Such an effort to redefine society in a more complex way has been started by Thompson: "The classic assumption in both ecology and social science is that there is a one-way transition from state A to state B." Models of change are often temporary and uni-directional. This is hardly our daily experience and not how facts nor the belief structure would project change going forward. So why are we constantly subject to making this mistake?

If we accept that human activities take place within environmental complexity, a multidisciplinary approach suggests several contextually valid views. In a paper that brings together the concepts of "relative surprise" from theoretical ecology, "cultural bias" from social anthropology, and the investigation of decision rationality, Thompson suggests that one's view of any change has as much to do with the individual's point of view (i.e., his or her psychology and environment) as it does with the validity of the change:

> When people argue from different premises they will, in all probability, fail to agree.... Attention is focused not on the facts of the matter but on the facts of the disagreement.... In other words, the discerning spectator begins by granting legitimacy to all these sets of contradictory premises. Nor does the fact that they are contradictory cause him any dismay. On the contrary, he sees social life as a process that depends for its very existence on the perpetual contention between these different sets of convictions about how the world is.

For example, a physicist's world has resources in abundance, since matter is neither created nor destroyed, while an ecologist's world has limited resources. Thompson goes on to outline a set of cultural relationships to nature that inevitably define the individual's approach to facts and opinions. And such a model might be a useful tool for environmentalists and ecologists as well.

As the environmental model of the planet begins to take hold in the culture, a new set of social classes will emerge based on the individual's view of nature. Thompson hypothesizes that "there are just five distinct cultural biases each of which has associated with it a distinct idea of nature."

Social Being	View of Nature
The Ineffectual	Lottery Controlled Cornucopia
The Hierarchist	Isomorphic Nature
The Hermit	Freely Available Cornucopia
The Entrepreneur	Skilled-Controlled Cornucopia
The Sectist	Accountable Nature

Our views of our environment, its politics, sciences, and arts, are filtered through a cultural screen. An act may be considered rational if it is consistent with the actor's idea of nature. This relativism reflects the political reality of our culture. But if we view culture not as a set of habits of mind, but as a continually renegotiated set of social relationships, we can establish what Thompson calls "a cultural construction of nature."

Thompson proposes that the new model resist the urge to remove complexity, goal ambiguity, contradictory certainties, conflict, institutional inertia, and temporal change from our culture. He suggests conceiving policies to preserve their "historical contingency" (which is perhaps a bit vague). The arts and sciences can understand their processes as evolving with the imperfections inherent in any cultural unit. While we cannot make much progress in specialized knowledge without a rigorous taxonomy of knowledge, we cannot make much progress in our relationships in society or nature without arts and sciences that accommodate the peripheral views: belief and fact. Yet while we cannot argue from these peripheral views, they are a result, existing at the edges that define change, not the habits of day-to-day engagement.

The implications of this concept for policy, for art and for integration in the sciences show us an approach "to moderate specific debates so as not to erode general consent." The disputes today between conservative and liberal political views, between scientific disciplines and environmental sciences, between traditional and risk-taking arts may benefit from this analysis of nature. In any case, they will become more and more prominent as environmental change drives social change.

One more point is that there is a fundamental conflict between planetary nature taken as a whole and the survival and flourishing of any one species or group of species. Without such analytic tools as Thompson, Goodwin, and others provide, we cannot manage our successes. Not only does our success as a species doom many others, it may, in retrospect, have been our own undoing. Thompson asks a fundamental question that many of you are no doubt asking as well: how do we treat humanity and nature together as a single complex system?

The great irony of our age appeared as soon as humanity grasped the possibility of getting out from under nature's boot—plague and privation. At this very moment, we see that we have gone too far: global warming, ozone deterioration, resource depletion, and general discontent with the political hierarchy. Can we use the analytic tools of arts and sciences interactively for the purposes of a policy of a less invasive approach to global domination? Or is it possible that the American global trading empire, integrated by balance sheets and capital movement, represents the less intrusive way of which I am speaking? Is such a "military" venture possible?

At this point, the contradictions in capitalism are being managed through controlling labor by moving capital around the globe. And conscious globalism, the irony of Marx's panacea, is for the first time a possibility. While many, from technologists, to investment bankers, to religious fundamentalists, will claim credit for globalization, the ability to mediate difference/diversity will be the measure of its success in the future. I continue to be less concerned about how we got here than about the nature of our continuity. As such, I want to represent what I consider important distinctions that condition action, rather than suggest convenient courses of action as the first step.

The fear is that we need to act right away, or with planning by "my" group, or never. The fear is that change cannot be predicated on facts. The fear is that...each of us has one or many of these fears and they modify our actions. And then there is self-interest modifying our judgments.

What I'm suggesting in this niche of ideas is that we start looking at our planet through a different scrim than the humanist or deist. Just go away from those divisive perspectives and start looking at the situation from our view of nature. See if you can identify yourself. That may be where you start making decisions that matter.

> Asymmetry provides the centrality/peripherality
> Criterion that serves to separate the prescribing
> Entrepreneur from the prescribed ineffectual.
> A personal strategy aimed at the deliberate
> Avoidance of all three types of order in nature
> Can also result in a viable conjunction
> Of social context and cultural bias—the hermit.
> The author does not take it literally,
> But the reader materializes it with her reading.

Aurora Afro-Americana

── TRACIE MORRIS ──

I've always had notions of identity in my work. No way to get around it. No need to: so much of it came to *me*, voluntarily or involuntarily. The chances of gender, race, economic reality, culture, context, or geography being erased from my purview are not even desired. The facets of what these notions mean, how they mean, and which of them takes priority over the other lap and elapse like the protocol of fingers waving hello (or goodbye). The tension between issues of rights and sacrifice, the experience of day-to-day living, and themes of metaconsciousness, is no more apparent than in the consideration of race and the environment. Of course, the compounded discussion of environmental racism has received exposure, but that topic is, depending upon who is doing the talking, framed as either part of eco-politics or racial politics. It is a subset, in context of whatever discussion in which it's raised. In either setting, the tangibility of the need is the focus of the commentary.

The dust particles of New York after 9/11 coated and obfuscated the markers of all city inhabitants that day: the wind currents united boroughs and the tristate area that had been fractured in sentiment, if not by name, for at least 100 years.

Whatever identity is, "traditional" concepts of it in the U.S. can't be ignored because of the eco-emergency we face. (Katrina has demonstrated that certainly. The doors granted that Cain-seeming mark of what? God's wrath? Man's wraith? The "genus" of our "human family"? The only moment of being equal. How FEMA, absorbs both the Fe[male] and the Ma[le], lets the flood take them all, lets the sun bake all the bodies brown). Fundamental nihilism is ingrained in the prejudice of the elite of the elite (the base).

I sought to dog-paddle through this swirling environment of "equal opportunity trauma" (~~including 9/11~~) in an experimental poetry theatre piece I presented at New York City's Kitchen Performance Space in the spring of 2003. Two and a half years before Katrina made me want to, in some ways, take it back, *Afrofuturistic* incorporated the premise that, if there were no earth, our other political debates would become "debatable," or actually "not debatable." I guess the corollary to that assumption is that before that point, our debates about identity most *certainly were not*.

How do marginalized groups negotiate this no/ation? That ID isn't important? (Marginalized groups always show ID). We can't turn in every physical marker for a green fig leaf, but … the absence of leaves, of life, is some no "we" can't get past. One of the pieces in the play explores this idea using Af-Am vocab/refs:

Apology to Pangaea

I seent you
blue: silk on a peacock feathered eyelet
corona around pupil of the old
Dye with expensive tastes:
red — corpuscles of the dyers.
In the underbelly of current,
coffin canoes heavily down.

And here we be with capes, spandex and big hair
hieroglyphs spelling superduper, people who made atoms,
his momma, molecules before mourning.
Dat was me with the buck dance and chicken head.
Me, making Grits gris-gris, wif.
Can I say sorry for dem sweep yo feet, Mam?
Do I throw coarse salt over ma shoulder?

My effort here was also to negotiate the ambivalence about the origins of Black in this *particulate* land, our ancestors' inescapable involuntary landscape, as well as the involvement of all humans in the harm done to the planet through consumerism and passive voice...a whisper.

I remember hearing something: a dark-matter eco-experience in pop, back in the day (when we had seasons in the Northeast). It was the astounding/underrecognized theme album, *Journey Through the Secret Life of Plants,* by our green giant Stevie Wonder. I recall hearing "Race Babbling":

This world is moving much too fast
They're race babbling

This world is moving much too fast
The end's unravelling

Man's production
Life's corruption
World destruct

Help me people
Save you people
God's induction
Life's construction
These instruct
Will save every living thing
Can't you see that
Life's connected
You need us to live
But we don't need you

This world is moving much too fast
They're race babbling

This world is moving much too fast
They're race babbling
This world is moving much too fast
The end's unraveling
This world is moving much too fast
You can't conceive the nucleus of all
Begins inside a tiny seed
And what you see as insignificant

Man's production
Life's corruption
World destruct

Help me people
Save you people

God's induction
Life's construction
These instruct
Will save every living thing
Can't you see that
Life's connected
You need us to live
But we don't need you

This world is moving much too fast
This world is moving much too fast
They're race babbling
This world is moving much too fast
They're space traveling

This world is moving much too fast
They're race babbling
This world is moving much too fast
The end's unraveling
This world is moving much too fast
This world is moving much too fast
This world is moving much too fast
They're race babbling
This world is moving much too fast
They're space traveling

Wonder's renown for boldly tackling racial issues has been well-earned, especially when considering that this album was distributed in 1979.[1] He incorporated then-new digital technology throughout the conceptual album and the vocalizations on this track were processed electronic sounds (except for the repeated refrain). In a

---

1 | I would add that Mr. Wonder's "Village Ghetto Land," on *Songs in the Key of Life*, references pollution and the depressed environmental landscape of

way, they call for saving the human race through a technologically displaced voice that could also be interpreted as the voice of another species of being, the *plants'* voices.

The deliberate fluidities rooted in Wonder's afrocentrism didn't address our ending environment in the same way that Marvin Gaye's "Mercy, Mercy, Me (The Ecology)," released eight years earlier in *What's Going On?*, did. Gaye's explicit lament as he forged his new path in Motown's catalogue implied an end to humankind.[2]

> Woo ah, mercy mercy me
> Ah things ain't what they used to be, no no
> Where did all the blue skies go?
> Poison is the wind that blows from the north and south and east
> Woo mercy, mercy me, mercy father
> Ah things ain't what they used to be, no no
> Oil wasted on the ocean and upon our seas, fish full of mercury
> Ah oh mercy, mercy me
> Ah things ain't what they used to be, no no
> Radiation under ground and in the sky
> Animals and birds who live nearby are dying
> Oh mercy, mercy me
> Ah things ain't what they used to be
> What about this overcrowded land
> How much more abuse from man can she stand?

---

1. | ghetto life, but this would be an example of a racial commentary with an environmental reference (e.g., "Children play with rusted cars/ Sores cover their hands / Politicians laugh and drink-drunk to all demands").

2. | The unusual spiritual chanting at the close of the piece is as cumulative and dystopian as Orff's version of *O Fortuna* in any number of horror masterpieces. This haunting sound at the end of Gaye's song is often cut off during commercial radio play. I guess the "play" is underscored in "commercials."

Oh, na na...
My sweet Lord...No
My Lord...My sweet Lord

Gaye's text is set as a jewel in a string of political wrongs addressed. The Hue-Man's (to reference Harlem texts) hue and cry, in the larger scope of the album, frames Blackness, anti-humanism, and eco-critique. No need to choose who here. No here, no who, and this particular who hears into the future.

These two guideposts, tunes to the ghost of childhoods past, lend fully formed ecological assertions that may have been the echo to my later apology. These previous notes call: cultural failsafes that ask us to secure the earth as ourselves. The earth's turns concern discrete concate/nation of humans, and other beings, to save. *Green is peeking out under/ the garish day-glow/of useless things*[3].

---

3 | From the poem "Mother Earth" by Tracie Morris ©2003.

Poetry, Ecology, and the Production of Lived Space

—— LAURA ELRICK ——

PART 1

In 1825, the great utopian socialist Charles Fourier "announced
that he would be home at noon every day to await a wealthy bene-
factor who would be willing to provide funds for the founding of
his new society."[1] This new society was to be based upon the idea
of the *phalanstère*, a self-contained but non-oppressive community
unit that would encourage the practice of something called *joyous
labor*—quite a far cry from the society we now know as industrial
capitalism, of which Fourier wrote scathing critiques, claiming it
bred a poverty "born of superabundance itself."[2] Such ideas were
among his most astute, and Marx would later develop them into a
more systematic critique of capitalism. But Fourier also made some
much more *fantastic* claims as to what would constitute the new
paradise on earth: "androgynous plants would copulate, the North

---

1 | John Bellamy Foster, "The Renewing of Socialism," *Monthly Review*, Vol. 57,
No. 3, 2005, pp. 2-3.

2 | Quoted in Foster, p. 2.

Pole would be milder than the Mediterranean, the oceans would be made of lemonade, and the world would contain 37 million poets equal to Homer."[3] Needless to say, Fourier waited and waited, eating his lunch alone for 12 long years before finally checking out.

Yet strangely, from the vantage point of the early 21st century, it now appears that the production of social spaces based on mutuality and the fulfillment of physical, material, intellectual, and spiritual needs is the far more fantastic notion, farther than *ever* from realization, while the seemingly *outrageous* ideas Fourier put forth are at least conceivable, if not just over the horizon. Indeed, androgynous plants do copulate (if you can call blasting the cells of one into another "copulation"); the Arctic ice shelf is melting at an alarming rate (so the North Pole *just might* become warmer than the Mediterranean); the oceans may soon enough be made of lemon-scented toilet bowl cleaner, if not Fourier's more delightful sounding "lemonade"; and there are probably *at least* 37 million poets on the eastern seaboard of the United States *alone,* though it is undoubtedly a subject for debate just which "Homer" we should be compared to.

But seriously, what might our torquing capitalist "utopia" mean for an ecologically motivated poetry?

---

3 | Steven Kreis, "Lecture 21: The Utopian Socialists: Charles Fourier," *The History Guide: Lectures on Modern European Intellectual History,* www. historyguide.org/intellect/lecture21a.html.

To begin to answer this question, I'd like to turn toward the "field" of culture itself, and specifically, to the explosion of cultural production that has occurred since the middle of the last century. Geographer David Harvey relates that in New York in 1945 only "a handful of galleries" existed, with "no more than a score of artists regularly exhibiting." However, roughly between 1975 and 1985, over *150,000* artists began exhibiting "at some *680* galleries, producing *more than 15 million artworks*" and this in New York City alone.[4] Clearly this trend has continued in the 20 years since 1985, and though the specific figures here relate to the visual arts, I think we would all agree that a similar trend has occurred in poetry.

Interestingly, at the same time we are seeing this huge proliferation in cultural production, we are also seeing a dramatic disappearance of species on the planet. Barthes' "scriptors" (the authors, of course, having died...along with everything else at the top of the food chain) are born through the increasing visibility of the mass(es) of their language products. But this correlation is not only one for the texts. In fact, the current biodiversity crisis is so severe that it is being called the "Sixth Extinction" (the fifth having occurred about 65 million years ago when the dinosaurs disappeared). It is by far the fastest-occuring mass extinction in Earth's 4.5 billion year history, happening now at a rate of approximately 30,000 species per year, a loss of about three species per hour.[5] Yet the coldness

---

4 | David Harvey, *The Condition of Postmodernity* (Oxford: Basil Blackwell Ltd., 1989), p. 290.

5 | E.O. Wilson quoted in Niles Eldredge, "The Sixth Extinction." ActionBioscience.org, www.actionbioscience.org/newfrontiers/eldredge2.html.

of numerical representation does little to underscore the intensity of the tragedy.[6]

Finally, we should note the dramatic shift in the modality of rule that occurred around the early to mid '70s with the birth of global neoliberalism. Some of the changes that accompany neoliberal rule include a delinking of currencies from mineral standards, the consequent explosion of finance capital, horrifically violent structural adjustment plans, growing disparities of wealth and poverty, and a new mode of production called flexible accumulation, in which the Fordist factories of the past are replaced with far-flung fragmented or "spatialized" factories all over the globe. Because of flexible accumulation, your TV might have had its parts made in six different countries. In short, industrial production begins to leave the U.S. at the same time cultural production skyrockets.

During this period, we experienced decreases in democracy at the workplace, decreases in access to healthcare and to quality public education, a slow but steady corporatization of the media, and an upsurge in covert military operations. Concurrently, the striking rise in world temperatures, speed of deforestation, rate of species extinction, and air, water, and soil pollution, might lead one to question whether the upsurge in the number of young people throwing in their lots with poetry is related to a democratization of literature when everywhere else democracy is shown to be a scam. Is it a free-

---

6 | For a more poetic treatment of this see Juliana Spahr, *Gentle Now Don't Add to Heartache* (Sub-Poetics Self Publish or Perish, 2004).

dom or a relegation? And for what and for whom? Perhaps this is the classic situation of obtaining a formal freedom, a good thing in its own right, in place of the freedom to participate in the collective determination of the material practices of social life, to decide democratically what will be produced, how it will be produced, and how and where it will be distributed.

At the risk of stating the obvious, I'll suggest here that the link binding all the changes I've mentioned is the brutal extension of the reign of profit into every area of the globe, and not only into physical spaces such as forests, glaciers, and oceans, but also into every facet of social life. Recognizing our collective participation in this extension might bring about new ways of engaging in the practice of poetry, a poetics, in short, that points less toward a fetishistic valorization of "the text" as object (form & content) and more toward an investigation of mediated textualities that intervene in (and experiment through) the mode of production, circulation, and exchange.

PART II

One way of avoiding an artificially narrow approach to ecology and poetics is to ground it in an analysis of space. Here again I turn to David Harvey's argument in *The Condition of Postmodernity* that it is exactly this maniacal drive for increased profit that has transformed our perception of space-time over the last 30 years, and to such an extent as to have practically annihilated the experience of real space through the speeding up of time.[7] Satellites, cell phones, and Internet technologies, in addition to changing how each of us moves in the world (oftentimes in a positive sense), *also*, if not *primarily*, speed up the transactions of capital. In short, as capital tries to deal with the recurring crises of over-accumulation (in which it has become so efficient at creating vast caches of consumer goods that there are not enough markets to buy them up), it seeks ways to decrease the time between production and turnover into profit, so as to get an increasingly narrower "leg up" on the competition. In this hyper-competitive world, satellite information transfer renders 500 miles virtually the same as 500,000.[8] Such exponential compression is also experienced in all its disorienting effects culturally, socially, and subjectively.

In this sense, the global profit imperative is a deciding factor not only in specific environmental contexts, but also in every facet of our lives as they are lived in space and time. Profit constitutes our physical and social horizons, the limits of what can be conceived of as "possible." It creates scenarios that force our own participation in the "pragmatic" decisions already bounded by the disarticulating agency of its power.

One such example is the way in which globally reproduced national discourses about the need to demolish "the welfare state" have

---

7 | Harvey, pp. 284-307.

8 | Ibid., p. 293.

translated into a decision by local governments in the northwest U.S. to sell their publicly owned old-growth forests. This might indeed seem a truly bizarre causal chain (especially because *social* welfare in the U.S. is essentially nonexistent) until one realizes that scarcity is a useful method to get people to discipline themselves. It works like this: public schools are strategically underfunded under the guise of "accountability," only increasing the by now very real perception that "our schools are failing"; privatization is sincerely offered as an alternative to the ineffective government use of "our" tax dollars; corporations then receive government monies to create private for-profit schools. To avoid The Gap High School from coming to your community, you can sell off public lands, if you wish, to fund the corpses of public education. Either way, corporate logic has made an incursion into what was once collectively determined social space, effectively creating *new spaces* for accumulation—what Jeff Derksen has called the production of "nonsite."[9] Nonsite is created by international electronic manufacturers in Tijuana who dump their chemical waste on the street instead of building proper disposal and treatment facilities, and by ExxonMobil's 30-year policy of silence around their 17-million-gallon oil spill in Newtown Creek that created a toxic underground lake beneath 55 acres of

---

9 | It is in the face of such contexts that Derksen warns against fetishizing localist discourses of resistance since "the particularisms of a place/site and its histories are not just the oppositional force to globalization (or the corrective to dominant historical narratives), but an aspect of place that can be utilized by globalism." Focusing on the way place is constituted through "a dialectic of local and global, or site and nonsite (if a place is imagined as siteless in its loss of particularities due to globalization)" is one way to avoid the mystification of this operative nexus of power. Jeff Derksen, "'Text' and the Site of Writing." *Biting the Error: Writers Explore Narrative* (Coach House Books, 2004), p.110.

residential homes in Greenpoint, Brooklyn, and by developers who have succeeded in making many "places" in the US indistinguishable from one another.[10] To get concrete then requires us to also think through abstraction. Our place (the place of our bodies and minds) is no longer locally determined.

The colloquial shrinking world of globalization—the "annihilation of space through time"—is the culmination of a rationalized abstract space, the space of developers and surveyors who posit it as an empty container, a Cartesian plane on which isolated objects can be moved around, as if on a blank template.[11] This is the power that arbitrarily slices up swaths of land into grids, represented on maps as mathematically arranged fragments, that become homogenous and universal in their qualities, literally parcels of space to be bought and sold as commodities. This is the divvying up of Africa (for European gain) into arbitrary states having nothing to do with already existing linguistic and cultural groupings, as well as the flattening of hills and the draining of creeks for the Wal-Mart parking lot. This is the production of space for and through private property, which not only pulverizes the land, but also our bodies, turning

---

10 | For information on school funding and public lands see "State Trust Lands," State Biodiversity Clearinghouse, a project of Defenders of Wildlife, www.defenders.org/states/factsheets/statetrust.html. On the environmental impact of maquiladoras in Tijuana see "Border Toxic," Environmental Health Coalition, www.environmentalhealth.org/pubs-factsheets.html. On the Newtown Creek oil spill see Deborah Gilbert and Genia Gould, "Class Action Suit Filed for Greenpoint Oil Spill Victims," *Greenline: The North Brooklyn Community News*, Vol. XXX, No. IX, Nov 4-30, 2005, pp. 1, 20.

11 | Jill Magi investigates the ideologies of such a space in her chapbook *Cadastral Map* (Portable Press at Yo-Yo Labs, 2005).

them into a compendium of features and parts that are function-alized for various tasks according to their category. Penis, vagina, breast, ass. Wrist, elbow, finger. And as Monique Wittig has writ-ten, "[w]e are compelled in our bodies and our minds to correspond, feature by feature, with the idea of nature that has been established for us."[12] Instead of conscious organism, our experience of the body has become one of inventory.

In short, if we are to combat this spatial and temporal regime of profit, "[w]e must," as Neil Smith has so succinctly written, "face squarely the production of nature by human hands and defy the conventional, sacrosanct separation of nature and society."[13] Conceptually, this is significantly different from saying that the environment is manipu-lated by human hands, since it suggests a reorientation away from the environment as separate, as exiting already outside us. In this sense, an ecological cultural project would work not so much to *save*, but to intervene in what kind of nature will be *produced*.

PART III

So where does this leave us poets as "cultural workers"? Does the recognition that the structures of capital, the mode of production,

---

12 | Monique Wittig, "One Is Not Born a Woman." *The Straight Mind and Other Essays* (Boston: Beacon Press, 1992), p. 9.

13 | Neil Smith, *Uneven Development: Nature, Capital and the Production of Space* (Oxford and Cambridge: Basil Blackwell, 1990), p. xvi. Also available online at web.gc.cuny.edu/ pcp/about_uneven.html.

played a pretty big hand in us being here together relegate us to a reactive cynicism? Are we agents of agency-less-ness? And anyway, you might ask, isn't poetry essentially a textual practice?

The problem is that if we state that our goal is to create an ecologically minded poetry based exclusively on formal textual maneuvers (such as a further dismantling of the I, or writing from a non-human stance, for example) then we risk replicating the mistakes of Romanticism, which in many respects served as the "rhetorical screen" behind which the economic, political, cultural and material devastations of industrialization occurred.[14] But equally (as Marcella Durand warns in her talk "The Ecology of Poetry"), a poetry that simply "delineate[s] the battles between bulldozer and bird" (that thinks of ecological poetry as a political rhetoric) skips the difficult process of creating new "grounds" that can encourage the formation of new social relations, instead relying on a never-ending "demand" for outside intervention.[15]

So as we attempt to negotiate between what Lefebvre has called "the abyss of negative utopias, the vanity of critical theory which works only at the level of words and ideas" on the one side, and the "highly positive technological utopia, a realm of prospectivism, of social engineering and programming" on the other, perhaps it is

---

14 | Barbara Novak quoted in Smith, p. 13.

15 | Marcella Durand, "The Ecology of Poetry," Small Press Traffic, www.sptraffic.org/html/ news_rept/ecology.html. Also published in *Ecopoetics* 2, 2002, pp. 58-62, www.factoryschool.org/ecopoetics.

necessary to shift our emphasis altogether.[16] Perhaps Charles Olson meant to suggest just such a shift when he wrote that "what we [poets] have suffered from, is manuscript, press, the removal of verse from its producer and its reproducer, the voice."[17] But by this I don't mean to propose a return to speech or a poetics of breath per se, but rather to suggest a possible grounding of poetics in spatial practices that challenge the "nature" of capitalist space, a practice that rejects the separation of our *bodies* from the *spaces we inhabit*.

There are a number of people already attempting such projects. Heriberto Yepez' anonymous (yet somehow mysteriously personal) project posting image and text signs near the Mexican-American border; Kaia Sand and Jules Boykoff's work with signage in southern Maryland, and collected in *Landscapes of Dissent: Guerrilla Poetry & Public Space*; Mark Nowak's call to become conscious of ourselves as part of an industry, as well as his readings and performances at labor halls, which challenge ideas of "proper places" for difficult poetry; Juliana Spahr and Stephanie Young's naked "paper" given at a recent conference in Los Angeles; Jonathan Skinner's incipient "poetry of walks"; David Buuck's works under the rubric of BARGE (Bay Area Research Group in Enviro-Aesthetics); Jeff Derksen's theoretical-creative work on re-articulatory practices, globalization and scale-shifting; Rodrigo Toscano's recent explora-

---

16 | Henri Lefebvre, *The Production of Space* (Oxford: Blackwell Publishers, 1991), p. 60.

17 | Charles Olson, "Projective Verse." *Collected Prose*, eds. Donald Allen and Benjamin Friedlander (Berkeley and Los Angeles: University of California Press, 1997), p. 245. Also available online: www.angelfire.com/poetry/jarnot/olson.html

tions and actions around "body-movement poems" and the formation of practicing communities through the Collapsible Poetics Theater; Joel Kuszai and Bill Marsh's "moveable architectures" of institutional intervention; and Steve Benson's improvisational movement-based performances all interrogate and redefine the space of, by, and for the poietic acts of bodies.[18]

I would like to suggest further, as a possibility for poetry, the exploration of what Henri Lefebvre has called "rhythm analysis," which would investigate "spatio-temporal rhythms of nature as transformed by a social practice."[19] Such a poetry would not engage in descriptions of space, nor in the classical musicality of the individual breath or line. Rather, it would enact an analysis of "space as social morphology,"[20] linking embodied experiments in and on social space to a protean poetics, a poetics committed to the cre-

---

18 | For Yepez see "Context and Signs of an Urban Visual Poetics." *Tripwire: a Journal of Poetics*, No. 4, Winter 2000-01, pp. 102-111, and images at Backlight Gallery at Factory school at factoryschool.org/backlight/yepez/ yepez.html. For Sand and Boykoff see their "Southern Maryland Sign Project." *Chain 11: Public Forms and Landscapes of Dissent* (Palm Press 2008). For Nowak see *Workers of the World Unite and Fight!* (Palm Press, 2005) and *Shut Up Shut Down* (Minneapolis: Coffee House Press, 2004). For Spahr and Young see the text of the paper at people.mills.edu/jspahr/foulipo. htm. For Skinner see the excerpt from "Sites of Writing: from Frederick Law Olmsted to Robert Smithson" at epc.buffalo.edu/authors/olson/blog/ SkinnerOlson.pdf. For Derksen see *Transnational Muscle Cars* (Vancouver: Talonbooks, 2003), and recent collaborations and projects at and www. springerin.at/dyn/ heft_text.php?textid=1317&lang=en. For Toscano see *Collapsible Poetics Theater* (Fence Books, 2008) and poeticstheater.typepad. com. For Benson see *Open Clothes* (Berkeley: Atelos, 2005) and sound files at www.writing.upenn.edu/pennsound/x/Benson.html.

19 | Lefebvre, pp. 117, 205-206, 405.

20 | Ibid., p. 94.

ation of textualites truly mediated by moments of embodied risk. Through attention to acoustic (both linguistic and non) and gestural movement (clusters, breaches, chains, gaits and even physiological "drives"), especially the way they are traversed, "mobilized, carried forward and sometimes smashed apart" by institutional power and the state, such a poetics would develop the non-formal knowledge of social bodies.[21]

And here I mean "the body" not as discursive site, but as practice— in a non-Cartesian space of being-becoming, bodies are the generators and producers of spatial reality through their movements repeated over time, both in terms of labor and in terms of ritual/cultural practices. Here, instead of "minds that move the bodies they inhabit," we are embodied cognition.[22] We are *sub*personal in the sense that we are neither free-willed isolated subjects nor completely determined, since we act in, on and through the shared manifold of the world.[23] Here we might truly speak of "vectors of co-participation" as we act to constitute each other.

---

21 | Ibid., pp. 87, 216, 405-407.

22 | Michael Steinberg, *The Fiction of a Thinkable World: Body, Meaning, and the Culture of Capitalism* (New York: Monthly Review Press, 2005), p. 41. Similarly, Lefebvre writes of "animated space" in *The Production of Space* (Oxford: Blackwell Publishers, 1991), p. 207.

23 | The term "subpersonal" comes from the work of Susan Hurley, and "shared manifold" comes from Vittorio Gallese, both neurologists whose work theorizes the implications of mirror neurons. See Vittorio Gallese, "The 'Shared Manifold' Hypothesis." *Journal of Consciousness Studies, No. 8,* 2001, pp. 33-50, available online at www2.unipr.it/~gallese/Gallese%202001.pdf; and Susan Hurley, *Consciousness in Action* (Cambridge: Harvard University press, 1998).

A poetry that challenges the relegation of cultural activity to the page or stage, one that engages and attends to the production of lived *and* abstract space, analyzing and intervening in the naturalization of such processes, contributes to the production of an ecology for living things.

Spatial Interpretations:
Ways of Reading Ecological Poetry

—— MARCELLA DURAND ——

The space between things has the form of my words.
PAUL ÉLUARD

SPEAKING FOR THINGS equals
A RECOGNITION OF WORDS.
FRANCIS PONGE

A necessary rather than an arbitrary relationship
between a word and the object or event it represents.
CRATYLUS

When objects consist of endangered cormorants, tree frogs, and ferns, and events consist of the disintegration of the Ross Ice Shelf, chemical spillage on a highway, the population explosion of a spruce-eating beetle—what words will be necessary? What spaces will occur between those words? What spaces and words will readers and writers carry with them into a world natural and unnatural? When the observer is actively impacting the observed, how does a poem come into being as something other than a recording of objects and events?

Defining the relationship of the observer to the observed has been one of the most problematic aspects of writing a poetry linked to its environs. This problem has persisted through that poetry's various manifestations as pastoral poetry, nature poetry, and its latest incarnation as ecological/environmental poetry.[1] At this point, it is interesting to explore how the way we *read* such poetry is also shifting. As the way we write changes, so does the way we read. After all, reading is another form of observation—of exiting the *I* to enter the *you*, the world, the other, even as the *I* is changed through this interaction.

I. READING FRANCIS PONGE

In Francis Ponge's The Making of the Pré[2], his writerly interaction with a particular sort of space unfolds in a very raw, exposed sort of creative linguistic process. The *pré*, which means in French "meadow," is a green space, a natural space, but also a human-caused transitional space.[3] Ponge's writing and the *pré* concurrently proceed in uneven patterns, curling back on themselves, or cutting forward: apprehension of space develops as the *pré* itself changes.

---

1 | I intentionally vacillate between using eco-/ ecological/ environmental poetry to describe whatever it is that I'm talking about. It's *not* a School—it's more an interest or at best, a process.

2 | Francis Ponge, *The Making of the Pré* (La Fabrique du Pré). Translated by Lee Fahnestock, University of Missouri Press, 1979.

3 | Meadows are typically old farm fields in the process of reverting to woodlands; in order to keep a meadow a meadow, maintenance is usually necessary.

Above (from the spot where we were, the spot where we happened to be, from which we overlooked the scene, where I saw it, for the first time saw, conceived) (21)

From looking, conceiving and from conceiving, revision and in revision, the spaces between observer and observed *must* be investigated, even if they are never answered, just as an atom that has eight electrons is *inert*, then an atom with missing electrons is always searching to change, meet, collaborate, become.

Here is another excerpt:

Prepared, longed for, crossed in flight as if by a bird, by the flash of a rapid bird, flying low *in direction counter to the writing* (reversing the sense, 'in misconstruction') (such is the acute accent). (57)

Ponge is not bound to "description" of the *pré*; rather, the poetry can run counter to the bird, even as the bird flies counter to the writing—the poem becomes itself an active and creative element, catalyzed by observation and investigation of the *pré*. The acute accent to which Ponge refers is the one over the final "e" in *pré*, a word he has been deconstructing with the help of the dictionary over preceding pages. The dictionary is uninformative enough, or so deeply erroneous in its rigid logic, that it leaves large enough gaps in its supposedly closed sphere for Ponge to reach into: he says, "It seems more and more bizarre to me that près and proche are not close" (39). *Près* and *proche should* be close, since they both mean close and near; the dictionary is mistaken to order them within an alphabetical index of words. By being close to each other, as they both mean close and near, they come closer to the content they signify—becoming more denotative, while yet never becoming the actuality of what they mean. Poems should also not be indexed, but rather understood through a spectrum of scientific and emotional knowledge, including common-sense intuition, which is the amalgamation of all sorts of knowledge and *vocabulary*, gathered from reading newspapers and watching television, from watching how water pours into a sink, or from adjusting one's body to walk down a street. This way a poem can enter the spaces between observer and observed in a more *necessary* way.

II. READING JACK COLLOM

Here is an early poem by Jack Collom[4] that seems particularly to lend itself to an ecological reading:

7-25-70

once again by the waters of left hand creek
the humps remain while their substance
moves on by.
white water
again & again

flanked by ponderosa pine
one
partway up the hill, bright fox-red
beautiful in death

---

4 | *Red Car Goes By: Selected Poems 1955-2000,* Jack Collom, Tuumba Press, 2001.

nat runs thru water
kicks it up in arcs that sparkle.
studying this
I throw a rock. it is
part of the creekbed—land
& the splash still trails
globed in a rhythm, flashing light.
the rock & the rockies
etc doing the same,
spaceshapes

nerves
project a like weightless muscle
like the water of left hand creek
twisting in a thin permission
of ground & gravity
splashed out
condensing to spheres.
the humps remain
"remain," like the creek, or creeks, or "creek,"
substance moves on by.

The poet here is scientist/naturalist, watching water move by and noticing that while the water (the "substance") changes, the way in which it changes (the "humps") remain the same, no matter if it is a creek, creeks, or "creek." While a literary critic could "interpret" the poem one way—perhaps focusing on how the dead tree is beautiful in that kind of interpretation that tethers poems to other books or emotional situations outside the poem's own reality—a physicist would have a different interpretation, using her or his knowledge of wave action to note how substance moves past while the process remains the same. Or one might look at how the structure of the poem follows the structure of the wave, in that the movement at the beginning of the poem ("the humps remain while their substance/ moves on by") foreshadows the end, while yet the poem retains an exploratory movement—there is a sense of the poem taking form as it is written. The poet throws an investigative rock and continues with words—the spaces between poet and word and creek are truly active, creative. A quote to interject here is from John Ashbery, "I think I am more interested in the movement among ideas than in the ideas themselves, the way one goes from one point to another rather than the destination or the origin."[5]

III. READING TINA DARRAGH

In Tina Darragh's ongoing project "Opposable Dumbs," she explores, in the form of a play (and it is two characters, Guido and Cytut, who utter the following in unison), an oblique and certainly more prickly branch of the ecological activist family—animal rights activists.[6]

> If all that business hopes to gain
> hides behind what's well or ill
> proclaiming rights of animals and man
> means more of both are sure to be killed

---

5 | Interview with John Ashbery, *The Paris Review*, "Art of Poetry XXXIII: John Ashbery" Interview by Peter Stitt. *Paris Review* 90 (1983).

6 | In fact, some would argue that animal rights activists are not part of the ecological movement at all. I find it thrillingly rebellious to include them as such and would be inclined to argue that their concern (although certainly often inarticulate and sentimental, or even misanthropic and violent) for the "other" and the awareness of animal consciousness and behavior would qualify them.

[10 seconds of silence]

slow wo hopes our gain stalls wide
behind the sill of spell and rook
sizing (an)I mal no vi
sults more ru than lore of reel

[10 seconds of silence]

if care of health is labor-bound
while labor binds to none
no local plan can make a deal
that's ever really won

[10 seconds of silence]

universal _____care
animal & hu_____care
un_____iversal care
animal & labor _____care
un(vers)_____care

[10 seconds of silence]

Boycott Clinical Trials Until The Taft-Hartley Act Is Repealed!
un(vers) _____care
Boycott Clinical Trials Until Health Care Is Not-for-Profit!
un(vers)_____care
Suspend Animal Experiments Until Animals Have Health Care!
un(vers)_____care[7]

---

7 | *Opposable Dumbs: A Play,* Tina Darragh, The Tangent Pamphlet Series #3, 2002.

Darragh takes the difficult language of animal rights activism,[8] which shadows human rights activism, and breaks it down, placing literal gaps between animal and human. But Darragh also brings in the question of capitalism, in that it exploits both animal and human (now, where did those gaps between the two go?) for even the seemingly most casual (i.e., cosmetics testing) of uses. Darragh also questions how human language—protest language—can enter a "poem," and if it does, how the structure of a poem changes. Much poetry has traditionally been written in a sort of elevated tone not often associated with the activist language of the streets, but how can that activist language also be investigated? Do "chestnuts" such as "Power to the People" and "The World is Watching Us"[9] still have the *puissance* that they did in the '60s? Or are they just easy markers of a certain stance? Does protest language need a poetic refreshing, as well? Are protesters really saying what they want to be saying? Once again, it is a poet who can explore these questions—linguistic, philosophical and social—as well as the links between animal rights activist, ecologist, scientist (using animals to experiment), doctor, and health care workers. But poetry also needs active readers who will follow it in word and *structure* (or, if you prefer, "form"). The animal rights activists need to read Darragh, just as poets need to read (investigate and use) the language of the protesters.

---

8 | In an additional complication, animal rights activists are "speaking for" animals.

9 | At a recent rally in New York City against the eviction of an entire building's worth of rent-stabilized tenants, one of the speakers began attempting to lead the crowd in a series of these chants. Unfortunately, the crowd, which only moments before had been enthusiastically clapping, almost immediately fell silent. There was an almost palpable collective sigh of boredom, a "here we go again" feeling.

IV. Conclusion that is not a conclusion

The interesting thing is that no matter where I open Ponge, my eye falls upon something necessary. For *this* essay, I had planned a more organized selection of excerpts, but then found that I had accidentally opened it at "*conclusion*," which actually is only midway through the book. Ponge's "conclusion" is no conclusion at all. So it's not to say that *The Making of the Pré* is such perfection it rotates to meet my linguistic needs at any point, but that it is truly a seven-ringed atom, a transitional space of poetry and environs, interior and exterior, process and system, that catches on to the reader and makes of him or her a poet/observer as well. It is in itself a *pré* of the movements among ideas, the shape formed by water moving by.

> *Conclusion:*
> Therefore nature, on our planet,
> *Our nature,*
> so proposes to us (procures) the *prés*.
> (Our nature, that is to say, as well,
> *what we are*
> what, each morning on awakening,
> we are).
>
> x
>
> To *our nature*, that is to say,
> To what each morning,
> we are, what on awakening we are.
>
> *Our nature*, that is as well
> the nature on our planet,
> what is offered to us for (by) our planet,

To *our nature*, therefore,
our nature
each morning proposes (procures), offers the *prés*.

                                                            x

Code (in the past tense):
Our nature has prepared us (for) prés.

Peter Lamborn Wilson asks in an essay on the German Romantic
Novalis, "[b]ut if the human body remains part of nature or *in* nature, then even a consistent materialist would have to admit that
nature is not quite yet dead."[10] This prepositional mystery echoes
the Bible[11]: Christ is *in* the world, but not *of* it. We live in the world,
but we are not *of* it. We live *in* nature, but are not *of* it, but why?
Because we are human? Is what we make (manufacture) intrinsically set off from nature, because it came from our heads and hands
(and machines, with machines begetting machines)? Where does
the line between us and nature begin and end? Is a city-dweller
part *of* nature or *in* nature? Natural systems are part of engineering
a McMansion, but is the McMansion part *of* nature or *in* nature?
When a car accident occurs on a highway, traffic patterns are affected for hours afterward, with "waves" of congestion persisting up
and down the highway. Is that part *of* nature or *in* nature? These are
questions that poets can bring to poetry, and have been bringing

---

10 | "The Disciples at Saïs: A Sacred Theory of Earth" by Peter Lamborn Wilson,
     printed in *Capitalism Nature Socialism*, Volume 15, Number 2 (June 2004).
     The essay will also be appearing in *Green Hermeticism*, edited by Chris
     Bamford and published by Lindisfarne Books.

11 | "They are not of the world, even as I am not of the world." John 17:16, *The
     Holy Bible: King James Version*. 2000. Peter Lamborn Wilson writes in a
     personal letter that he has "also heard of it as definition of Sufism!"

for centuries, with that part of poets that collects information and shapes it through the process of writing a poem. The information may be random, or arcane, pertinent or impertinent, but no matter which, it will still reveal unexpected sides of itself as it is written through a poem. The prepositional mystery of *of* and *in* continues to persist—and which preposition denotes a more transitional space?

Ultimately, it doesn't matter what "formula" a poet follows to write so-called "ecological poetry"—there is really no definition for it, only explorations and conjectures. Ponge's "spot where we happened to be" may be mountain range, middle of the woods, lumber yard, industrial park, bookstore, art opening, or the inside of one's own eyelids. I'm interested in the investigative process of writing ecological poetry, but I'm also interested in how to develop alternative interpretive structures that include physics, biology, geology, sociology. The raw material for pastoral poetry has been altered by humans, including poets (just using a computer to write impacts the environment, as well as your own health; look "PBDEs" up on the Internet sometime). Therefore, we have to both *write* and *read* through these deep changes and, as Thoreau did, keep looking and looking into the darkness until our pupils enlarge.[12]

---

12 | Henry David Thoreau, *Cape Cod*, Parnassus Imprints, 1984.

Thinking Ecology in Fragments:
Walter Benjamin & the Dialectics of (Seeing) Nature

— CATRIONA MORTIMER-SANDILANDS —

CAVEAT

This text is most certainly a work in progress: it should be understood as an entry point, a step to a larger project of thinking with Benjamin toward a "critical ecology." More accurately, perhaps, it is a reconnaissance mission. I have been involved in the field of environmental cultural studies (including environmental literary criticism) for many years; my work in this field has been to think through a practice of "reading" environments and human/ more-than-human relationships in a way that not only reveals the power relations informing and reformed by particular intersections of culture and nature (if you will temporarily pardon that bifurcating shorthand), but that also initiates the possibility of finding new ethical—and political— ecological relationships from *within* that constellation of practices. In that sense, I have been in the terrain of "critical ecologies" many times before; as a *reconnaissance* then, the thoughts that follow constellate a *re*-entry into the landscape of "environmental cultures," a process of coming to know an already well-trodden (and well-contested) landscape with a different kind of critical intimacy.[1]

---

1 | Indeed, I have actually walked this landscape with Benjamin once before (see "A Flâneur in the Forest? Strolling Point Pelee with Walter Benjamin," *Topia* 3 [Spring 2000]: 37-57). Although that trip was a useful one insofar as it helped me develop the idea of parks as "ecological arcades," the considerable flaws in that paper are part of what has prompted me to go back to Benjamin in a more thoughtful and thorough way.

Perhaps I might even follow Benjamin and offer this collection of thoughts as an *exposé* in the dual sense of the word: an initial exposure of something (usually sordid) and a presentation of facts. What I would like to "expose" is Benjamin's extraordinary potential to animate a critical ecological practice of "seeing" nature in the (sordid) age of the nature-commodity, an ecological analytics—and, as I shall suggest, poetics—that rescues the possibility of the ecological fragment from the commodified web of relationships in which that fragment is ensnared—indeed, by which it is both produced *and* obscured. Thus, the presentation of facts/initial exposure that follows attempts to develop a relationship between a nature in fragments, and a reading of Benjamin that, while clearly preliminary, enacts his potential to transform the fragment into something (I hope) more enduring.

INTRODUCTION

In Cape Breton Highlands National Park—specifically, near the Chéticamp Visitors Centre in the southwest corner of the park—there is one of those standing plywood caricatures with a hole cut in the face into which visitors can insert their heads for the sake of a campy picture or two. This one is actually made up of three human figures: There is a faceless Scotsman, complete with mandatory Nova Scotian tartan kilt and bagpipes; there is a moccasin-clad, presumably Mi'kmaq person with a hooked fish in his right hand, a spear in his left, and a limp, dead mammal in his belt; and there is, in the middle, a female figure with an earthenware jug, white cap and apron, and large crucifix who must, at least by subtraction, be Acadian. Slightly off to the right is a fourth image: a brightly painted fishing boat chugging across a calm sea, complete with what are probably dolphins playing in the foreground. "How tacky," one might think. The cosmopolitan traveler to Cape Breton, en route to one of the park's many hiking trails, campgrounds, scenic vistas or beaches, would be forgiven for scoffing at this rather anachronistic fragment of tourist kitsch: the "real" nature of the park is, after all, to be found elsewhere, in its imposing billion-year old geology, its mountainous and densely forested interior, its dramatic views of the Gulf of St. Lawrence on the west side or the Atlantic Ocean on the east, all now thankfully preserved by the park "for the sake of future generations."

But consider this: the flat piece of manicured lawn on which that cosmopolitan tourist stands as she scoffs was either seasonal or permanent Mi'kmaq territory well into the mid-18th century, at which point the British, no longer worried about allied French/Mi'kmaq military threat, placed the latter forcibly on reserves. Consider this as well: the Acadian population of western Cape Breton consists largely of the descendants of families who had fled the Acadian expulsions from mainland Nova Scotia, also in the mid-18th century. To facilitate the park's establishment in 1936, the lands, homes, and livelihoods of several Acadian families living in the community of Cap Rouge — more or less exactly where our tourist is standing — were expropriated in a second "expulsion" that moved them mostly to nearby Chéticamp Island. In light of then-premier Angus MacDonald's renowned "Tartanism,"[2] in which Nova Scotia, Cape

---

2 | The phrase is from Ian MacKay's "Tartanism Triumphant: The Construction of Scottishness in Nova Scotia, 1933-1954," *Acadiensis* XXI. 2 (Spring 1992): 5-47. For a fuller discussion of the establishment of Cape Breton Highlands National Park, see Alan MacEachern, *Natural Selections: National Parks in Atlantic Canada, 1935-1970* (Montreal: McGill-Queens University Press, 2001).

Breton "Highlands" included, was systematically Scottified in the interests of a coherent public presentation, the assumedly happy National Park coexistence of Scotsman with Acadian with Mi'kmaq is somewhat galling. And let's not even talk about what the decimated fisheries have meant for that happy little fish boat. In short, our kitschy little caricatures are more than a tiny bit guilty of obfuscating a profoundly colonial, racist, and ecologically exploitative history.

But let's look at them again, this time with a little bit of help from Walter Benjamin. I would argue that the faceless figures are fragments in a different history, a history that revolves around the fact that in all four caricatures, the actual face we see surrounded by the painted plywood is that of the park visitor. The tourist is the figure around whom the landscape of the National Park is arranged, the figure whose natural and cultural consumption violently renders all earlier identities and relations—Mi'kmaq, Acadian, Scot, and fishery alike—to nature in the land that is now park the stuff of the past, the stuff of nostalgia. Looking at her own face repeated among the caricatures of history, the tourist sees only her own visually consuming relations to the landscape, here wrapped in particularities that have, it seems, been rendered mere sartorial footnotes along the path of progress toward ultimate "emparkment." The park is thus an attempt to break with the history it presents; it visibly celebrates the fact of its rupture with that past and becomes, precisely in its placement of Scot with Acadian with Mi'kmaq with boat, a gesture toward its own desire for a nature beyond history. On the one hand, there is a distinctly utopian element to this celebration. All particular pasts, identities, social natures, and modes of extraction are irrelevant, and the park stands as a utopian gesture toward benevolent preservation, permanent and unimpeded access to nature for "future generations," universal appreciation of a natural world that transcends and must transcend particular identities and economies, and perhaps even the possibility of an aesthetic reconciliation with nature in which extractive domination is no longer the primary axis of human/more-than-human interaction. On the other hand, of course, in the dream-state that is capitalism, even this rupture, this wish-image of equality and reconciliation, remains firmly embedded in a set of commodity relations by which nature is rendered fetish and, with it, all histories of non-consumer relations to nature for this place. It is not so much that historical particularities are eliminated from the park; it is that they are violently wrestled from their places to be re-placed on sale in a marketplace, a phantasmagoria of natures and "traditions" that are all equally arrested and eviscerated in order to be consumed. And it is certainly not that history has been made irrelevant through preservation; rather, all history has been turned to the task of a far more barbaric consumption. To put it differently, the caricature that is not only the plywood, but also, metonymically, the park itself, appears to represent the ultimate achievement of bourgeois history, a state of universal nature appreciation from which the park consumer can look backward and congratulate herself at having reached the confident position in which the specific history of the place has led to a benevolent present: nature has, at last, achieved salvation from history.

Viewed as a dialectical image, however—via Benjamin—the same caricature, and the same park, stands as a reminder of the violence of the commodity form itself, in *precisely* its ability to transform life into phantasmagoric fetish, to absorb history into the self-congratulation that is the bourgeois present of nature-consumption. Our task in dialectically *seeing* the caricatures is then to wrest the transitory truth of nature *from* this history, to blast the images out of the historical continuum that seems to bring them so inevitably to their commodified present—to interpret, in other words, the fragment of truth against the historical grain of capitalist triumphalism.

Fetish, phantasmagoria, wish-image, dream-state, history, commodity, fragment: these concepts form the constellation of what I understand as Benjamin's most significant potential contributions to a critical ecology. There are certainly other possibilities: Mick Smith, for example, has written quite extensively about the implications of Benjamin's critique of progressivist history for a revitalized sense of environmental responsibility, about his insistence on the cultivation of a discontinuous relationship with history as a model of ecologically ethical remembrance, and about his underexplored philosophy of language and mimesis as a place from which to begin to think about the expressiveness of the material world.[3] My intent, however, is to consider Benjamin more specifically through his (admittedly iconoclastic) historical materialist trajectories as an exemplary figure with whom to think through the politics of ecology

---

3 | See, respectively: "Ecological Citizenship and Ethical Responsibility: Arendt, Benjamin and Political Action," forthcoming in *Environments* 33.3 (2007); "Environmental Anamnesis: Walter Benjamin and the Ethics of Extinction," *Environmental Ethics* 23.4 (2001): 359-376; "Lost for Words? Gadamer and Benjamin on the Nature of Language and the 'Language' of Nature," *Environmental Values* 10 (2001): 59-75.

in the age of the nature-commodity. Focused on his magnificent unfinished *Passagen-Werk* (*The Arcades Project*), but necessarily including texts that were embedded in that larger project such as the often-cited "Theses on the Philosophy of History," and the rather less-cited "On Some Motifs in Baudelaire,"[4] my ongoing project is to take up Benjamin's "dialectics of seeing" as a way of wresting nature from the bourgeois historical narrative that finds its self-congratulatory victory in the park, the nature-store, the eco-tour, the IMAX wildlife documentary, the hybrid SUV—even in the fisheries management strategy, the new Canadian Green Plan, and the global biodiversity initiative.

In so doing, of course, I am heavily influenced by Susan Buck-Morss, for whom *The Arcades Project* is not simply philosophic but pedagogic. In my view, Benjamin's work in the *Project* is a political and deeply *poetic* enactment of its central philosophical precepts, organized to affect the reader emotionally and physically—at the very least, to incite something like shock—in its presentation of commentary against quotation, interjection against aphorism, interpretive kernel against caption, announcement, fragment. As Buck-Morss argues, the very subject matter of the *Project* was integral to Benjamin's desire not only to write *about* the phantasmagoria of the arcades, but also to offer in its empirical pre-

---

4 | Both in *Illuminations*, ed. Hannah Arendt (New York: Schocken Books, 1968): 254-264; 155-194. Also of considerable importance to my project are Benjamin's more autobiographical essays, e.g., as collected in *Reflections*, ed. Peter Demetz, trans. Edmund Jephcott (New York: Schocken Books, 1978), in which Benjamin enacts a poetics of destructive/creative staticization as a way of wresting life from bourgeois memory.

sentation a poetic and pedagogic experience that might shock the reader into thinking beyond the mythic, bourgeois history in which both arcades and reader are located. The Paris arcades of the 19th century—then the "fairy grottos" of spectacular consumption, but already neglected and ghostly by the time Benjamin started writing about them in 1934—were, in Buck-Morss' words, "Benjamin's central image because they were the precise material replication of the internal consciousness, or rather, the unconscious of the dreaming collective. All of the errors of bourgeois consciousness could be found there (commodity fetishism, reification, the world as 'inwardness'), as well as (in fashion, prostitution, gambling) all of its utopian dreams."[5] In other words, "the way the past confronted one" in the actual experience of the arcades "was as an external experience that paralleled the internal, mental experience of 'involuntary memory,'"[6] those flashes of unexpected and often visceral recognition that, as Benjamin describes in his essay on Baudelaire, not only exceed, but challenge "what has been experienced explicitly and consciously"[7] as formal remembrance. Thus, echoing the arcades, Benjamin's carefully constructed montage of often-contradictory fragments and insights seeks to provide a collective version of that involuntary memory in order to shock the reader *out* of the voluntary memory that is the mythic progression of bourgeois narrative history. At the same time as Benjamin

---

5 | Susan Buck-Morss, *The Dialectics of Seeing: Walter Benjamin and the Arcades Project* (Cambridge, MA: MIT Press, 1989): 39.

6 | Ibid., 38.

7 | Benjamin, "On Some Motifs in Baudelaire," 160.

certainly understood the *Project* as a work of philosophical history (*Geschichtsphilosophie*), "committed to a graphic, concrete presentation of truth, in which historical images made visible the historical ideas…without providing a totalizing frame,"[8] he also understood this dialectics of seeing as a pedagogy, a practice by which "to educate the image-creating medium within us to see dimensionally, stereoscopically, into the depths of the historical shade."[9]

If you'll forgive my considerable (and perhaps controversial) insistence on Benjamin's poetics as integral to his philosophical history and politics, allow me to return more directly to the role of the dialectical image in the cultivation of a critical ecology. In the spirit of Benjamin's poetics, let me offer his beautiful passage from "Theses on the Philosophy of History" in which he writes of the Paul Klee painting "Angelus Novus":

> This is how one pictures the angel of history. His face is turned toward the past. Where we perceive a chain of events, he sees one single catastrophe which keeps piling wreckage upon wreckage and hurls it in front of his feet. The angel would like to stay, awaken the dead, and make whole what has been smashed. But a storm is blowing in from Paradise; it has got caught in his wings with such violence that the angel can no longer close them. The storm irresistibly propels him into the future to which his back is turned, while the pile of debris before him grows skyward. This storm is what we call progress.[10]

---

8 | Buck-Morss, op. cit., 55.

9 | Benjamin in Ibid., 292.

10 | Benjamin, "Theses on the Philosophy of History," 258.

Two theses down, Benjamin makes a related point that is not so often cited: the "progress" that is the storm of bourgeois historical inevitability includes the working class' own regard for capitalist "technological developments as the fall of the stream with which it thought it was moving."[11] Moreover, these technological developments fuel and are fuelled by a view of labor that "recognizes only [its] progress *in the mastery of nature*, not the retrogression of society, [and thus] amounts to the exploitation of nature, which with naïve complacency is *contrasted* with the exploitation of the proletariat…. Nature, which…'exists gratis,' is a complement to the corrupted conception of labor."[12]

From the perspective of Benjamin's angel, the single catastrophic wreckage that bourgeois history narrates as "progress" visibly includes the wholesale exploitation of nature. Paradoxically, however, precisely the progress that lays waste to the natural world is understood, even experienced *as* nature in bourgeois thought, as "the stream" in which the working class "thought it was moving." One need only think of Social Darwinism (and, more recently, evolutionary psychology) here: in this mythic form, the ideological fusion of nature and history affirms not only the position of the dominant class, but a "natural" history of the achievement of that dominance, and "where we are" is not simply an historical present but an evolutionary destiny. The seamless insertion of nature into

11 | Ibid., 258.

12 | Ibid., 259, my emphases.

bourgeois history thus affirms the very progress by which nature is violently degraded; for Benjamin, any genuine reconciliation with nature is only possible once humanity has broken with this evolutionary "prehistory" and realized "the social *promise* of technology, the beginning of a truly human history."[13] Thus we can read his expressed appreciation in "Theses on the Philosophy of History" of Fourier's utopian views on nature in light of Benjamin's equally utopian desire for a reorganization of nature and labor in specific *opposition* to exploitation, perhaps even including an explicit recognition of the social processes of production and reproduction in the "natures" we might encounter outside of that exploitation. Writes Benjamin:

> According to Fourier, as a result of efficient cooperative labor, four moons would illuminate the earthly night, the ice would recede from the poles [!!], sea water would no longer taste salty, and beasts of prey would do man's [sic] bidding. All this illustrates a kind of labor which, far from far from exploiting nature, is capable of delivering her of the creations which lie dormant in her womb as potentials.[14]

For Benjamin, the *Arcades Project* dialectically develops this view to a "new" nature by *juxtaposing* nature with bourgeois history in a non-narrative montage in order to reveal and increase the semantic gap between the one and the other, not only to "polemicize against the still-barbaric level of the modern age, but…to disclose

---

13 | Buck-Morss, op cit, 64.

14 | Benjamin, "Theses on the Philosophy of History," 259. One could fruitfully juxtapose Benjamin's views on prostitution with the gendered sexualization of nature apparent in this passage.

the essence of the 'new nature' as even more transient, more fleeting than the old."[15] To oversimplify and overcondense, Benjamin thus understood a significant part of his project as one of natural history, of recovering and dehistoricizing fossils of a prehistoric commodity culture, in order to pull from these petrified and decaying fetish-fragments exactly the fleeting quality of truth that signals the possibility of the redemption of the monadic fragment against the commodity "progression" that gave rise to it. The fleeting truth is contrasted to the "new" that is the naturalized barbarism of capitalist prehistory; the latter functions as fetish and compels us eternally to return to the same; the former is the flash that redeems the truth in the object beyond its overdetermination as commodity. Buck-Morss puts it rather better: "If petrified nature and decaying objects provide the imagery adequate to allegory, the imagery of the symbol that would show fleeting matter in a redeeming light is...organic nature, active and live, and for that reason unalterably passing."[16] For better or worse, this is an ecology of the ephemeral, the monadic, the truth revealed in the fragment.

Dialectical images, then, are made of the "rags and refuse" of commodity culture, each scrap endowed with the almost-alchemical potential of becoming-truth. Such images are, however, neither arbitrary and subjective nor ready-made; in the words of literary critic Diane Chisholm, they are "*exemplary* material embodiments of the

---

15 | Buck-Morss, op. cit., 64.

16 | Ibid., 18.

contradictory forces of history and, therefore, objects of explosive recognition. Their potential to incite political awareness is ontologically imminent but not epistemologically transparent, since obscured by commodity phantasmagoria."[17] But their dialectical qualities are, nonetheless, immanent; in this respect, they act as allegories rather than as symbols or fantasies, in that their meaning resides in their particularity, and their truth lies not in their reflection of an overarching historical regularity, but in their relationships to one another revealed in careful collection and juxtaposition. Benjamin understood these as "constellations of awakening," as pieces of detritus the value of which is dramatically re-rendered through a process of blasting and assembling, creating singularities—monads—out of processes. As allegories and as monads, dialectical images allow Benjamin to "make visibly palpable the experience of the world in fragments"[18] ; as carefully collected constellations, they allow the reader an *experience* of awakening in the midst of the phantasmagoric dream that is commodity capitalism.

Whether or not my plywood caricatures precisely qualify as dialectical images, I do think parks and other public nature spectacles— zoos, live animal safari parks, marine amusement centers, and the like—are fruitfully understood as arcades of our ecologically consumer age along the same lines as Benjamin understood the 19th-century Parisian fairy grottos of early consumer capitalism. For

---

17 | Diane Chisholm, *Queer Constellations: Subcultural Space in the Wake of the City* (Minneapolis: University of Minnesota Press, 2005): 81, my emphasis.

18 | Buck-Morss, op. cit., 18.

in 2006 Nova Scotia as in Benjamin's 1934 Paris, national parks are already decaying; the nature-ideals they represented through the mid-20th century are increasingly irrelevant. The wider and more technologically mediated array of potential "natures" available on reality television, in video games, and in niche tourist experiences that organize travel around ever-tinier fetish nature-moments, renders the utopian desire of publicly available nature "beyond" economic interests an increasingly obvious fossil. The wish-image of a universally consumable nature "beyond" history is one whose mythic moment is increasingly part of the past; indeed, for the tourist as much as for the materialist historian, it is not the utopian moment of the park that returns to us in the present, but instead its quality as a fetish, as a commodity. The fossil, in constellation with our present gaze upon the fossil, speaks of the consistency of the commodity form that has not only organized the aesthetic history of this place against the livelihoods of the Mi'kmaq and the Cap Rouge Acadians, but which has also captured *us* in the endless return of the same. The tourist's face among the caricatures reminds us perfectly of this relationship; the utopian moment of cohabitation in which all identities and economies might find equality or reconciliation in the landscape is lost in the phantasmagoria by which the face of the consumer, the reduction of nature and history to consumption, is reflected everywhere.

The park, like many other institutions that claim to "save" nature—and these are technological, scientific, and political, as well as spatial (even if we should speak of the particular power of the physicality of this particular eco-Arcade)—is founded exactly on the bourgeois narrative by which nature has led us to the present moment. All other histories, from this point of commodified park-nature, are reduced to the status of interesting historical diversions en route from the geological time of the cliffs to their preservation in Cape Breton Highlands: these natures seem now to have achieved protection, even fulfillment, as items in a catalogue of places to see. Such is the triumph of the commodity. What Walter Benjamin offers such a place—and, I would argue, a variety of other nature-fragments that might incorporate other variations on this theme of the fossilized fetish—is the possibility of seeing it differently. With his dialectics of seeing, the act of violently blasting a fragment of social nature from its naturalized status in self-congratulatory bourgeois narrative holds the possibility of shock, the possibility of revelatory allegory, the possibility of an actual experience of the world in fragments: in short, the possibility of a poetically shaped philosophic awakening from the dream-world of the eco-phantasmagoria.

Epilogue[19]

In the dialectical image, what has been within a particular epoch is always, simultaneously, "what has been from time immemorial." As such, however, it is manifest, on each occasion, only to a quite specific epoch—namely, the one in which humanity, rubbing its eyes, recognizes just this particular dream image as such. It is at this moment that the historian takes up, with regard to that image, the task of dream interpretation. (N4,1)

---

19 | Italicized passages are from Walter Benjamin, *The Arcades Project*, ed. Rolf Tiedemann, trans. Howard Eiland and Kevin McLaughlin (Cambridge, MA: Harvard University Press), 1999: 464.

Park Objectives: To protect and preserve the representative resources and processes of the Maritime Acadian Highlands Natural Region including examples of the landforms, features, and ecosystems of the Boreal, Taiga, and Acadian Land Regions of the Park with their representative, rare, and significant plant and animal species.[20]

The expression "the book of nature" indicates that one can read the real like a text. And that is how the reality of the [twentieth] century will be treated here. We open the book of what happened. (N4,2)

---

20 | *Management Plan Summary for Cape Breton Highlands National Park* (Ottawa: Environment Canada, 1987): 2.

Nature is a Haunted House: Ecopoetics & Scientific Epistemology

—— KAREN LEONA ANDERSON ——

Nature is a Haunted House—
but Art, a House that tries to be Haunted.
EMILY DICKINSON to THOMAS WENTWORTH HIGGINSON,
1876 (Letter 459A)

Americans have never left our destiny to the whims of nature,
and we will not start now… [These trials] remind us of
a hope beyond all pain and death—a God who welcomes
the lost to a house not made with hands.
GEORGE BUSH,
from a speech delivered in New Orleans, September 2005

Writing in two different centuries, Emily Dickinson and George Bush converge briefly in their response to St. Paul's promise of a heavenly "house not made with hands." But in this convergence, their differences also show most sharply. Dickinson asserts that art strains constantly toward a superior "Nature"; Bush, on the other hand, dismisses that same "nature" as violently whimsical and offers, as compensation to the newly homeless of New Orleans, the promise of heavenly housing. I do not want to suggest here that if Bush or his speechwriters were more sensitive or less cynical poets that such housing would suddenly appear, for I do not believe that literary reconceptualizations—and here I include ecopoetics—are the first, best, or only responses to real floods, real death, real politics. But what Bush's biblical allusion does show is that the repetition of tropes, that haunting of language's house by history's ghost, has a relationship to social and material issues. The call to respond to this repetition is also my justification for the focus in the following essay on historical rather than current or projected examples of ecopoetics.

I chose this historical lens because such tropes may be old and dusty, but they are still being used. For example, Bush and his speechwriters' descriptions of the "cruel and wasteful storm" whose destruction we must "overcome" support his administration's policies of building "higher" and "stronger" as they claim U.S. citizens did after the "great fire" in Chicago, the "great earthquake" in San Francisco, and those "first, terrible winters in Jamestown and Plymouth" (Bush). This personification of a "cruel and wasteful storm" *also* allows Bush and his speechwriters to compare U.S. preparation for the "challenge[s] of nature" to the "act[s] of evil men that could threaten our people"—and to proffer the solace of "a God who welcomes the lost to a house not made with hands" (Ibid.). The administration's arguments for private entrepreneurship, continuing tax cuts, unfettered development, relative inattention to environmental issues, and the religious acceptance of social injustice are at the very least buttressed by this version of "nature" in the almost entirely figurative guise of dangerous opponent to civilization, weak-minded terrorist, and temporarily harsh mother to God's ultimately gentle, housing-providing father.

So if I, very conventionally, would rather claim Dickinson's harsh contribution to ecopoetics than one that is gentler, or even one more overtly political, it is because I see it as a call to rhetorical arms when I hear Bush's retelling of the old story of a wayward mother nature who needs to be disciplined. Dickinson works for me because she works *with* the uncomfortable, uncanny repetitions of the stereotype of a female "Nature" to recall its absurdities. In the final two stanzas of a late poem, for example, she takes up the house of nature again, but this time with more threatening overtones:

> But nature is a stranger yet;
> The ones that cite her most
> Have never passed her haunted house,
> Nor simplified her ghost.
>
> To pity those who know her not
> Is helped by the regret
> That those who know her, know her less
> The nearer her they get.   (Franklin ed. 1433)

This is not an overtly political poem; however, as it reverses the representation of a whimsically violent but ultimately compliant female "nature," it also forestalls several commonly asked questions about poetry engaged with environments. Instead of prompting its readers to ask whether it represents the natural or whether it engages with or constitutes an environment that is socially salutary, the poem asks *how* we know what is around us and what we are. In other words, in her poetics' subversively symbiotic relationship to the commonsense language of a "nature" that is separate from us and our social concerns, Dickinson draws us into the question of epistemology.

One partial description of this epistemology, which I hope may be helpful for poets concerned with ecological issues as well as for understanding Dickinson, is that it intersects with the ways of knowing endemic to the sciences. If for Bush science and technology are tools with which human civilization beats the environment into submission, science also provides a basis for the counternarrative, both in Dickinson's poetry and in the application of environmental science. Scientific knowledge is part of what allowed the levees to be built, but it is also behind the data that enables environmentalists to show that storm surges around New Orleans are reduced by a foot for every 2.7 acres of wetlands that exist (Sullivan). How we might respond as poets to these disparate uses of science raises a whole host of unanswered questions around the issues of scientific epistemology and social responsibility. For example, what kind of politics does the word *ecopoetics* imply? How does it engage with environmental science? And what does it have to do with social justice? More specifically, if a rhetoric of science and technology such as Bush's severs environmental awareness from social justice, how might ecopoetics bring those concerns back into conversation? What, in this context, does socially contextualized science have to offer to ecopoetics?

I do not have a single answer to this question because I believe the understanding of science as socially shaped offers us danger as well as hope. Evidence of this danger comes in the form of a Michael Crichton novel, *State of Fear* (2004), which depicts global warming as an environmentalist conspiracy and tells the tale of the scientist-hero who thwarts various "ecoterrorists." This narrative is buttressed by Crichton's bibliography of articles on environmental science and an essay calling for independent assessments of biased science. Based on his own research, Crichton guesses "the temperature increase over the next century will be about 0.812436 degrees Celsius" and adds that "[t]here is no evidence that my guess about the state of the world one hundred years from now is any better or worse than anyone else's." In September 2006, Crichton's book won him an invitation by Republicans to testify as an expert witness on global warming in front of the U.S. Senate; however, as Senator Hillary Clinton pointed out, most climate scientists disagree with his assessments (Wilson). But more indicative of the problems with Crichton's thinking are the final two sentences of his author's message: "Everyone has an agenda. Except for me" (573).

Crichton's book may be recent, but his claim to be objective is another old story. Since Bacon's 17th-century corrective to scholastic explanations of the world based on faith or speculation, some part of the cultural perception of science has been its promise of the clean, unbiased fact, nature in the buff; and since Bruno Latour's late '70s *Laboratory Life*, we have been aided by the perception that to view any and all scientific endeavors as being guaranteed by this objectivity is to ignore how science is culturally shaped. It is also to miss all the richness and potential of science as a cultural tool, a way that hypotheses admittedly produced by biased minds and tested still might produce surprises; it is an epistemology, in other words, that might be of help when we can acknowledge that we *all* have agendas.

The use of socially shaped science as a tool that may be liberatory or destructive is exactly what I find in my second historical example of an ecopoetic practitioner, Lorine Niedecker. For me, it is not that Niedecker notices how science can be productively social and constructively indeterminate, but what she makes of that inherent indeterminacy that could be a model for ecopoetics. One of her longest poems, "Wintergreen Ridge," was composed about the time Latour was working out his own conclusions about the social implications of science. Here, she celebrates the conservation of a Wisconsin ridge and the categorization of its resilient, amazing plants, their value made clear through the lens of scientific understanding:

> Bedeviled little Drosera
>   of the sundews
>   deadly
>
> in sphagnum moss
>   sticks out its sticky
>   (Darwin tested)
>
> tentacled leaf
>   towards a fly
>   half an inch away
>
> engulfs it
>   Just the touch
>   of a gnat on a filament
> stimulates leaf-plasma
>   secretes a sticky
>   clear liquid   (Niedecker 252)

"Bedeviled" as these plants may be, they are highly functional in comparison with the increasing human industrialism that threatens the plants and makes victims of those humans who are caught within it:

```
home town
        second shift steamfitter
                ran arms out

as tho to fly
        dived to concrete
                from loading dock

lost his head
        Pigeons
                (I miss the gulls)

mourn the loss
        of people
                no wild bird does                    (Niedecker 257)
```

Ultimately, for Niedecker, the "wild bird[s]" have the ability to see through the illusion of human superiority. By the end of "Wintergreen Ridge," it is clear that things and ideas and organisms are not necessarily getting better as time goes on; in fact, the worship of commodified newness hinders our ability to see that it is "lichens," not humans, that "may survive the bomb." According to Niedecker, our environment gives us a choice: we can choose to acknowledge our interdependence on the fluid world around us, or we can simply become extinct—that vulnerability to change and chance is the real revelation of Darwin's natural selection. The test of poetry, for Niedecker, becomes whether it can be of use to humans who are, whether they admit it or not, just another component of an environment. Her hero is the sunflower, who replaces the mad suicide of the steamfitter with a productive self-sacrifice as its seed-heavy head falls forward:

Old sunflower
    you bowed

to no one
    but Great Storm
        of Equinox   (Niedecker 257)

Many contemporary poets and critical writers are pursuing a similar social contextualization of the scientific ideas that shape our understanding of the environment: I think here of Elizabeth Willis' *Meteorite Flowers*, Brenda Iijima's *Around Sea*, Ed Roberson's *Voices Cast Us Out To Talk Us In*, or work written by the other members of this spring's ecopoetics panel, Jill Magi, Laura Elrick, and Evelyn Reilly. This poetry is important to the future of ecopoetics, I would say, precisely because it forms a part of a literary and social past, a history that is richer than the droning repetition in speeches like Bush's of the dusty tropes of human superiority and exceptionalism reinvoked in an attempt to convince us that they are simply truth, agenda-less facts.

I have only begun to sketch out here how science as a social phenomenon might be one of the invisible links between us, our environments, and our poetics; in accordance with the tentative status of my argument, I want to conclude by mentioning another new, as yet unproved hypothesis. Described in a recent book called *The Plausibility of Life*, this theory posits that there is a strong selection for organisms that can adapt, that is, whose bodies have the capacity to tolerate large mutations. As the authors explain it, the development of vertebrates' limbs into "fins, wings, legs, paddles and flippers" (171) depends in part on the tolerance of bodies for "exploratory processes" that allow, for example, the muscles and nerve cells to follow along as the bones take one of a number of shapes (172-174). If we understand this theory as both plausible and culturally contingent, might it also be a useful model for eco-poetics? When, for example, we decide to use poetry as a response to the rhetoric of environmental injustice, and whether we do so by exposing the contingencies of epistemologies, like Dickinson, or by illuminating their social effects, like Niedecker, I hope for an ecopoetics that can accommodate such epistemological mutations. If ecopoetics is flexible enough to borrow from other disciplines without surrendering its social and critical focus—without trying to sell metaphorical, heavenly houses in place of real ones—then we may be able to grow beyond our own ghosts.

WORKS CITED

Bush, George W. Remarks on Hurricane Katrina Recovery. 15 September 2005. New Orleans, LA.

Crichton, Michael. *State of Fear.* New York, New York: HarperCollins, 2004.

Dickinson, Emily. *The Letters of Emily Dickinson.* Ed. Thomas H. Johnson. Cambridge, MA: The Belknap Press of Harvard University Press, 1958.

Dickinson, Emily. *The Poems of Emily Dickinson.* Ed. R. W. Franklin. Cambridge, MA: The Belknap Press of Harvard University Press, 1998.

Kirschner, Mark, and John C. Gerhardt. *The Plausibility of Life: Resolving Darwin's Dilemma.* New Haven, CT: Yale University Press, 2005.

Niedecker, Lorine. *Collected Works*, ed. Jenny Penberthy. Berkeley, CA: University of California Press, 2002.

Sullivan, Bob. "Wetland erosion raises hurricane risks." MSNBC.com. 19 September 2005. http://www.msnbc.msn.com/id/9118570/

Wilson, Jamie. "Novel Take on Global Warming." Guardian.co.uk. 29 September 2005. http://books.guardian.co.uk/comment/story/0,16488,1580591,00.html

Ecopoetics and the Adversarial Consciousness:[*] Challenges to Nature Writing, Environmentalism, and Notions of Individual Agency

— JILL MAGI —

WHY CONSIDER ECOLOGY?

According to Neil Everndon, in "Beyond Ecology: Self, Place, and the Pathetic Fallacy," a small male fish called the cichlid regards the circle of territory around its own physical limits as part of itself during the breeding season. It responds to invasions of that territory with as much ferocity as it does to attacks on its actual skin. The lesson is about territory, boundaries. The self is not the self you see and feel and can outline—edge of skin meeting air. The little fish turned fierce is evidence of the self as a field of experience and of "a mutualism in which the fate of two (or more) organisms has become so intertwined as to make them appear inseparable" (Everndon 94). Evernden posits that

> the really subversive element in Ecology rests not on any of its more
> sophisticated concepts, but upon its basic premise: inter-relatedness.
> But the genuinely radical nature of that proposition is not generally

---

[*] | "Strengthening the Adversarial Consciousness" is from a comment by Susan Sontag on the purpose of art.

perceived, even, I think, by ecologists. To the western mind, *inter-related* implies a casual connectedness. Things are inter-related if a change in one affects the other. So to say that all things are inter-related simply implies that if we wish to develop our "resources," we must find some technological means to defuse the interaction. The solution to pollution is dilution. But what is actually involved is a genuine *intermingling* of parts of the ecosystem. There are no discrete entities (93).

This radical ecology, which isn't about preservation, altruism, or morality, but about interrelation, says it is hard to draw the line between one creature and another. This radical ecology, denying "the subject-object relationship upon which science rests" (93), has the potential to teach us about language and maybe even how justice is won.

In contrast, values of purity, utopia, disembodiment, the separation of self and other, self and land, head and heart are persistent civilizing notions (read: white, successful, efficient) that allow citizens to entertain ideas of freedom right alongside traditions of enslavement, genocide, and war. I want, as a citizen, artist, and writer, to push against these notions of so-called civility and purity.

WHY AN ECOPOETICS?

An ecopoetics potentially operates in an oppositional mode, creating performances of language that point out literature's role in perpetuating power, and its role in erasure. An ecopoetic practice may result in writings that resist commodification, defying traditional measures of effective communication, yet not always embracing experimentalism uncritically. Finally, if I am to use the term, I would have to take ecopoetics to be a continued critique of ecology, nature writing, and environmentalism—mainstream environmentalism: a movement that has largely ignored race, class, and labor, and has, in typical liberal fashion, concentrated on legal means of change, as if the legal system is designed, in the first place, to work for us all.

LANDSCAPES WRITTEN, LANDSCAPES "SAVED"

Nature writers are "the children of Linnaeus," according to John Elder and Robert Finch, editors of the *Norton Book of Nature Writing* (19). Establishing the genre in a very specific liberal, educated class, and taxonomic tradition, the editors continue to describe nature writing in North America an act of "exploration," not conquest. They describe this writing as "escapist" in a positive sense and they praise the voice of "prophetic anger" from early environmentalists. These editorial demarcations are indicative of the ideology of nature writing: that nature writing ties curiosity to a well-developed moral sense, linking this sense to North American adventure and individualism. Conceptualizing nature writing in this way fails to articulate the link between the abuse of peoples and the abuse of land and literature's role in those abuses.

Traditional nature writing is evidence of the persistence of Enlightenment thinking. And is environmentalism evidence as well? Yes. Occupying a moral high ground, retreating into the rhetoric of protecting the earth, separating out nature and species-advocacy from issues of labor, race, class? Yes. Supposedly born of light, nature writing side-lights history, creating long shadows and severe blind spots. Environmentalism, the child of nature writing, is closely related to notions of preservation and separation and has its blind spots too.

David Mazel, from his essay "Literary Environmentalism as Domestic Orientalism":

> Our reading of environmental literature should help us realize that the concerns are not exclusively of the order of "shall these trees be cut?" or "shall this river be dammed?"—important as such questions are—but also of the order of "what has counted as the environment, and what *may* count? Who marks off the conceptual boundaries, and under what authority, and for what reasons?" (143).

In "Landscape, History, and the Pueblo Imagination," Leslie Marmon Silko writes:

> [T]he term *landscape*, as it has entered the English language, is misleading. "A portion of territory the eye can comprehend in a single view" does not correctly describe the relationship between the human being and his or her surroundings. This assumes the viewer is somehow *outside* or *separate from* the territory he or she surveys (265-266).

The (My) Pastoral

After September 11, 2001, I found myself writing often about the sky, birds, trees, small houses with porches and shutters. From the Psalms of the Bible, from a religion I had left a long time ago, these words came echoing: "I will lift mine eyes unto the hills, from whence cometh my help." And even Rogers and Hammerstein: "I go to the hills when my heart is lonely." Rather than moving away, I decided to rethink my own tendency toward equating nature with escape. Inspired by an event that signaled the connectedness of all of corporeal, intellectual, emotional, and material territories, I needed to research and rethink the (my) American pastoral.

The name of my childhood town in northwest New Jersey is Allamuchy. Nearby rivers are the Pequest and the Musconetcong. There is Lake Hopatcong. There are towns called Independence and Liberty. Names, evidence of the uprooting/routing of peoples. An arrowhead pops up out of a freshly plowed field after a soaking rain. It rests against the spines of my childhood books. Familiar with the concept of a subway thanks to my mother who grew up in the city, I envisioned the underground railway rumbling beneath fields. Above ground, the crumbling foundations of slave-quarters, the unspoken truth of slavery in the north. The Estonian forests of my father's childhood harbored nationalist fighters, the Forest Brethren, heroes. Those same forests, sites of extermination camps where thousands of Jews were killed. When I once asked my father if he knew about the camps and he said he had no idea.

TREES OF THE SAME FOREST HOLD DIFFERENT STORIES.

The land is left to cover something or we dig, looking for a full history. The land is peaceful or a haunted witness to human cruelty. The forest, site of desperate escape.

Janie Crawford's grandma, in Zora Neale Hurston's novel *Their Eyes Were Watching God*, relates the story of escaping into the forest with Leafy, the mother Janie Crawford never knew: "In de black dark Ah wrapped mah baby de best Ah knowed how and made it to the swamp by de river. Ah knowed de place was full uh moccasins and other bitin' snakes, but Ah was more skeered uh what was behind me" (18).

Joy Harjo: "The landscape of the late twentieth century is littered with bodies of our relatives." "Violence is a prevalent theme in the history of this land" (19).

Leslie Marmon Silko: "You are never the first to suffer a grave loss or profound humiliation. You are never the first, and you understand that you will probably not be the last to commit or be victimized by a repugnant act" (274).

I want writing to acknowledge the legacy of North American whiteness—whiteness in the way that critical race theory sees race as "products of social thought and relations" (Delgado and Stefancic 7). I think of white consciousness, even if liberal, as the investigating self, separate from what is seen, the upward-pointing morals, the body as ocular and rational above all else. The accompanying psychosis of power, of possession, of ownership: utterly restless, always in search of the new. Literature unwinding itself from this tradition—is it possible?

So-called "alternative" ways of being and conceptualizing language, of course, exist and always have. Harjo: "I think of Bell's theorem which states that all actions have a ripple effect in this world. We could name this theorem for any tribe in this country as tribal peoples knew this long before we knew English or the scientific method" (34).

Zora Neale Hurston's Janie, upon end-of-her-story reflection: "She pulled in her horizon like a great fish-net. Pulled it from around the waist of the world and draped it over her shoulder. So much of life in its meshes! She called in her soul to come and see" (193).

Brenda Hillman, from "12 Writings toward a Poetics of Alchemy, Dread, Inconsistency, Betweenness, and California Geological Syntax": "A single body is not big enough to hold an experience" (277).

Juliana Spahr, in *This Connection of Everyone with Lungs*: "There is space in the room that surrounds the shapes of everyone's hands and body and feet and cells and the beating contained within" (4).

Lyn Hejinian, in *Happily*, writes, "One is stung by a bee and it is noticeable that the whole body is involved/ Why isolate part of the field?" (231).

The preceding can be read as ecopoetic—opposing a tradition in literature that rewards self-containment, digestible epiphanies, rehearsed forms, consumption, and the separation of inner and outer worlds. This stance may be inclined to describe and inscribe while conscious of the structures that train the eye, and conscious that literature is never neutral.

A CRITIQUE OF ENVIRONMENTALISM

What about the real problems of pollution, water shortages, natural resource depletion, endangered species? An ecopoetics would begin by exposing the hegemony of environmentalism.

David Mazel:

> Any politically actionable environmentalist discourse...requires two creations of difference, both of which can be construed as thoroughly political. First is the discrimination of an outside from an inside. Such discourse also requires a secondary discrimination, a marking off of some graspable portion of the remaining totality. But what part? Such a selection requires a prior determination of what shall count as environment. This is the source of the second layer of politics, for not everyone will agree on what matters (142).

Ted Nordhaus and Michael Shellenberger, in their essay "The Death of Environmentalism" posit that "[w]e can no longer afford to address the world's problems separately" (28). For example, Michel Gelobter, et al, in "The Soul of Environmentalism," urge us that discussions of land use should be about "exposing sprawl as a symptom of race and class segregation, not its cause" (19).

Appealing to the legislative body on single issues has been environmentalism's persistent strategy since the '70s. This strategy's effectiveness relies on the act of separating issues, providing a focused, singular presentation on an aspect of "environment," meaning "nature." Individuals are organized remotely to comment through letters, emails, faxes, and donations of money toward the singular issue. In this model, the citizen stands opposed to the legislative body, connected by an invisible cord called "communication." Letters probably come back in reply, emails get a response. And because the loop is closed, we are satisfied that we have agency for the moment.

But have there been resulting policy victories as a result of these communication rituals?

Nordhaus and Shellenberger:

> Over the last 15 years environmental foundations and organizations have invested hundreds of millions of dollars into combating global warming. We have strikingly little to show for it. From the battles over higher fuel efficiency for cars and trucks to the attempts to reduce carbon emissions through international treaties, environmental groups repeatedly have tried and failed to win national legislation that would reduce the threat of global warming (6).

Michel Gelobter, et al:

> The problems facing environmentalism today are eerily similar to those faced by the Civil Rights Movement two decades ago.... Both movements started out as social uprisings that were visionary and com-

munity- and systems-oriented. Both lost popular support as time went by. Both narrowed their advocacy increasingly to legal interventions. Both shifted from winning broad mandates to fighting specific political, regulatory, and legal battles (12).

An ecopolitical practice may articulate connections between people, institutions, and issues, and resist single-issue thinking and branding. (No discussion of environmental issues without discussion of campaign finance reform. Global warming legislation needs to have labor on its side; it *is* about jobs. Any discussion of environment should include a discussion of access to health care and the cost to companies of providing benefits. Disaster relief and poverty is a foundational part of any global warming concern.)

A ROLE FOR POETRY AND POETS?

What is interesting for me as a writer is the potential of poetry to denaturalize language, to insist on language beyond the scale of mass-communications and dictums. As Jonathan Skinner suggests in his "Editor's Notes" to *ecopoetics* no. 3, "[i]magining endangered species is a useful act of language; writing that decenters the habitual configurations, enough to see who's endangered, may be more useful."

Poetry, as a subversive element of ecology, may resist the ritualized emptiness of "efficient" and "effective" communication in its insistence on individual utterance and on a non-standardized performance of language. Poetry is a language with no measurable market effect. As a poet, this is my lullaby: "no measurable effect." The difference (if any) made by a poem cannot be measured. This state of not knowing creates an inherently oppositional mode within a post-capitalist information age. It is within this mode that I want to operate.

Édouard Glissant proposes such a modality in his *Poetics of Relation*:

> [T]he poetics of Relation remains forever conjectural and presupposes no ideological stability. It is against the comfortable assurances linked to the supposed excellence of a language. A poetics that is latent, open, multilingual in intention, directly in contact with everything possible. Theoretician thought, focused on the basic and fundamental, and allying these with what is true, shies away from these uncertain paths (32).

In our political climate, with the record of losses on the left, are artists nervous about exercising quiet, nervous about being ineffectual or out of touch? Perhaps the very health of our society depends, to some degree, on our art-making acts of reflection. In *Pedagogy of the Oppressed*, Paulo Freire writes, "[i]n dialectical thought, world and action are intimately interdependent. But action is human only when it is not merely an occupation but also a preoccupation, that is, when it is not dichotomized from reflection" (35).

ART AND ACTIVISM

To advocate for the union of art and politics assumes that the two realities are separate. For many artists in this country and all over the world, there has been no separation between art and politics, between experiences of daily life and larger social structures. While some in society notice and count the macroaggressions of wars and visible violence, many experience daily microaggressions, often race- and/or gender-based and evidence of the nonexistence of equality and of the failure of rights and the law. For many, daily living and political issues are not separate spheres.

There may be for many no need for the word ecopoetics. I would define ecopoetics as a practice aware of the context of its own terminology.

One of the most powerful liberatory possibilities humans possess is to accept distinction and inclusion at once. This is the domain of art, making art inherently relational, and, therefore, political. Given this, the arts of language need not decide to be either conceptual/ abstract or narrative in order to be "political."

Inscription is always an act of abstraction, impression, power, and limitations—it is impossible to extract "the political" from writing when thought of in this way, which is not how Enlightenment thinking and most liberal educators conceptualize inscription. Their notions of literacy center around civilizing and betterment and might ignore power. Therefore, if inscription is considered inherently po- litical, down come crashing the hierarchies of taste and purpose that would rank the hermetic above the demotic, high art over low art.

Though ecopoetics might be grounded in literary experimentalism, whose traditions have included a deep skepticism of traditional grammar, narratives, and "telling," I believe an ecopoetic stance may be wary of the fixity of that aesthetic and conceptual position, recognizing, as feminism and critical race theory has, the necessity of storytelling and the historical fact of artists and intellectuals shaping their texts for distinct political purposes. Direct narratives employing plain speech, or what could be called a demotic rhetoric, may be necessary tools to bridge gaps in knowledge, experience, and to forge empathy. Stories, always more complex as versions emerge, are personal *and* communal, performed *and* revised, inviting utterances that result in more utterances, signaling relation and interconnection. Silko points out, "[t]he ancient Pueblo people sought a communal truth, not an absolute.... For them, this truth lived somewhere within the web of different versions..." (269).

Agency and the Individual

Is it enough for me to write poems? I'd like, I must admit, for the answer to be "yes" and this desire finds its roots my own history— one that includes working in community-based organizations and liberal education programs for many years only to see them fold or take misguided turns before the work is done. I sometimes rest on the fact that I still teach and the classroom is a transformative space and maybe that's enough. But even if I didn't teach, I might still want to think of art-making as a practice, not as an outcome, and as a way of navigating daily living not necessarily.

While it's true that many of my own writing projects begin with a personal response to a larger social structure, I still believe that to import an agenda for social change onto the work is to run the risk of denying the power in what Audre Lorde calls "the erotic" found in writing, in creating something. In her essay, "Uses of the Erotic, the Erotic as Power," she writes, "[i]n touch with the erotic, I become less willing to accept powerlessness, or those other supplied states of being which are not native to me, such as resignation, despair, self-effacement, depression, self-denial" (58). This erotic sense of writing and inquiry is not, for me, programmatic, individualistic, and apolitical.

Consternation over the use of "I" in our writings might only signal that too much is being made of the idea of our own individualism. To me, the intensely personal first-person perspective does not arouse suspicion any more than does the unidentified author, attempting to mask a point of view.

Additionally, social change has never resulted from an isolated individual action. Perhaps some concern over solipsism in our writings has to do, at root, with an overestimation of the effectiveness of individuals. The story of Rosa Parks comes to mind; she is celebrated for her individual act of courage. But the full story is that she attended trainings at the Highlander Center/Folk School in Tennessee; her actions were part of a group plan. She was chosen because she was trained, because of her light skin color and the possibility that her actions would not be met with as much violence as those of her darker sisters, and because she was a player in the strategy of a larger movement. Knowing this about her story doesn't mean that a hero has fallen and we should get depressed about agency; to me it means that individual agency is one small part of large-scale social change.

Right now I need to question the notion that "incrementalism and step-by-step progress" (Delgado and Stefancic 3) is good enough. Instead, I am interested in the practice of imagining a sea change, a radical practice that "questions the very foundations of the liberal order, including equality theory, legal reasoning, Enlightenment rationalism, and neutral principles of constitutional law" (3). Those of us who call ourselves word-workers are positioned to reject flaccid utopian thinking and Band-Aid activism, creating a space for reflection, study, and intuition: how and why are things as they are? How, then, to really change them?

Finally, back to our small fish and the self as field of experience. Joy Harjo says that some people are born with nerve endings "out to there," beyond their physical bodies. So poets and artists may have been, and others too. And we may write from that experience, that stance of beyond-borders, beyond momentary agency. If I believe this, will the networks of nerves grow, might the deadening of the entire organism, of which I am a part, subside? Regardless of how I answer, and whether or not I think of my answer as part of an ecopoetic movement, I remember this: "[t]he single complicated human becomes a wave of humanness and forgets to be ashamed of making the wrong step" (Harjo 51).

This essay comes out of a talk I gave at the Segue Foundation Reading Series in January of 2006 entitled "The Problem of Edges." Thanks to Brenda Iijima and Evelyn Reilly for inviting me to participate. I am deeply appreciative of Brenda Iijima whose Portable Press at Yo-Yo Labs published my chapbook *Cadastral Map*, one of the fruits of this investigation. I also owe a debt of gratitude to Jonathan Skinner, Marcella Durand, and Juliana Spahr for their work of a couple years ago that inspired and helped to shape my considerations of an ecopoetics.

WORKS CITED

Delgado, Richard and Jean Stefancic. *Critical Race Theory: an Introduction.* New York: New York University Press, 2001.

Elder, John and Robert Finch. Introduction. *The Norton Book of Nature Writing.* New York: Norton,1990.

Evernden, Neil. "Beyond Ecology: Self, Place, and the Pathetic Fallacy." *The Ecocriticism Reader: Landmarks in Literary Ecology.* Eds. Cheryll Glotfelty and Harold Fromm. Athens, GA: University of Georgia Press, 1996.

Freire, Paulo. *Pedagogy of the Oppressed.* New York: Continuum, 1995.

Gelobter, Michel, et al. "The Soul of Environmentalism: Rediscovering Transformational Politics in the 21st Century." <http://www.rprogress. org/soul/soul.pdf>.

Glissant, Édouard. *Poetics of Relation.* Trans. Betsy Wing. Ann Arbor: University of Michigan Press, 1997.

Harjo, Joy. *The Woman Who Fell From the Sky.* New York: Norton, 1994.

Hejinian, Lyn. "Excerpts from *Happily.*" *American Women Poets in the 21st Century: Where Lyric Meets Language.* Eds. Claudia Rankine and Juliana Spahr. Middletown, CT: Wesleyan, 2002.

Hillman, Brenda. "Twelve Writings toward a Poetics of Alchemy, Dread, Inconsistency, Betweenness, and California Geological Syntax." *American Women Poets in the 21st Century: Where Lyric Meets Language.* Eds. Claudia Rankine and Juliana Spahr. Middletown, CT: Wesleyan, 2002.

Hurston, Zora Neale. *Their Eyes Were Watching God.* New York: First Perennial Classics, 1999.

Lorde, Audre. *Sister Outsider.* Berkeley, CA: The Crossing Press, 1984.

Mazel, David. "American Literary Environmentalism as Domestic Orientalism." *The Ecocriticism Reader: Landmarks in Literary Ecology.* Eds. Cheryll Glotfelty and Harold Fromm. Athens, GA: University of Georgia Press, 1996.

Nordhaus, Ted and Michael Shellenberger. "The Death of Environmentalism: Global Warming Politics in a Post-Environmental World." 2004. <http://www.thebreakthrough.org/images/Death_of_Environmentalism.pdf>.

Silko, Leslie Marmon. "Landscape, History, and the Pueblo Imagination." *The Ecocriticism Reader: Landmarks in Literary Ecology.* Eds. Cheryll Glotfelty and Harold Fromm. Athens, GA: University of Georgia Press, 1996.

Skinner, Jonathan. "Editor's Notes." *ecopoetics* no. 3, Fall 2002.

Sontag, Susan. Interview. "The Art of Fiction No. 143." *The Paris Review* no. 137, Winter 1995.

Spahr, Juliana. *This Connection of Everyone with Lungs.* Berkeley and Los Angeles: University of California Press, 2005.

Eco-Noise and the Flux of Lux

—— EVELYN REILLY ——

1.

An ecopoetic silence fills the page as the *Pequod* descends to the ocean's depths. The deranged captain has been destroyed. The polyglot crew (excepting, of course, Ishmael) is about to meet its end. Perched on the top of the mast, Tashtego, a descendent of the tribe that first encountered the Pilgrims, is the last to disappear, and along with him, a compendium of benighted metaphors: whiteness as soul, leviathan as human overreaching, beast as mirror of the darkness in the human heart. In this exceptionally strange piece of post-enlightenment writing, all such figures, if they were ever truly light, go implacably dark.

Only a few years ago, people would ask me, "what is ecopoetics?" and no answer seemed to stick. I'd explain that it's an investigation into how language can be renovated or expanded as part of the effort to change the way we think, write, and thus act in regards to the world we share with other living things, and they'd say, "oh, updated nature poetry." I'd assert that it has nothing to do with nature poetry, the separation into genre being a symptom of the disease. Still, they would file it under "species political poetry, subspecies nature," before turning to other, more urban, social, linguistic "literary" concerns, even as I'd insist that all concerns are concerns of our being or doing as nature, that there is nothing more social, urban, post-humanist and po-mo-post-lang-po than "eco." Happily, this has begun to change.

So, ecopoetics: an exploration of what human use of the word "n/ Nature" makes and has made possible—starting perhaps with the history of naming and separation, with the concept of original sin reinterpreted as the self-separation of humans "from." For with naming, comes the subject-who-names as well as the object-that-is-subjected-to-naming, and the cost, as Adorno and Horkheimer put it, to the namers, who "pay for this increase of their power with alienation from that over which they exercise their power."[1]

Thus, self-expulsion from the garden, via our divorce from the rest of nature (in one story).

Thus, shipwreck of the self-separated in delusions of transcendent grandeur (in another).

Thus, ecopoetics as a search for a language congruent with a world that is not filled with objects or subjects, that is not "the context,"

---

1 | Theodor Adorno and Max Horkheimer, "The Logic of Domination," reprinted in *The Green Studies Reader: From Romanticism to Ecocriticism*, edited by Laurence Coupe, Routledge, 2000, p.77.

nor "the setting" for subjects or objects, but that is a permanent state of flux between subject-objects and object-subjects.

In some ways ecopoetics is a correction, an amendment, a set of rejections. A rejection of compensatory notions of nature as retreat and of our role as consumers of consoling description. An investigation that naturally engages many current poetic and ethical concerns, such as the crisis of the "lyric I"; the recuperation of cultural, industrial, and political erasures; the dismantling of dichotomies of self/other, nature/culture, indigenous/alien and central/peripheral—bringing them all into a larger, trans-species arena of investigation.

Ecopoetics: a search for language that coheres with evolution, with our destiny as animals among other plants and animals. A search for a poetry that is firmly attached to earthly being and that is thus *dis-enchanted*, in the sense of being free of the mesmerizing spell of the transcendent. For ecopoetics reflects yet another in a series of human decenterings, as from an ecological perspective, the self dissolves into the gene pool and the species into the ecosystem.

In fact, ecopoetics requires the abandonment of the idea of center for a position in an infinitely extensive net of relations. Thus, it connects to Objectism and the poetics of vector relationships as articulated by Charles Olson:

> Objectism is the getting rid of the lyrical interference of the individual as ego, of the 'subject' and his soul, that peculiar presumption by which

western man has interposed himself between what he is as a creature of nature . . . and those other creatures of nature.[2]

At root (or stump) what *is*, is no longer THINGS but what happens BETWEEN things, these are the terms of the reality contemporary to us—and the terms of what we are."[3]

This is a relational poetics, one that reflects the shift from a classification biology obsessed with naming, to an ecological biology with its emphasis on processes of interaction and change, and, on the molecular scale, with randomness and contingency. Ecopoetics points to a poetry that attempts to trace the kinetics of whole systems, and to enact connections rather than to mark distinctions. As such, ecopoetics might be called democratic in the most aspirational meaning of the word:

> Nature is not a form, but rather the process of establishing relations. It invents a polyphony: it is not a totality but an assembly, a "conclave," a "plenary session." Nature is inseparable from processes of companionship and conviviality, which are not preexistent givens but are elaborated between heterogeneous living beings in such a way that they create a tissue of shifting relations, in which the melody of one part intervenes as a motif in the melody of another (the bee and the flower). Relations are not internal to a Whole; rather, the Whole is derived form the external relations of a given moment, and varies with

---

2 | Charles Olson, "Projective Verse," *Selected Writings*, New Directions, 1966. Others have interpreted passages of Olson's essays within an ecological framework, including Jed Rasula in *This Compost: Ecological Imperatives in American Poetry*, Rosmarie Waldrop in *Dissonance (if you are interested)*, and Jonathan Skinner in his essay in this volume.

3 | Charles Olson, *Human Universe and Other Essays*, quoted by Rosmarie Waldrop in "Charles Olson: Process and Relationship," Ibid., p.60.

them. Relations of counterpoint must be invented everywhere, and are the very condition of evolution (Deleuze).[4]

Thus, perhaps, too, there is a connection to recent interest in the American philosophical tradition of pragmatism,[5] in which language is seen as a set of tools rather than a mode of representation,[6] and philosophy is, as Dewey once described it, not "in any sense whatever a form of knowledge," but instead "a form of desire, of effort at action."[7] For the pragmatist, language is no more and no less than a biological adaptation for human interaction with the world, and the "truth" of any particular "instance of language" is a matter of how useful it is in terms of successful integration with the environment, meaning, in the largest sense, communal well-being and ecological sanity.[8]

This view makes possible a cautious embrace of both rationality and of critiques of essentialist views of language in that from a pragmatist point of view, language/logic/truth evolves with our relation to a changing environment. For poets, a "pragmatic ecopoetics" puts

---

4 | Gilles Deleuze, "Whitman," *Essays Critical and Clinical*, University of Minnesota Press, 1997, p.59.

5 | Examples of pragmatist literary criticism include Michael Magee's *Emancipating Pragmatism: Emerson, Jazz, and Experimental Writing*, Cornel West's *The American Evasion of Philosophy*, and Richard Poirier's *Poetry and Pragmatism*.

6 | This view is articulated in depth by the philosopher Richard Rorty in *Contingency, Irony, and Solidarity*, Cambridge University Press, 1989.

7 | John Dewey, quoted by Magee, Ibid., p.1.

8 | For a discussion of the implications of pragmatism for the decrease of human suffering, see Rorty, Ibid.

experimentalism at the heart of the endeavor and ties it to a larger social and environmental project. It connects to both Hejinian's notion of poetry as the "language of inquiry"[9] and Retallack's concept of "poethics."[10]

All this proposes a poetry that is not one of retreat and meditation, but of engagement and innovation—one that is not rural, regional, or pastoral, but is of a world in a continuum of crisis and ecological in scope, a community of communities. It calls for a poetics that is also an ethics, because, as Aldo Leopold famously wrote, "[e]cology is the science of communities and the ecological conscience is therefore the ethics of community life"[11]—a formulation in comparison with which the golden rule seems meager.

2 .

So what might an ecopoetic poetry be? Many poets have been trying to directly or indirectly answer this question, as has the journal *ecopoetics*, edited by Jonathan Skinner since 2001. Agreeing, however, with Marcella Durand that ecopoetics is less of a school than an interest[12] (although I'm wishing it to be a passionate, a necessary interest),

---

9 | Lyn Hejinian, *The Language of Inquiry*, University of California Press, 2000.

10 | Joan Retallack, *The Poethical Wager*, University of California Press, 2003.

11 | Aldo Leopold, *A Sand County Almanac*, Oxford University Press, USA, 1968.

12 | Marcella Durand, "Spatial Interpretations: Ways of Reading Ecological Poetry," included in this volume.

I've been taking note of poetry that seems to point in an ecopoetic direction. In doing so, I've become more and more convinced that it isn't something that can be *aimed at,* but that instead *happens* as poets participate in realizing the full implications of our position as language-using animals in a world composed of interconnection.

I've also been noting directions that I *don't* think are particularly helpful, including writing that simply expands the arena of natural description to include landfills and polluted streams, or that devises yet more astute metaphors based on carbon cycles and energy flows. While these tactics might have their uses, I think that ecopoetics must be a matter of finding formal strategies that effect a larger paradigm shift and that actually participate in the task of abolishing the aesthetic use of nature as mirror for human narcissism.

In the case of Olson, this ethos is manifested most dramatically in the opening of the page both topo- and typo-graphically as a surface for juxtapositions, transforming it into a kind of MapQuest program, capable of being manipulated to investigate adjacencies in any direction, and in which any apparently peripheral element can be moved to a central position. In addition, his use of open parentheses made it possible to turn a poem into a theoretically endless branching diagram, in which any word or phrase can become the jumping-off point for an entirely new set of diagrammed relationships.

Through such means, Olson at his best wrote poetry that could encompass the history of nature, as well as our own kinetics of place, exemplifying Dewey's notion of history, which "takes in rivers, mountains, fields and forests, laws and institutions…the purposes and plans, the desires and emotions, through which these things are administered and transformed."[13] Olson himself called this clearing out "the gunk/ by getting the universe in (as against man alone/& *that* concept of history."[14]

In *The Maximus Poems*, the human species, the town, and its inhabitants *occur* as a piece of the natural world, so that "An American/ is a complex of occasions,/ themselves a geometry/ of spatial nature"[15] and Merry, the drunken would-be matador, "sought to manifest/ his soul" just as "the stars/ manifest their souls":

> <u>subterranean</u> and celestial
> primordial water holds
> Dogtown high
>
>   And down
> the ice holds
> Dogtown, scattered
> boulders little bull
> who kills
>
> Merry
>   who sought to manifest
> his soul, the stars
> manifest their souls
>   my soft sow the roads

---

13 | John Dewey, "Philosophic Method," *Experience and Nature*, Dover, 1958, p. 9.

14 | Charles Olson, "A Later Note on Letter # 15, *The Maximus Poems*.

15 | Charles Olson, "Maximus to Gloucester, Letter 27 [withheld]," Ibid.

of Dogtown trickling like from underground rock
springs under an early cold March moon[16]

Later, in the Gravelly Hill section of *Maximus*, the Olsonian
"I," which has, up to this point, stood for both singular poet and
communal amanuensis, merges with, and even "disappears" into
geophysical history—

> . . . Gravelly Hill says
> leave me be, I am contingent, the end of the world
> is the borders
> of my being

which leads in turn to a very Emersonian notion of selfhood:

> . . . the end of myself,
> happens, on the east side (Erechthonios)
> to be the beginning of another set
> of circumstance.[17]

The Maximus Poems—one of those big flawed important works that
emerge now and then from the culture of this big flawed country—
manages to make visible many invisibilities of nature, even while
notably participating in other erasures, particularly of women, who
appear primarily as either mythic statuary or sexual receptacle. For
this reason, it is a happy fact that in the hands of a poet such as

---

16 | Charles Olson, "Maximus, from Dogtown—1," Ibid.

17 | Charles Olson, "'at the boundary of the mighty world' H. (T)620 foll.," Ibid.

Susan Howe, Olson's poetics have since been extended and further elaborated in the service of yet another "reading" of the New England landscape—as topography scarred by race- and gender-based exclusions and elisions.

Perhaps the most famous example of this is "Thorow,"[18] a work that begins its explorations by means of a fairly decorous grid/stanza form within which certain understandings lead to a startling abandonment of that same form. The poet's introduction to the work points to the conundrum of the writer's position on the shores of a history in which notions of the "wild" stimulated a thicket of gendered metaphors of growth, sexuality, and exploitation.

> I thought I stood on the shores of a history of the world where forms of wildness brought up by memory become desire and multiply.

> Lake George was a blade of ice to write across not knowing what She.

An early passage acknowledges/reclaims/mourns the gathered invisibles, who have been rendered so by the strictures of containing social/historical forms:

> Dear Seem dear cast out
> Sun shall go down and set

> Distant monarchs of Europe
> European grid on the Forest

---

18 | Susan Howe, "Thorow," *Singularities*, Wesleyan University Press, 1990.

so many gether togather
were invisible alway Love

As the poem proceeds, this elegiac approach gives way to a more confrontational tone at the same time as Howe's project takes on definition.

Elegiac western Imagination

Mysterious confined enigma
a possible field of work

The expanse of unconcealment
so different from all maps

Spiritual typography of elegy
Nature in us as a Natural

These lines are soon followed by "I pick my compass to pieces," a line, it turns out, that will serve as a detonator, blowing the traditional form to smithereens on the very next page (see figure 1).

In this and the following pages, words abut words in mirrored inversions, fragments of lyric stanzas (surveyors' grid) oppose, overlap, juxtapose, and crisscross fragments of a contested natural, cultural, and military history. Treaties and war songs battle and confront each other in equality with lily roots, swamps, mud, water bugs. Even the margins of the page, the place where Howe so often finds poetic redemption, are seen as insufficient, as she expresses, in the center of one of these disrupted fields, what might be called an in-

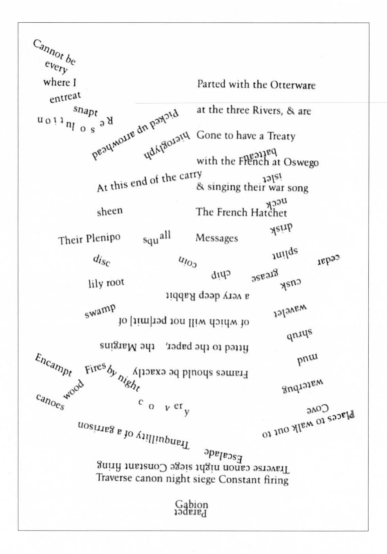

Figure 1

| *Eco-Noise and the Flux of Lux*

completely fulfilled ecopoetic desire: "paper, the Margines/of which will not per[mit] of/ a very deep Rabbit". Through such acknowledged desires and exploratory disruptions, Howe's work particularly succeeds in one aspect of the ecopoetic project—the inclusion of nature within history and history within nature.

The subject of the poetic use and abuse of animals is too large to take on here, but in some poetry the presence of/meditation upon nonhuman animal life does indicate an enlarging ecopoetic sympathy, as in the work of George Oppen, which took note of "the little amoeba at the heart of things"[19] and posed the question: "Humanism: Because people exist. What other things exist?"[20]

Pragmatically, Oppen viewed poetic language as an investigative tool: "Prosody is a language, but it is a language that tests itself.... It tests the relations of things..."[21] Often in his poems, humans coexist in an interanimating egalitarianism with each other and with the nonhuman living world. This is especially the case when the poet's sense of "being numerous" includes "the world, weather-swept, with which/one shared the century,"[22] and when he asks what a newborn child, who made herself "cell by cell," will think of "a world...of

19 | George Oppen, *Selected Prose, Daybooks, and Papers*. University of California Press, 2007, p.62.

20 | George Oppen, Ibid., p.61.

21 | George Oppen, "Statement on Poetics," Ibid, p.49.

22 | George Oppen, opening section of "Discrete Series," *Collected Poems*, New Directions, 1975.

which she is made."[23] It is also apparent in poems in which cultural history blurs into natural duration:

> O, the tree, growing from the sidewalk—
> It has a little life, sprouting
> Little green buds
> into the culture of the streets.
> We look back
> Three hundred years and see bare land.
> And suffer vertigo
>   (from "The Building of the Skyscraper")

That his poetry transcended some of the limiting bigotries of the era,[24] especially that of excess anthropocentrism, I think is due, partly, to his pragmatist stance:

> Does philosophy burden itself unnecessarily with the terms "mind" and "subject"? Is it not possible simply to hold that the world contains, among other things, living organisms? The problem of knowledge would therefore reduce to psychological or physiological problems. It would result, I would suppose, in a pragmatist solution, since it is clear that the reason cannot judge its own reasonableness except by its results in action.[25]

Many writers on ecopoetics have talked about the qualities that differentiate the poetry of John Clare from his supposedly "greater"

---

23 | George Oppen, "Sarah in her Father's Arms," in "The Materials," Ibid.

24 | This ecopoetic expansiveness, along with an engagement with issues of class and race, is found in both the poetry and prose, but sadly stands side-by-side with a dismaying sexism and homophobia in the recently published *Daybooks*. For a few examples, see *Daybook I*, p. 59 and *Daybook II:I*, pps. 72-73.

25 | George Oppen, *Daybook II.III*, Ibid, p.88.

Romantic contemporaries,[26] most especially, Clare's restraint from using his powers of local observation as a springboard to transcendent abstraction—a form of early environmental humility. This refusal to "go vertical," to exit the earth, can also be found in the work of Lorine Niedecker, who shared with Clare a laboring person's suspicion of moves that abandon the local in the name of "higher" purposes. In her case, such skepticism was also probably due to a life spent on a floodplain with its continual obliterations of human "improvements."

"North Central" is a poetic sequence that addresses the natural history of Niedecker's northern Midwest and its history of "exploration" by Joliet and Marquette, the latter a Jesuit missionary. Its first lines assert:

> In every part of every living thing
> is stuff that once was rock
>
> In blood the minerals
> of the rock

A few lines later she exercises her characteristic irony —

> The water working together
>   internationally
> Gulls playing both sides

---

26 | See Jonathan Bate, *The Song of the Earth*, and Angus Fletcher, *A New Theory of American Poetry: Democracy, the Environment, and the Future of Imagination*.

and then juxtaposes cultural symbol against natural imperfection, favoring the latter.

> Through all this granite land
> the sign of the cross
>
> Beauty: impurities in the rock

In "Traces of Living Things," Niedecker effects a trans-species inversion that makes the reader ask, just who is meeting whom here?

> Having met the protozoic
>   Vorticellae
>   here is man
> Leafing toward you
>   in this dark
>   deciduous hall

Finally, in the poem "Darwin," Niedecker makes her case against "intelligent design" via the extraordinary comparison of a god-like, but "brutish" designer and the chance-embracing laws of nature:

> the universe
>   not built by brute force
>   but designed by laws
>
> The details left
>
> to the working of chance

It is interesting to compare Niedecker's poetry with that of Ronald Johnson, another Midwesterner with acute powers of natural observation. In his epic work *Ark*, a fascinating tension exists between an ecopoetic impulse and the tendency to use nature as vehicle for extraterrestrial aspirations. Although artistically embedded in the landscape of his native Kansas, Johnson actually drew his formal inspiration for *Ark* from the spires of the Watts Towers, and the poetry is literally in-"spire"-d, in that its dominant gesture is to point up, away from the world.

On one hand, this is a poet with a stunning perceptiveness, scientific proclivities, and an extraordinary ear:

> When the light walks, clockwise, counterclockwise,
>   atoms memorize the firefly's wing
> > > (from Beam 21, 22, 23, *The Song of Orpheus*)

> > hare electric
> > lone deer poise encalded of antler
> > > (Arc 57, *Rungs II, The Gaia Spire*)

> mind is a revelation of matter
> > > (Beam 12)[27]

But Johnson is also a poet of "Eternal, *interior, not ocular, vision*" (Beam 21, 22, 23, *The Song of Orpheus*). This is a quality that emerges most strongly when he exercises his "concrete" aesthetic, with its predilection for ecstatic symmetries and a pressing toward exaltation.

---

27 | *Ark*, Living Batch Press, Albuquerque, 1996.

In one section, this semi-concrete poem, or "Beam," as he called the sections of *Ark*:

eartheartheart
eartheartheart
eartheartheart
eartheartheart
eartheartheart
eartheartheart

"any piece of counterpoint includes
a silent part
for the rhythmic movements of heart and
lungs"

(lilacs)

(Beam 24)

is followed by the line "prosper/ O/ cell" and an illustration of the mitotic cell. But in another section, the scent of chrysanthemum is lost in the eternal sanctities of a "chrysos-anthemon," and the very changefulness of the word "flux" is lost to iconic stasis in a perfect square of "lux":

CHRYSOS
anthemon

f lux f lux f lux f
lux f lux f lux f l
ux f lux f lux f lu
x f lux f lux f lux
f lux f lux f lux f

(Beam 13)

In the end, *Ark* is primarily a religious work preoccupied with refracting light into Light. This is not to say that ecopoetics must be set against a religious impulse, or, for that matter, against a social idealist impulse, but that it is troublesome when such desires fixate the gaze of language onto utopian elsewheres of little use in reforming an imperfect here.

All these examples, of course, predate the notion of ecopoetics, which is beginning to consciously and unconsciously color the work of more and more poets. In addition to explicitly ecopoetic projects by writers such as Jack Collom, Lisa Robertson, Jonathan Skinner, Christopher Dewdney, Brenda Iijima, Tina Darragh, and Marcella Durand, evidence of an expanding ecopoetic sensibility abound. It can be found in Mei Mei Berssenbrugge's *Endocrinology*, with its exploration of the body as both "space of culture" and as "material, of non-negotiable contingency," in Robert Kocik's investigations of the "sociochemical" nature of bodily existence in *Rhrurbarb*, and in Sina Queryas' permutational exploration of one of the oldest tropes of all in "A River By the Moment."

Maybe it's a sign of the times that Queyras' book *Lemon Hound* and Robertson's *XEclogue* both use lines from Gertrude Stein as cautionary epigraphs (and as versions, possibly, of Raymond Williams' statement that "nature is perhaps the most complex word in the language"[28]):

---

28 | Raymond Williams, quoted by Laurence Coupe in *The Green Studies Reader: From Romanticism to Ecocriticism*, p. 3.

What is nature.
Nature is what is ...
but is nature natural.
No not as natural as that. (Queryas)

Nature is not natural and that is natural enough. (Robertson)

Which brings us back to Ishmael, floating in his cradle-like coffin, in the wake of an exercise in factory-hunting gone terribly awry. The only silence, of course, is that of the machinery of slaughter. What actually fills the air is the noise of a world larger than the self-reflecting symbols we, Ahabs all, would make of it:

Now small fowls flew screaming over the yet yawning gulf; a sullen white surf beat against its steep sides; then all collapsed, and the great shroud of the sea rolled on as it rolled five thousand years ago.[29]

---

29 | Herman Melville, "*Moby-Dick, or, The Whale*," chapter CXXXV, "The Chase—Third Day."

Metamorphic Morphology (with gushing igneous interlude) Meeting in Language: P as in Poetry, Poetry Rhetorical in Terms of Eco

——— B R E N D A   I I J I M A ———

Input output—economic imperialism surges networks with zeros and ones. Industrial production paradigms infiltrate and attempt to totalize ecologies and make for one compressed top-down world saturated with itself. Part of this process involves rearranging bodies by dividing and subdividing social life, poisoning both internally and externally, razing to the point of no return, gutting diversity. Factors of race, class, and gender figure into the calculation of ecological positioning. Being is converted into abstractions of zeros and ones with decimal points to signal gross and net values. Has it come to this: where the "horizon is qualified by capitalism's total investment of life: by a biopower colonizing and occupying the entire biopolitical fabric of history and society…(so that) we circulate within an absolutely fetishized and commodified world"?[1] This architecture creates a myopic mono-view. Blurriness sets in when the system confronts intricacies beyond direct outcomes like profit margins and bottom lines: "official estimates of toll/ have been suppressed for purposes of

---

1 | Negri, Antonio. *The Porcelain Workshop.* Cambridge & London: MIT Press, 2008. p. 78. Here Negri outlines the positions of Jean-François Lyotard, Jean Baudrillard and Paul Virilio.

piece/ by piece attention to belief./ authorization to the area/ is given as is birth to myriads."[2] Poetries are social documents that express relationships within ecosystems. I like to think this process (poetry) recalibrates the social—how we function dynamically in space, in time, with each other—communally, communicational.

There's a teeming microlevel that hasn't been reaped for profit— molecular bits and particulates but also the minisystems that are the building blocks for larger entities and conditions—worlds within worlds might exist here, syntaxes, poetics—language opening and in-terrelating additionally. New possibilities for imagining embodiment coalesce around these shape-shifting micro-energies. Tonya Foster, from *(In) Somniloguy*: "This hive of sound: base-buzz, engine-crank, voices laugh/ seal the sonic cracks." [3] Close proximities, frictions, melding. When I acknowledge that my body is intimately connected to your body (we affect each other), we can no longer categorize indi-vidual disabilities. Bodies are *about* and *between* bodies—that is to say, bodies extend beyond physical selves. Empathetically we are incorpo-rated into/by each other. A politic of not disparaging bodies—and I'm not speaking humanocentrically (or anthropocentrically) because this must extend to all sentient beings, and the formation of beings must be considered too, so matter itself must be cared for. Thom Donovan, in a talk on disability, reminds that "dis-ability is a term used by Martin

---

2 | Roberson, Ed. "from news continued release," published in *Every Goodbye Ain't Gone: An Anthology of Innovative Poetry by African Americans.* Tuscaloosa, AL: The University of Alabama Press, 2006.

3 | Foster, Tonya. "(In) Somniloguy"
http://www.mipoesias.com/EVIESHOCKLEYISSUE/foster_t.html.

Heidegger to indicate a situation of anti- or non-instrumentality."
He says, "For to disable is finally to show how something works by
how it doesn't—it is 'knockout' as [Robert] Kocik puts it; more so,
however inadvertently or fortuitously, disability posits the subject at
the indiscernible points, the blind spots, where a technology—that
which works, or functions all-too-well—has failed to maintain its
instrumentality in relation to a user for whom the existence of that
technology would otherwise recede in use."[4] In conversation with par-
ticipants of the Nonsite Collective Kocik made the following query:
"Can a poetics that opposes the ableist environment by pursuing
or revering novelty, extremity, permutation, atypia, incongruity, sequence deletion, breakage, disfiguration, etc. possibly (paradoxically)
be beneficial? What about 'transfiguration' as a third term in the abil-
ity/disability discourse?"[5] I'd like to propose the term *re-enable-ment*
to join what Donovan, Kocik and others have initiated. Instead of
thinking in potentially polarizing terms, I'd suggest that function and
dysfunction are impossible to pin down—there is a wavering among
these terms. It isn't just that what is functional in one context might
not be in another. Rather, it is impossible to know the variousness of
function and dysfunction—they often go hand in hand. Dysfunction
can bring about different sorts of functionality that rebel against cat-

---

4 | Donovan, Thom. *Allegories of Disablement* (talk).
   http://whof.blogspot.com/2008/08/allegories-of-disablement-talk.html.

5 | "Nonsite is a framework for self-organized pedagogy in which participants
   collaborate to create 'curricula,' or sets of inter-linked inquiries. This pedagogical
   dimension is explicitly affirmed and promoted in constellations of events,
   discussions, and documents all related, more or less loosely or determinately, to
   ongoing investigations." http://www.nonsitecollective.org/node/664.

egorization. Furthermore, many functional technologies come with side effects that can cause dysfunction. Re-enable-ment speaks of the body thought to be powerless or problematic or disabled and how this body asserts itself in a burgeoning dynamical interplay along a spectrum of possible logics. I'm interested in recuperation, which signals that differences are embraced. Amber Di Pietra's thoughts and responses to Bhanu Kapil's talk (also a part of the ongoing Nonsite Collective discussion) offer a bountiful reexamination of disability, "I think of the other, more functional version of the word disable in our society. It means to stop the code, to break the chain of computation, to disable and allow for your own programming, a different kind of conveyance than what has been set up....To write new code at the most autonomic level and allow for greater of syncing across physical histories. Compacted/impacted is also being completely contained while witnessing that container as one in a set of shifting exteriors to other containers."[6] This has everything to do with poetry since poetry is a social document, an acknowledgement of interrelations.

The basis of animate substances is the miniscule writhing sub particle, the string—perpetually in flux, operative, it agitates at an imperceptible level, in motion-filled conjunction with the more evident

---

6 | Di Pietra, Amber. *Compacted Notes* (blog entry). http://www.nonsitecollective.org/node/489#comment-140. Bhanu Kapil, as a prelude to her talk asked the following, "My question, then, for writers/artists working through a poetics of disablement—towards hybrid works, in particular—is there any language we can think through together, about the experience of hybridity/fusion in the body—and how might this affect our transgressive relationships to the space of the book, the territory of document, our ability to attain the kind of couplings/intensifications/resonant physical gestures that further the limit of what a book is? I feel as if there is another kind of book I am only beginning to imagine. What about you?"

forces shaping the environment (or has this theory been disproved?). This is how I see language functioning, the way thinking functions, at microlevels, in body-brain, (a semi-autonomous system contained in a helmet of skull and skin that filters, links, agitates)—creative, aware, proactive—changeable—attuned to the surrounding environment where it submerges with the political, the social, the emotional, the local. It is libratory to conjure the numerosity of the subatomic, as Michio Kaku points out in his book, *Hyperspace: A Scientific Odyssey Through Parallel Universes, Time Warps, and the 10th Dimension*, "[t]he deeper we probe into the nature of subatomic particles, the more particles we find."[7] The cellular level is a memory bank, it is a prosthetic device, a trace, a synapse. Read M. Nourbese Philip[8]:

       the smallest cell
                  remembers
           a sound
       (sliding two semitones to return
   home)
        a secret order
        among syllables
               Leg/ba
               O/shun
               Shan/go
       heart races
       blood pounds
       remembers
             speech

---

7 | Kaku, Michio. *Hyperspace: A Scientific Odyssey Through Parallel Universes, Time Warps, and the 10th Dimension*. New York: Anchor Books, 1995. p. 153.

8 | Philip, M. Nourbese. *she tries her toungue, her silence softly breaks*. London: The Women's Press, 1993.

Poems can ooze like sludge, suck (as interesting as gravitational pull!)—syntax dangling thickly in clumps, slimy, greasy—hungry. Green up verbs to be. Lyrical Is (plural of I) join rocks in igneous, sedimentary, and metamorphic processes. Contentious histories heat the fortified walls of denial's antechambers. Language intermingles. Diction can express the health of earthworms, microbes, intestinal flora, etc., (additional meanings of culture grow). Landfills belching methane offer us a cross-section of the sublimated quotidian—the consumer burial mounds where the discarded nouns of our lives lie wasting. Refuse lingual—new processes for poems to undergo. Words, dirt, filtration—rich, moist soil in the works. O dirt, expansive erogenous depth! CAConrad reminds,

> Filth is another word for pollution, for garbage, for the bacteria-laden STINK we sweep out the door to become someone else's problem, some other environment's stinking problem. Garbage is on the streets all over Philadelphia and sometimes I see it and feel an affinity. It feels important to not only admit this affinity, but to examine how and why there would be. It's not surrendering to the total breakdown, but accepting and understanding that IT IS ME the breakdown, as much as it is all of us. The garbage on the street is who we are."[9]

Conrad's poetry is some of the least alienated work I know of because of his care, sensitivity and intimacy. Here's a brief description of his practice in an interview we conducted for ON: Contemporary Practice.

---

9 | Conrad, CA. Interview in ON journal edited by Thom Donovan, Kyle Schlesinger and Michael Cross, New York and Seattle: Cuneiform Press, 2008.

The Body, somatic, is FROM dirt, and is walking ON dirt. Spirit is Soma. This is a poetry conducted through the Soma and Somatic, literally, by manipulating our bodies and other anatomies of our physical world to connect our spiritual centers for a more holistic poetry. The brain has too much rule over our lives the more mechanized our world becomes, pushing us further and further into forgetting THE DIRT we come from, THE DIRT WE ARE. (Soma)tic Poetics relocates the intelligence of the physical and spiritual worlds and alerts and alters other aspects of our lives as a result, keeping us tuned into the frequencies of wood, toenail, blood, sleet, all the neighboring carbon, gentle AND NOT.[10]

Language is a matrix. Everything is pertinent to language and it is the impetus of language to pertain to the environment in interchange, nothing excluded. Beyond being merely mimetic of an outside reality, language is a conduit for bodies to articulate explicitly—meanings travel and exchange in every conceivable spatial direction. Language enacts. Language is a biological function as much as it is a technology. Biorhythms and metabolic functions coincide with language as it is rendered, conveyed, and received. Thoughts and utterances become bodily substance as encoded matter that imprints and sheds itself in worlds. Sueyeun Juliette Lee, from *Perfect Villagers*:

> imagination can be secreted. sweat makes an outline around the body when we dance. many instances converge slowly on the minute, and through hand bashes mouth or strikes a face down, we rise without repenting, stand tersely for the cue.[11]

---

10 | Ibid.

11 | Lee, Sueyeun Juliette. *Perfect Villagers*. Lincoln, NE: Octopus Books, 2006.

The brain (which is body), simultaneous to all other responses, encompasses language, engages with multifaceted simultaneous ability. Language takes this cue and act like bodies (that emit it)—is the becoming of the body (as cells store sensory data). Language expands beyond representation as an initiating and responding energy. The recombinant aspects of sounds and syntax enter consciousness and have altering effects on the material body much the same way as matter does when it is digested, experienced. Meanwhile a phoneme choir led by dancer/healer Daria Fain and architect/poet Robert Kocik is conjuring amorphous energies able to recalibrate and conduct collective psychophysical temporalities. Phonemes sung in group formation create a swarming, buzzing swell of sound dimensions. Language feels liquid and particulate. The blend and dissonance of voices is a body organ engulfing a body surround. Rhythmic dance is choreographed within the voiced vibrations. Other projects of Kocik's include designs for the Preemptive Peace Place (an agency devoted to the permanent peace movement) and the Prosody Building (a building entirely attuned to the prosodic). M. Mara-Ann's *Containment Scenario: DisloInter MedTextId entCation: Horse Medicine* is a multimedia project that engages music, theater, and dance to evoke data from the Intergovernmental Panel on Climate Change, the Global Green USA & Green Cross International policy report and the United Nations Kyoto Protocol to the United Nations Framework Convention on Climate Change, but it also is manifested as a book published by O Books in 2009. The book presents an overload of cascading data. Animals and biomes are enmeshed in the data. The data here is on the changing environment. Threats to the habitats of animal-humans are audible within the data. An epic shift of presence occurs through the multiple frequencies in which the work articulates itself (itself in this case is the saturated environment).

Julia Kristeva writes, "John Paul Sartre chooses nausea as an emblem of existence. Nausea and not grace is the metaphor of the unfulfilled and the open, of the negative and the impossible, of being and the other."[12] Sartre is on to something when he suggests the mental impacts the physical through and through. If only one could cough up the toxicity! The endless breakdown of other into other others (or is it others *unothering* others?), the wars, genocides, racism, poverty, pollution, and psychic duress obscure the life pulse, (yet, it must be noted, since 1965 the human population has managed to double itself while, simultaneously, the environment is well along into its 6th total extinction according to zoologists and others who track and study the biodiversity crisis). Gilles Deleuze makes the case that the formation of the instinct is inseparable from historical and social conditions. To quote Deleuze, "[o]ur words reach us only as far as the instincts, but it is from the other agency, that is, from the Death Instinct, that they receive their sense."[13] I don't find much concordance with Freud's death drive per se, for one, because of its built-in idea of limited reflexivity: tension does not automatically signal aggression or a kind of abject, relaxed calm, the so-called nirvana state. These states don't necessarily mean system failure. I

---

12 | Kristeva, Julia. *The Sense and Non-Sense of Revolt: The Powers and Limits of Psychoanalysis*. New York: Columbia University Press, 2000. p. 160.

13 | Deleuze, Gilles. *The Logic of Sense*. New York: Columbia University Press, 1990. p. 326

submit the contrary is often the case. Freud continued to adjust his take until he claimed destrudo energy was the desire to return to an inanimate state—devoid of instinct. It is reassuring that Freud's theory was constantly in flux. Everything molecular is animate—earth and all it consists of is molecular, therefore it is animate, in transition! On earth one could say, "vegetative state" or "catatonic" but this is not the same as being inanimate—even when the body dies the material substance is still pulsating with energy. The death drive as a psychoanalytical trope has been written too staunchly on the body (or projected at bodies). My desire is to override it with flows of energy that don't have a polarity—at the subatomic level the string is simply flickering—neither positively nor negatively. It's a utopian fantasy to imagine that the Furies might come along and compost or recycle the death drive. To make it a psychosocial prerequisite only exacerbates the situation. This forces forward an eschatological attitude, a negativized plentitude championed, for instance, by the evangelical right. Then again, this doomsday outlook of inevitability is scripted into Western consciousness. The Judeo-Christian concept that there is a savior (divine individual male figure) who miraculously comes along to rectify the injustice and turmoil returning life to a state of grace isn't all that feasible, from my point of view. The synchronicities, multiple presents, overlapping futures, budding present states, and friction of the un—as in unrecognized, unrealized, unheard, unsung—claiming, being, singing burgeon conductive realities. Registers that beckon, intersect, trisect, swarm, and surge—it is a pulsating riddle. An example of such poetry is Jennifer Scappettone's work in *From Dame Quickly*[14] where she constructs and deconstructs at a rapid-fire pace capitalism's illusions and concretized tropes/forms, sending up a storm of spectral dust from these micro-explosions and implosions. The energy in these poems reverse themselves and clash into themselves repeatedly with so much agitation that it causes questions to sprout not only along fault lines but the entire epidermis of the social. There is no stable term here. A discussion of Socratic *pharmakons* could be one trajectory to pursue. Jacques Derrida describes the function of the pharmakon as that which "alternately and/or all at once petrifies and vivifies, anesthetizes and sensitizes, appeases and anguishes."[15] As Marco Giovenale says of Scappettone's work, "[d]isorientation and fragmentation are guerrilla warfare: they are the ultimate movements to impress upon the net of references and texts setting free and affirming the untold (always told) in Western history—the way it is now, as it wounds, is wounded, and regards us."[16] *From Dame Quickly* is a heady critique of thingness. Carla Harryman and Judith Goldman's work functions similarly. Here's an excerpt of Harryman's prose poem essay, *Regard for the object rather than communication is suspect*:

> Hurricanes flare up impatiently, flinging our furniture and debris onto our concrete identities. Our roles in society are attacked by what we

---

14 | Scappettone, Jennifer. *From Dame Quickly.* Brooklyn: Litmus Press, 2009.

15 | Derrida, Jacques. *Dissemination.* Chicago: University of Chicago Press, 1981. p. 119.

16 | Blurb for Jennifer Scappettone's, *From Dame Quickly*

own. It is hard in this context to stand up and be simple, to have a body dependent on other bodies, a being contiguous with other beings.[17]

Poetry can actively engage blind spots—where conditioning, de-naturalization, and denial for instance, have buttressed the status quo, politically, socially, spiritually, and environmentally, leading to a degraded ecosystem that places terrestrial well-being, everyone's well-being, all living organisms, oceans, forests, etc., in jeopardy. This is a challenge of a magnitude where every subtle gesture could support holism. Joan Copjec's essay, *The Tomb of Perseverance: On Antigone* reminds me firstly that Freud also proposed a concept of perseverance, *Haftbarkeit*—and emblematic of such persever-ance is Antigone, "Antigone's perseverance is not indicated by her remaining rigidly the same, but by her metamorphosis at the moment of her encounter with the event of her brother's death and Creon's refusal to allow his burial."[18] Death can bring forth empathy through grief—a provocative, generative state. Simon Critchley quotes Judith Butler in his book, *Infinitely Demanding: Ethics of Commitment, Politics of Resistance*: "[i]n grief, we are held in thrall by the other." He continues by paraphrasing Butler, "[i]n grief and mourning we undergo an experience of affective self-dispossession or self-undoing that can provide the motivational force to enter into a political sequence. It is this meta-political moment that propels one into facing and facing down a wrong or

---

17 | Harryman, Carla. *Adorno's Noise*. Athens, Ohio: Essay Press, 2008. p. 25.

18 | Copjec, Joan. "The Tomb of Perseverance: On Antigone," in *Giving Ground: The Politics of Propinquity*. London: Verso, 1999. p. 258.

confronting a situation of injustice, not through sovereign legal norms backed up with the threat of violence, but through an ethical responsiveness to the sheer precariousness of the other's face, of their injurability and our own."[19] Political awakening and social action involves coming out of quietude, out of waiting, shedding latency—Antigone voices. This, from Kamau Brathwaite's shimmering book, *Middle Passage*:

> to be blown into fragments. your death
> like the islands that you loved
> like the seawall that you wished to heal
>
> bringing equal rights & justice to the bredren
> that the children above all others would be like the sun.
> rise.
>
> any where or word where there is love there is the sky & its blue
> free
> where past means present struggle
> towards vlissengens where it may some day end[20]

Seated prominently on the upper food chain are the language-user-human-primates Embedded systems of commerce, government and communication cloak the extremity of the ecological situation. Obfuscation is the norm via a lulling stream of commercialized media din and the reassuring cheer generated out of the ideology of progress—this was pretty much the case until the recent economic

---

19 | Critchley, Simon. *Infinitely Demanding: Ethics of Commitment, Politics of Resistance.* New York: Verso, 2007. p. 120.

20 | Brathwaite, Kamau. *Middle Passages.* New York: New Directions, 1993.

downturn—note the term toxic assets and its ecomorphology. Rob Halpern's work addresses these predicaments:

> These conditions barely speak to the changeless mould that has come upon us. Perhaps there's nothing worse than 'mere murmur of dissent.' Unable to sing the pure and expressive note, we fall visibly shaken by it all—in fact we become quite ill—performing full body spasms, merely hinting at the rictus.[21]

Language that engages these pressing realities can be viewed as extreme, sensational—or sanctimonious. Poetry, because of its compression and condensed energy, is a potent form of expressiveness. Because poetry inclines language to its most agile and expressive potential, it can be effective as a means to create and articulate alternative strategies for living. Cognition and language involve the body's participation, the very body subjected to an increasingly hazardous set of environmental circumstances. Tyrone Williams points out, "[a]ttention to relation itself, to the networks that sustain capital, demands we recognize our own interpellation as subject-positions, as flexible and moveable as the feast of production and consumption."[22] Here is an excerpt from Taylor Brady's "To Be Low-Density Fieldwork":

> Pores in a sprained body
> are relief
> of standing water.
> I speak for the trees, for shade

---

21 | Halpern, Rob. *Rumored Place.* San Francisco: Krupskaya, 2004.

22 | Williams, Tyrone. (talk) "Apparently I am picking fights: Cultural Studies and Poetics Mix It Up in Taylor Brady's Yesterday's News." Delivered at the MLA, 2006.

zones out the mixed-use tract.
from[23]

In its National Water Quality Assessment, the U.S. Geological Survey found that a sampling of the nation's streams contained two or more pesticides 90 percent of the time. It estimates that one billion pounds of pesticides are used each year in the United States.[24] The distressing effects of these industrial effluents as they enter the ecosystem have gone unmonitored until very recently. Since World War II it is estimated that 200 new synthetic compounds have been introduced into the environment with unknown effect (and thus, 200 potent words enter the language stream). It is troubling that each chemical compound on its own has adverse effects, but even more alarming is how these agents mix to form a toxic brew. The hazardous effects of agrochemicals (only one aspect of the chemical aggregations of cosmetics, medical waste, solvents, etc.,) on nontarget organisms (plants, animals, and humans) have only begun to be a concern for study—a risk assessment for use of these compounds has yet to be thoroughly executed.[25] The only way I have of sharing this provocative informa-

---

23 | Brady, Taylor. *Yesterday's News*. Ithaca, San Diego, San Francisco: Factory School, 2005.

24 | This data is from a report titled, "Pesticides in the Nation's Streams and Ground Waters 1992-2001" http://water.usgs.gov/nawqa/pnsp/.

25 | http://www.nrdc.org/onearth/06win/chem3.asp
http://www.nrdc.org/onearth/06win/chem1.asp
http://www.nrdc.org/health/pesticides/natrazine.asp
http://www.nrdc.org/health/science/ijsscience.asp
http://www.nrdc.org/media/pressreleases/020415.asp
Collins, Terrance J. and Chip Walter. "Little Green Molecules." *Scientific American*, March, 2006.

tion with you is through language! Images alone would not suffice.

Rachel Carson warned us 30 years ago in her eloquent book, *Silent Spring*, about the poisoning effects of pesticides, insecticides, and herbicides. Chemicals designed as weapons in WWII are now being used as insecticides. Consider for example DDVP. A toxic herbicide, atrazine is one of the nation's most common and widely used weed killers—approximately 80 million pounds is applied annually in the U.S. alone. A study conducted in 2002 by Dr. Tyrone Hayes showed that atrazine distresses the endocrine system and reproductive system, causing anatomical changes in frogs. Another study showed that workers at an atrazine manufacturing plant had elevated incidence of prostrate cancer. Dr. Hayes' website states,

> It has become clear that the adverse effects of atrazine extend beyond amphibians. Through endocrine-disrupting mechanisms identical to those acting in amphibians, atrazine produces effects in other animals, including prostate and breast cancer and decreased fertility in laboratory rodents. These same effects are associated with atrazine exposure in humans. In addition to the scientific interests, this issue is one of environmental justice. Citizens in lower socio-economic classes and, in particular, ethnic minorities are less likely to have access to this information, more likely to be employed and live in areas where they are exposed to pesticides, less likely to have access to appropriate health care, and more likely to die from what are already the number one cancers in men in women (prostate and breast cancer, respectively), with cancer now being the number one cause of death.[26]

---

26 | http://www.atrazinelovers.com/m4.html.

An insidious saturation from industry's laboratories is presented to consumers as lifestyle enhancement and/or part and parcel of general subsistence. From Yedda Morrison's poem sequence, "The Amazing Race (Prime Time Vision Quest)" in her book *girl scout nation:*

> in the coveted midst of the little flame
> Scout will never complete her catalogue of atrocity
> Giant lucidity marshaled into duckweed
> Sits plotting, and in plotting endures[27]

Language unifies us as human animals—other species use language as well, but there is a rift in mutual communication. Consciousness is embedded in language and becomes more nuanced and interactive when there is heightened perception and acknowledgement of the polyrhythms that exist in combination with social bodies, environmental social bodies, political environmental social bodies— the string can be extended as long as there are combinations to be recognized. "the whole earth together/dirt/controls/clouds/holding up air/water flows/a surface bent in/as made…to smash the/head/ on out/on the tree for you/years turn stone/it's geology"[28]—Larry Eigner, from *Things Stirring Together or Far Away*. The impossibility of a solitary body, also…. ": unfamiliarity with the edges of one's body"[29]—Eileen Tabios, from *The Secret Lives of Punctuations*, Vol. 1. It is deceptive to see writing as a solitary act. Language acts along

---

27 | Morrison, Yedda. *girl scout nation*. Ann Arbor: Displaced Press, 2008.

28 | Eigner, Larry. *Things Stirring Together or Far Away*. Los Angeles: Black Sparrow, 1974.

29 | Tabios, Eileen. *The Secret Lives of Punctuations*, Vol. 1. Espoo: Finland, 2006.

generative routes toward, away and into, *as*: language is involved, so are you. *All there is* is bound up in the concept of environment. It is moot to conceptualize separation. Nothing can sequester itself from the environment—environment is all. Survival entails mutual agreements based on body consensus which is ultimately health—all organs in play (where death does not equate with annihilation).

Contributors

KAREN LEONA ANDERSON is the author of *Punish honey* (Carolina Wren Press, 2009). She received an M.F.A from the University of Iowa Writers' Workshop, an M.A. from Victoria University in Wellington, New Zealand, and her Ph.D. from Cornell University. Her work has appeared or is forthcoming in *ecopoetics*, *jubilat*, *Fence*, *Volt*, and other journals. She is currently an assistant professor of English at St. Mary's College of Maryland.

JACK COLLOM teaches at Naropa and in many elementary schools, writes crazy nature poems, and birds in Boulder, Colorado. His latest book is *Situations, Sings*, with Lyn Hejinian. He believes in variety and does the same things all the time.

TINA DARRAGH lives in Greenbelt, MD, and earns her keep as a reference librarian. Sections of "Deep eco pré," her collaboration with Marcella Durand, can be found in the online magazines *HOW2* and *Little Red Leaves*. Other publications include: *opposable dumbs: a project report* (summer 2007-Thanksgiving 2007), *dream rim instructions* (Drogue Press, 1999), *a(gain)2 st the odds* (Potes and Poets Press, 1989), *Striking Resemblance* (Burning Deck, 1989), and *on the corner to off the corner* (Sun & Moon, 1981). "Bad I.O.U.", her play about universal health care, was performed at the Yockadot Poetics Theatre Festival, Alexandria, VA, in May, 2007. Darragh's work has been included in several anthologies: *In the American Tree* (National Poetry Foundation, 1986), *"Language" Poetries* (New Directions, 1987), *From the Other Side of the Century* (Sun & Moon, 1994), *out of everywhere: linguistically innovative poetry by women in North America & the UK* (Reality Street Editions, 1996), and *Moving Borders: Three Decades of Innovative Writing by Women* (Talisman House, 1998).

MARCELLA DURAND's latest books are *AREA* (Belladonna Books) and *Traffic & Weather* (Futurepoem Books), both published in 2008. She has spoken on the intersections of poetry and ecology at Small Press Traffic, Naropa University, Kelly Writers House, Exit Art, and other venues. Her long collaboration with Tina Darragh involving Michael Zimmerman's *Contesting Earth's Future* and Francis Ponge's *The Making of the Pré* was recently published in HOW2's ecopoetics issue.

LAURA ELRICK's most recent poetic works have taken form outside the book: some audio pieces and an interview can be heard on the Ceptuetics radio program at ceptuetics.blogspot.com, and her video/poem *Stalk* (a dystopian urban cartography and spatial-poetic intervention) can be seen on blip tv. Previous books of poetry include *sKincerity* (Krupskaya, 2003) and *Fantasies in Permeable Structures* (Factory School, 2005). She lives and works in Brooklyn.

BRENDA IIJIMA is the author of *Around Sea* (O Books), *Animate, Inanimate Aims* (Litmus Press), *revv. you'll—ution* (Displaced Press) and *If Not Metamorphic* (forthcoming, Ahsahta Press). Presently, she is writing an informal encyclopedia on animals used as surrogates by humans. She is also a visual artist and the editor of Portable Press at Yo-Yo Labs.

PETER LARKIN works as a subject librarian at Warwick University. From 1988-2002 he ran Prest Roots Press. A collection of 10 years' work, *Terrain Seed Scarcity*, was published by Salt Publications in 2001. Since then he has published a chapbook-threesome, *Sprout Near Severing Close, What the Surfaces Enclave of Wang Wei, Rings Resting the Circuit* (The Gig, 2004) and *Leaves of Field* (Shearsman, 2006). A new collection, *Lessways Least Scarce Among* is forthcoming from The Gig. Recent work has appeared in *fragmente, Free Verse, Salt Magazine* and *Stride Magazine*. An interview with Edmund Hardy is available at *Intercapillary Space*.

JILL MAGI's books and chapbooks include *Threads* (Futurepoem, 2007), *Torchwood* (Shearsman, 2008), *Cadastral Map* (Portable Press at Yo-Yo Labs, 2005), and the forthcoming *Poetry Barn Barn!* (2nd

Avenue) and *From the Body Project* (Felt Press). Recent works have appeared in *Tarpaulin Sky*, *Miniature Forests*, and *Action Yes!*. She teaches at Goddard, Eugene Lang, and City Colleges.

TRACIE MORRIS is an interdisciplinary poet who has worked extensively as a sound artist, writer, bandleader and multimedia performer. Her installations have been presented at the Whitney Biennial and the Jamaica Center for Arts and Learning. Tracie is the recipient of numerous awards for poetry and performance and has contributed to, and been written about in, several anthologies of literary criticism. She holds an MFA in poetry from Hunter College and a PhD in Performance Studies from New York University. Dr. Morris is an Associate Professor of English and Humanities at Pratt Institute. She is completing two books: an academic work "WhoDo with Words" on the work of philosopher J.L. Austin and a poetry collection, "Rhyme Scheme."

CATRIONA (CATE) MORTIMER-SANDILANDS is Canada Research Chair in Sustainability and Culture at York University, Toronto. She is the author of *The Good-Natured Feminist: Ecofeminism and the Quest for Democracy* (Minnesota, 1999) and co-editor of *This Elusive Land: Women and the Canadian Environment* (UBC, 2005) and *Queer Ecologies: Sex, Nature, Politics and Desire* (Indiana, 2010). She is currently working on a manuscript on the work of lesbian novelist, essayist and activist Jane Rule.

JULIE PATTON is a sight and sound specific "make-up artist" who mixes words with action, spit, soil, sounds, found texts, leaf melodies and anything else she can get her hands on. *A Room for Opal*, part of the Olin Art Museum's (Lewiston, Maine) Green Horizons exhibition (see Jonathan Skinner's essay about Patton's project in ON: Contemporary Practice 1, November, 2008) is one of the many text-based "library installations" Julie has created in her practice as an X-Pat..., *Poverty native in the Americas. *Using Blue to Get Black* was just released in *Crayon: On Beauty* (Issue 5, October 2008), *Notes for Some (Nominally) Awake* was published by Portable Press at Yo-Yo Labs. On the "found-sound" side, Patton has collaborated with musicians Ralph Alessi, Uri Caine, Ravi Coltrane, Henry Grimes, Barnaby McAll, Nasheet Waits, and Paul Van Curen. Patton has been awarded the 2008 Acadia Arts Foundation Grant, the 2007 New York Foundation for the Arts Poetry Fellowship. As the Founding Director of the Dandelion Society, Let It Bee Gardens, Green Scouts and NeighborWoods, Julie extends her "pulp poetic practice" into collaborative, civic, and natural spaces with market garden, gleaning, urban prairie initiatives, sustainable artist-housing and green job skills for youth.

JED RASULA teaches at the University of Georgia. His most recent books are *Modernism and Poetic Inspiration: Shadow Mouth* (Palgrave Macmillan) and *Hot Wax, or Psyche's Drip* (Book Thug). In the works are a large anthology of early twentieth century vanguard poetry in translation, *Burning City* (Action Books), co-edited with Tim Conley, and *Jazzbandism*, which scrutinizes early interactions between jazz and the avant-garde.

EVELYN REILLY's *Styrofoam*, published by Roof Books, is a text-image meditation on notions of immortality (literary vs. environmental), so-called authentic vs. faux materials, and the ambiguities of plastic. Earlier work includes *Fervent Remnants of Reflective Surfaces* from Portable Press at Yo-Yo Labs and *Hiatus* from Barrow Street Press.

LESLIE SCALAPINO's newest book is *It's go in horizontal* from University of California Press; and *Floats Horse-Floats or Horse-Flows* is forthcoming from Starcherone.

JAMES SHERRY is the author of many books of poetry and criticism. His most recent work, *Sorry: Environmental Poetics* was published by Factory School in 2009. He is the editor of Roof Books and founder of The Segue Foundation in NYC.

JONATHAN SKINNER's poetry collections include *With Naked Foot* (Little Scratchpad, 2008) and *Political Cactus Poems* (Palm Press, 2005). Skinner edits the journal *ecopoetics*, which features creative-critical intersections between writing and ecology. His essays on the poets Ronald Johnson and Lorine Niedecker appeared recently in volumes published by the National Poetry Foundation and by University of Iowa Press. Skinner teaches in the Environmental Studies Program, at Bates College in Central Maine, where he makes his home.

TYRONE WILLIAMS teaches literature and theory at Xavier University in Cincinnati, Ohio. He is the author of two books of poetry, *c.c.* (Krupskaya Books, 2002) and *On Spec* (Omnidawn Publishing, 2008). He also has several chapbooks out, including *AAB* (Slack Buddha Press, 2004), *Futures, Elections* (Dos Madres Press, 2004) and *Musique Noir* (Overhere Press, 2006). A new book of poems, *the Hero Project of the Century*, was published in 2009 by The Backwaters Press. He recently completed a manuscript of poetry commissioned by Atelos Books. His website is located at the following link: http://home.earthlink.net/~suspend/.

Ecopoetics: An Incomplete Curriculum

JONATHAN SKINNER & BRENDA IIJIMA

Abram, David. *The Spell of the Sensuous: Perception and Language in a More-Than-Human World.* New York: Vintage, 1997.

Agamben, Giorgio. *The Open: Man and Animal.* Trans. Kevin Attell. Stanford, CA: Stanford University Press, 2004.

Allen, Austin. *Claiming Open Spaces.* Documentary film, 1994.

Baker, Steve. *The Postmodern Animal.* London: Reaktion Books, 2002.

Bataille, Georges. *The Cradle of Humanity: Prehistoric Art and Culture.* Trans. Stuart Kendall and Michelle Kendall. New York: Zone Books, 2005.

Brathwaite, Kamau. *Middle Passage.* New York: New Directions, 1994.

Browne, Sir Thomas. "*On the Gardens of Cyrus, or the Quincunx, Naturally Considered*" in *The Major Works.* New York: Penguin, 1977.

Buell, Lawrence. *The Future of Environmental Criticism: Environmental Crisis and Literary Imagination.* Oxford: Blackwell Publishing, 2005.

Carroll, Lewis. *Alice's Adventures in Wonderland and Through the Looking-Glass.* New York: Penguin, 1998.

Carson, Rachel. *Silent Spring.* Boston: Houghton Mifflin, 1962.

Davis, Mike. *Dead Cities.* New York: The New Press, 2002.

Descola, Philippe. *Par-delà nature et culture.* Paris: Éditions Gallimard, 2005.

Denes, Agnes. *The Human Argument: The Writings of Agnes Denes.* Ed. Klaus Ottman. Putnam, NY: Spring Publications, 2008.

Derrida, Jacques. *The Animal Therefore I am.* New York: Fordham University Press, 2008.

Feld, Steven. *Sound and Sentiment: Birds, Weeping, Poetics, and Song in Kaluli Expression*. Philadelphia: University of Pennsylvania Press, 1982.

Fletcher, Angus. *A New Theory for American Poetry: Democracy, the Environment, and the Future of Imagination*. Cambridge: Harvard University Press, 2004.

Glissant, Édouard. *Poetics of Relation*. Trans. Betsy Wing, Ann Arbor: University of Michigan Press, 1997.

Grosz, Elizabeth. *Chaos, Territory, Art: Deleuze and the Framing of the Earth*. New York: Columbia University Press, 2008.

Guha, Ramachandra. *Environmentalism: A Global History*. London: Longman, 1999.

Haraway, Donna. *The Donna Haraway Reader*. New York: Routledge. 2004.

Hinton, Leanne, Johanna Nichols, John J. Ohala, eds. *Sound Symbolism*. New York: Cambridge University Press, 1994.

Howe, Susan. *The Birth-mark: Unsettling the Wilderness in American Literary History*. Hanover, CT: Wesleyan University Press, 1993.

Hyesoon, Kim. *Mommy Must be a Fountain of Feathers*. Trans. Don Mee Choi. Notre Dame, IN: Action Books. 2008.

Kapil, Bhanu. *Incubation: A Space for Monsters*. Providence: Leon Works, 2006.

Kropotkin, Peter. *Mutual Aid: A Factor in Evolution*. London: Freedom Press, 1998.

LaDuke, Winona. *All Our Relations: Native Struggles for Land and Life*. Cambridge, MA: South End Press, 1999.

Lingis, Alphonso. *Dangerous Emotions*. Berkeley: University of California Press, 2000.

Lock, Margaret, Farquhar, Judith, eds. *Beyond the Body Proper: Reading the Anthropology of Material Life*. Durham, NC: Duke University Press, 2007.

Malinowski, Bronislaw. *The Language of Magic and Gardening (Coral Gardens and Their Magic*, Vol. II). 1965. Bloomington: Indiana University Press, 1935.

McClure, Michael. *Scratching the Beat Surface*. San Francisco: North Point Press, 1982.

Midgley, Mary. *The Essential Mary Midgley*. New York: Routledge, 2005.

Mithen, Steven. *The Singing Neanderthals: The Origins of Music, Language, Mind, and Body*. Cambridge: Harvard University Press, 2007.

Morrison, Yedda. *girl scout nation*. Ann Arbor: Displaced Press, 2008.

Nabhan, Gary Paul. *Gathering the Desert*. Tucson: University of Arizona Press, 1986.

Nash, Roderick. *Wilderness and the American Mind*. New Haven, CT: Yale University Press, 1967.

Olmsted, Frederick Law. *Civilizing American Cities: Writings on City Landscapes*. Ed. S. B. Sutton. New York: Da Capo Press, 1997.

Pèna, Devon G., ed. *Chicano Culture, Ecology, Politics: Subversive Kin*. Tucson, University of Arizona Press, 1998.

Philip, M. Nourbese. *Zong!*. Middletown, CT: Wesleyan University Press, 2008.

Rasula, Jed. *This Compost: Ecological Imperatives in American Poetry*. Athens: University of Georgia Press, 2002.

Richards, Deborah. *Last One Out*. New York: Subpress, 2003.

Rothenberg, David. *Why Birds Sing: A Journey Into the Mystery of Birdsong*. New York: Basic Books, 2005.

Rukeyser, Muriel. *U.S. 1*. New York: Covici Friede Publishers, 1938.

Schafer, R. Murry. *The Soundscape: Our Sonic Environment and the Tuning of the World*. New York: Knopf, 1977.

Schuyler, James. *The Crystal Lithium*. New York: Random House, 1972.

Smithson, Robert. *The Collected Writings*. Ed. Jack Flam. Berkeley: University of California Press, 1996.

Snyder, Gary. *The Practice of the Wild*. New York: North Point, 1990.

Solnit, Rebecca. *Storming the Gates of Paradise*. Berkeley: University of California Press, 2008.

Steingraber, Sandra. *Having Faith: An Ecologist's Journey to Motherhood*. Cambridge: Perseus Publishing, 2001.

Tedlock, Dennis, trans. *Finding the Center: The Art of the Zuni Storyteller*. Lincoln and London: University of Nebraska Press, 1999.

Thoreau, Henry David. *The Journal of Henry David Thoreau*. Ed. Lewis Hyde. New York: North Point Press, 2002.

Toomer, Jean. *Cane*. New York: Boni Liveright, 1923.

Werner, Marta. *"The Flights of A 821: Dearchiving the Proceedings of a Birdsong."* *Chain* 6: Letters. 1999.

Wheeler, Wendy. *The Whole Creature: Complexity, Biosemiotics and Evolution of Culture*. London: Lawrence and Wishart Ltd., 2006.

Wessels, Tom. *Reading the Forested Landscape: A Natural History of New England*. Woodstock, VT: Countryman Press, 1997.

Opal Whiteley. *The Singing Creek Where the Willows Grow: The Mystical Nature Diary of Opal Whiteley*. London: Penguin, 1995.

Williams, Raymond. *The Country and the City*. New York: Oxford University Press, 1975.

Portable Press at Yo-Yo Labs publishes poetic works: subtle and intense forms of public exchange and autonomous expressions—dynamic in awareness—luminous in form.

Emphasis: diversity and interconnection—social, cultural, environmental and aesthetic.

Nightboat Books, a nonprofit organization, seeks to develop audiences for writers whose work resists convention and transcends boundaries. We publish books rich with poignancy, intelligence, and risk. Please visit our website, www.nightboat.org, to learn more about us and how you support our future publications.

NYSCA

This book has been made possible, in part, by a grant from the New York State Council on the Arts Literature Program.